God's Tender Mercies

By Common Consent Press is a non-profit publisher dedicated to producing affordable, high-quality books that help define and shape the Latter-day Saint experience. BCC Press publishes books that address all aspects of Mormon life. Our mission includes finding manuscripts that will contribute to the lives of thoughtful Latter-day Saints, mentoring authors and nurturing projects to completion, and distributing important books to the Mormon audience at the lowest possible cost.

God's Tender Mercies

*Sacred Experiences
of a Mormon Convert*

David C. Dollahite

For information contact:

By Common Consent Press
4062 South Evelyn Drive
Salt Lake City, UT 84124-2250

ISBN-13: 978-0-9986052-6-5
ISBN-10: 0-9986052-6-3

10 9 8 7 6 5 4 3 2 1

The Lord is good to all: and his tender mercies are over all his works.
—*Psalms 145:9*

For the glory of the Father, and the blessing of His
children—especially the choice ones he has entrusted to Mary
and me: Rachel, Erica, Camilla, Kathryn, Spencer, Jonathan, and
Luke—and for the blessing of their children, to turn their hearts to
the Father.

Acknowledgments

It was my mother's practice of reading on topics far and wide that led her to accept and keep the copy of the Book of Mormon that I eventually read and which led to my conversion to the restored gospel of Jesus Christ. It was my father's quiet example of honesty that led me to act on the truth when I found it. Although they were quite unhappy that I joined the Church of Jesus Christ of Latter-day Saints and served a full-time mission, my parents tried to understand and support me in my new faith.

I am deeply grateful to LoDonna and Ray Leininger, my "Mormon Parents," through whose missionary zeal I came to know of and embrace the gospel. And it was their kindness, and generosity, that facilitated my ability to get into Brigham Young University (BYU). They helped me pay for my freshman year and my mission. A few years ago, when I was asked to speak at LoDonna's funeral, I did a little research and found out that through the faith and missionary efforts of those I have been blessed to teach the gospel to, thousands of people have accepted the gospel as a result of the one Book of Mormon she first gave to my mom. I look forward to seeing them on the other side of the veil.

I am extremely grateful to my beloved wife, Mary, for her constant devotion and willingness to bear with me as I try to become what our Heavenly Father and I would like me to be. She is, besides only my testimony of the restored gospel, the greatest tender mercy that God has blessed me with. I am thankful to my children for being willing to listen to their father tell of his spiritual experiences over the years and thus share "the things of my soul" (2 Nephi 4:15).

I am grateful for the many Latter-day Saints who have taught me, blessed me, led me, and borne with me as I have tried to learn and live the gospel. In telling about the experiences I have had I will use actual names most of the time. If, for some reason, I chose not to reveal the identity of a person I will use a pseudonym and will use an asterisk (*) next to his or her name. I apologize to anyone whose role in my conversion to and early years in the Church I may have neglected to mention or give proper credit to.

I am grateful to the good folks at By Common Consent Press, especially Steve Evans and Michael Austin for believing in this book and for their work at every stage of the process. I am grateful to Kathyrn K. Dollahite for her excellent copy-editing of the book.

I am eternally grateful to God, the Eternal Father, for kindly but clearly bringing me to know Him and His Son, Jesus Christ. In the forty years that I have been a member of the Church of Jesus Christ of Latter-day Saints, I have been blessed by the constant love, mercy, and guidance of the Father and the Son. I offer all that I have and am to them and their work.

* * *

Royalties from this book (minus tithing and taxes) will be donated to (1) LDS Charities which sends food, clothing, medical supplies, and other emergency relief assistance to those with urgent needs around the world and (2) the Student Fellow program of the American Families of Faith project which exists to discover and share research-based ideas about ways of being religious that can best (a) facilitate human joy and relational quality and stability, and (b) help religious individuals, couples, and families thrive in an increasingly secular culture (see <u>americanfamiliesoffaith.byu.edu</u>*).*

Introduction

The Lord has been extremely kind, generous, and merciful to me
throughout my life. However, there was a special abundance of divine
tender mercies during the two months I investigated the Church of
Jesus Christ of Latter-day Saints and in the first few years I was a
member of the Church—particularly on my mission and leading me
to my marvelous wife, Mary.

The winter of 2017 marks forty years since the events recounted
in this volume began to unfold. The Lord saved me from a path of
worldliness, nearly certain marital and family unhappiness, potential
addiction, and lifelong ignorance of Him and His purposes. In His
tender mercy and by His gracious love, he placed me on a path that
has led me to great happiness, deep peace, marital and family joy, and
joyful knowledge of Him and His ways.

He did this by giving me a clear and undeniable witness of the
truthfulness of the restored gospel through the power of His Spirit and
then through a series of sacred experiences that were marvelous to me
then and now. I have often wondered why it was that God blessed me
with such an abundance of sacred experiences when so many others I
have known, who are far better people and Latter-day Saints than I
was and am, have not seemed to be so richly blessed.

I have concluded that because of the powerful culture of
worldliness that I was raised in, and because of my own weaknesses

and foibles, the Lord needed to give me an extra measure of spiritual witnesses and sacred experiences to help me become a less unprofitable servant. Being raised in Marin County, California—one of wealthiest and worldliest places in the world—I was, in a sense, born and raised in Babylon. Thus, I think the Lord needed to bring me out of that strongly worldly culture with "a strong hand" (Exodus 6:1). Perhaps others who are more spiritually sensitive, humbler, and spiritually stronger than I am may not need as much or as many of those kinds of experiences to get and keep them on the path that leads to ultimate joy and peace. My spiritual heroes are not those who have been blessed with remarkable spiritual experiences, but rather those who stay faithful despite never having received an overpowering spiritual manifestation. However, I am eternally grateful to the Lord for His great kindnesses to me.

I begin with the sacred experiences that led to my conversion to the restored gospel and continue on through my baptism, early months in the Church, first year at BYU, two-year full-time mission, courtship, and early marriage.

In this book, I share a number of the most sacred experiences I have been blessed with. I do so with the understanding that we ought not to "cast [our] pearls before swine" (Matthew 7:6) nor lightly share deeply personal spiritual experiences indiscriminately. I wrote this account first and foremost for the benefit of my children and grandchildren but I hope and pray that it might be a blessing in the life of any person who reads it. I have carefully considered the inclusion of each and every one of the experiences I share. I offer them with the hope that they might serve to turn the hearts of my brothers and sisters in Christ as well as my friends of other faiths to their Father in Heaven and His Son, our Savior. I discuss the challenges of writing sacred experiences in APPENDIX A.

I hope and pray that my weak words might be made "strong in [the] faith" (2 Nephi 3:21) of all who read them. In four decades of hearing my fellow Mormons share their experiences in countless testimony meetings, talks, lessons, personal conversations and my interviews with Latter-day Saints as part of my research, it has been my observation that many active Latter-day Saints have the kinds of experiences and tender mercies that I share here. I share mine to encourage others to recognize, appreciate, and record theirs.

My hope is that the experiences I share here will be of value to my children, to other Latter-day Saints (both converts and those raised in the Church), and to my friends and family of other faiths who may read this account. Because I hope that this book might be given to our friends of other faiths—and to those who are not religious—I will do my best to report what I remember thinking and feeling as an outsider, then a newcomer, and then a relative novice in the Church of Jesus Christ of Latter-day Saints. I do this so that those who are not as familiar with Latter-day Saint (LDS) belief and practice will have some sense for how LDS beliefs, practice, and culture appeared to me at that time.

Additionally, in an effort to increase understanding and empathy among people of various faiths, here and there I provide some brief explanations of LDS belief and practice for the benefit of my friends of other faiths. I also provide some brief explanations of the belief and practice of other faiths for the benefit of my LDS friends. I do this in the text and, for somewhat lengthier explanations, in footnotes. My hope is that the things that I discuss will engender meaningful and edifying conversations between people of different faiths.

But, because I have had 35–40 years of life experience since most of the events and experiences I share herein, in addition to writing what I thought and felt then I also reflect on what lessons I learned from the experience and the way I now think about how and why the Lord showed me His tender mercies—even if I did not always realize those things at the time. That is, the first part of each chapter is told from the perspective of the young, ignorant, and overzealous person I was when the experience occurred. The second part of each chapter reflects on what I learned from those experiences or how I think about them now.

With encouragement from many who had heard me share my experiences, I had felt for many years that I should write about them for the benefit of my children and others. But I always felt that I lacked in two critical things: (1) the ability to write well and (2) adequate perspective on my experiences. Throughout my elementary and secondary education, I only read what I absolutely had to and avoided writing in all ways possible. I had absolutely no interest in academic things like reading and writing. My entire focus was on athletics, friends, and fun. But, in 1981, I returned from my two-year LDS mission with a desire to obtain the education needed to help families—and that meant learning how to write better.

It has taken me many years of training and experience and practice to learn to write. But because I have had to write a great deal in my profession as a BYU professor of family life, my writing has gradually improved over the years. I have also learned by hard but happy experience that good editors can work miracles with even the poor grammatical materials I provide and I thank all those who have been patient enough to work with me—particularly my wonderful and wise wife, Mary. I thank them all for taking my meager literary loaves and fishes and helping make them available to those who read this account. Like Nephi, I hope and pray that for those who read this account the "words which I have written in weakness will be made strong unto them" (2 Nephi 33:4).

Although by no means do I consider myself a great writer, I have at least developed enough confidence to make a record of the Lord's dealings with me that I hope will be of value to others. Like a number of those who wrote in the Book of Mormon, I feel frustration that my words cannot possibly convey the depth of my joy and the fullness of the Lord's goodness to me (see Helaman 8:3; Ether 12:24). Yet I do feel strongly compelled to give my best efforts in this regard. Thus, my first excuse no longer holds. The fact that forty years have elapsed since my conversion to the gospel means that I now have some perspective on life to bring to this account. So, my second excuse no longer holds either.

But even more than the evaporation of excuses, two things directly influenced me to undertake writing this account. In 2005, LDS Apostle Elder David Bednar gave a great talk, "The Tender Mercies of the Lord," in which he quoted Nephi's statement that he would "show unto you that the tender mercies of the Lord are over all those whom he hath chosen, because of their faith, to make them mighty, even unto the power of deliverance" (1 Nephi 1:20).[1] He then related a number of principles and personal experiences that brought me to a new way of thinking about these issues. Until that talk, I was not sure how to organize my thinking to bring so many diverse experiences together and write about them in a way that made sense. Elder Bednar's talk allowed me, for the first time, to bring all the experiences the Lord has blessed me with under the umbrella of one clear purpose.

---

1. David A. Bednar, "The Tender Mercies of the Lord," LDS General Conference talk, April 2005, lds.org/general-conference/2005/04/the-tender-mercies-of-the-lord.

The second major direct influence was a Sunday School (Gospel Doctrine) class on January 27, 2008, the day before the 30th anniversary of my conversion to the Church. Our instructor, Brother Louis Carr, mentioned that Nephi wrote the small plates as much as thirty years after the events that led to Lehi and his family leaving Jerusalem (see 1 Nephi 19). Something about this made a deep impression on me and I knew that the time was now right to make this account. I spent the next six months preparing the first draft of this book and have worked on it off and on since then. I pray that what is shared herein will lead others to glorify God, to remember and record their own spiritual experiences, and to share those experiences with others they care about—particularly their children and grandchildren.

By nature, and by choice, I am a positive, optimistic, and idealistic person. The things I remember, focus on, and choose to share tend to be positive in nature or in outcome. While I share some of the challenges and struggles I have faced, the majority of the experiences I share here are positive and "faith-promoting" in nature. In fact, I have been so greatly blessed in the forty years since I accepted the fullness of the gospel of Jesus Christ that there are not many negative experiences to relate. Of course, I have had my share of challenges and times that I have felt overwhelmed, discouraged, and confused. But my experience has been that as I turn to the Lord in faith and humility His tender mercies overcome any and all of those difficulties.

Some, reading this book, may mistakenly believe that the types of experiences I share herein occur regularly. Not so. This account collapses the most memorable and wonderful spiritual experiences from the first several years of my association with the LDS faith. By no means do I have these kinds of experiences every day and I certainly have my share of frustrations, seemingly unanswered prayers, failures, and times when things do not work out at all as I thought, hoped, or prayed they would. I am not a particularly spiritual or righteous person. But the Lord has been particularly kind and merciful to me and I happily and thankfully bear witness to His goodness and patience and wisdom in my life.

Like everyone else who strives to live a life of faith, I have had my spiritual "ups and downs" and periods when the heavens seem shut to me and the kinds of experiences I share came few and far between. Yet there is no question that during the times in my life when I was making my best efforts to fully live the gospel and turn to the Lord in faith, I have been blessed with the kinds of answers to prayers and spiritual experiences that I share in this account.

DCD
August 2017

PART I

Conversion
& Early Months in the Church

CHAPTER I

The Blue Book with the Golden Statue

I was 18 and a freshman at a junior college in Marin County, California. Raised an Episcopalian, I had not been to church since about age 12. I spent my youth playing with friends and playing baseball, basketball, football, and tennis. I cared nothing for books unless I thought they would help me with sports.[1]

The day before Thanksgiving in 1977 I was relaxing in our comfortable wing chair, watching TV, when I had the strangest thought: "I should read a book; on my own; voluntarily." And not one that dealt with sports. I thought that, since I was now a college student, I should begin to become an educated person and should read a book that was not assigned by a teacher (and those I mainly skimmed). This was a strange thought for me because the only book not required for school I remember reading before then was *The Inner Game of Tennis* (by Timothy Galway). I hoped to play professional tennis and then teach tennis for a living. So, I did not see much point in reading.

With this strange thought in mind I got up from the chair and went over to my mom's wall of bookshelves. My mother was an avid reader and the shelves were packed with books on a wide variety of subjects. I was feeling ambitious and so thought that I should read not just any book, but a big thick one. I perused a number of books

---

1. For information about my family and faith background and a little about my youth (when my religion was sports), please see Chapter 2.

including *The Rise and Fall of the Third Reich* (a thick book about Nazis with a large black swastika on the cover).

After a few minutes my eyes caught a little paperback book in the left-hand corner of the top shelf. I had a feeling that I should read that book. I pulled it down and looked at the Book of Mormon—a light-blue paperback with a gold statue of someone blowing a trumpet. I had a strong feeling to read the book. This surprised me since I had seen this book before and had had a negative reaction to it when I first saw it.

One day, months before, I had come home from school and seen that book sitting on the table. I rolled my eyes and thought, "Oh please, now my parents are reading the Mormon Bible." My mom worked with a woman named LoDonna Leininger who had been telling her about her Mormon religion for a couple of months and gave my mom a copy of the Book of Mormon. On those occasions that I ate dinner with my family it seemed to me that my mom spoke quite favorably about the things she was learning about the Mormon Church—things like how the Mormons took care of their own, had strong families, and sent their young people out on missions at their own expense.

None of these things were of any interest to me but it seemed like my parents were impressed. In fact, my parents had even attended some kind of pageant at some kind of Mormon temple and a church picnic. When my parents had invited me to go along I said, "No thanks. Please keep all that Mormon stuff away from me." Thus, when I had seen the Book of Mormon sitting on the dining room table a few months before, I assumed they were seriously interested in the Church. I teased my parents about joining this weird religion and told them that they should keep it to themselves—I was not at all interested.

So with this in mind I sat down and began to read this strange blue book. I glanced at the first several pages which had pictures of Jesus and someone called Joseph Smith along with a number of photos of gold plates, and ancient South American ruins. These were followed by some descriptive material about the book. Then I began reading from the beginning.

From the first verse of the book I felt a strange, but wonderful, feeling—a kind of tingling throughout my body. I had never felt this before and, at first, thought there must be a draft in the room. I checked the windows and doors but they were all shut tight. I checked the thermostat but it was quite warm in the room. I returned to the chair and the book and began reading. Again, I felt that strong, strange, and wonderful feeling and found myself deeply interested in what I was reading.

After about twenty minutes I realized that I had to get to work. I did not want to stop reading but I put the book down and drove to the Tamalpais Theatre for my evening shift. While driving along I thought about what I had read, and particularly about what I had felt while reading this book. I was not a religious person and did not give any thought to religious ideas or issues. In fact, although my early religious experiences were mostly positive, some recent experiences with religious people had not been.

After the movie began, I was sitting behind the candy counter and I began thinking that perhaps there was a God and perhaps I should look into religion. I was strongly impressed by that little blue book and the thoughts and feelings I had when I read it. Thus, I was looking forward to getting home after work to continue reading. In the midst of these thoughts I noticed an old man come out from the theater. Although there were a number of other people in the lobby, he walked straight up to me and pulled a pack of cigarettes out of his shirt pocket and, with no introduction whatever, said, "These are Kool cigarettes. I used to smoke Camels but God came to me and told me to stop smoking Camels and start smoking Kools." He then proceeded to tell me a number of very strange things that God had told him to do. The look in his eyes made it clear to me he was mentally ill. After a few minutes of this he stopped abruptly, turned away, and walked back into the theater.

My thought was: "What a complete nut. Religion makes people totally crazy." I thought about some of my other recent negative experiences with highly religious people: Our town had its share of "Jesus Freaks" or hippies who were on drugs and would preach to any who would listen (or to those who tried to avoid listening). I remembered some less-than-enjoyable encounters with some pushy members of other evangelically-oriented faiths. And my closest and longest girlfriend during high school was a devout Lutheran and while she was a wonderful person, her religious lifestyle meant she had many restrictions that I found bothersome.

But the most difficult experience I had was a couple months before that when my best friend and tennis doubles partner, Rob, had called me at work and tried to get me to accept Jesus as my savior. He had not been at all religious but told me that while he was in New York on a trip he had been mugged, beaten badly, stripped practically naked, and left in an alley. A minister had come by and taken him in and preached Jesus to him. Rob called to tell me about his experience and that he had been saved. He then said that if I did not accept Jesus I would burn in hell eternally. I told him I was glad he was okay and happy he had found something to make him happy (his father had died of a heart attack when Rob was young and that of course was very difficult for Rob). I told him I appreciated his interest in my eternal fate but I was not interested in Jesus. He said, quite stridently, and in a tone that

I had not heard from him, that I was a sinner and would burn forever unless I accepted Jesus. Again, I told him I was not interested but he continued to preach to me and would not let me change the subject. He became more insistent and I told him if he couldn't stop preaching Jesus at me I would hang up on him. He kept at it until I finally had to hang up on my friend. I thought at the time that he was a completely different person from the fun-loving guy I had traveled with around California, playing in tennis tournaments. In fact, Rob had changed so much I thought religion had "made him nuts."

These several thoughts led me to decide that since religion made people crazy I wanted nothing to do with it. I decided that I would not read any more from the Book of Mormon.

When I got home from work that night, at about ten o'clock, I was looking forward to going to sleep and went up to my room. But I had a strong feeling and thought that I should go downstairs, get the Book of Mormon, and read it. I said to myself, "I'm not going to read that book. Religion makes you crazy." The strong feeling came again with the suggestion: "You should read the book." I thought again, "No. Religion makes you crazy and I'm not going to read it." Again, I had a strong feeling with the thought, "You should read the book." I then thought that perhaps I would just read for a couple of minutes before going to sleep. So, I went down and got the book, brought it back up to my room, sat at my desk, and began to read.

Again, from the first verse I read, I began having the same strange but wonderful feelings. I wondered what this feeling was but continued reading, hour after hour. I was impressed with what I was reading although I did not understand many things. I came to certain parts of the book that I had a hard time understanding (for example, the Isaiah Chapters in 2 Nephi) but I had the feeling that I should just keep reading and not worry that I did not understand. Several times during

what turned out to be my first of two consecutive all-nighters reading
the Book of Mormon, I wanted to put the book down and go to sleep.
I was tired, my eyes were sore and my back ached. But I kept having a
strong feeling that I should keep reading. During that first long night,
more than once I thought to myself, "I should be asleep, not spending
all night reading. See, this proves it. Religion makes you crazy!"

I read through the night until about six in the morning.
Throughout that day (Thanksgiving) I thought about what I had read
and read for a few more hours. I was impressed with the prophets I was
reading about. They were strong men who I could look up to. When I
was younger I had developed the idea that religious people were weak.
I am now ashamed to say that I even thought that Jesus was weak.

There were three reasons for this. First, it seemed that most of the
sermons I heard focused on how Jesus taught that we should "turn the
other cheek" and that he himself allowed others to hurt and even kill
him. Second, the crucifixes that adorned the church I was raised in
and the Catholic churches I had been in showed an emaciated man
hanging on the cross and at that time to me this seemed the result
of weakness. Third, although I cannot say that I was an especially
observant boy, it seemed to me that most of the people who attended
Holy Innocents' Episcopal Church were older women. I remember very
few, if any, strong and athletic men at church and, like many young
boys with interest in sports, I admired strength and athletic skill above
all else.

Thus, by reading the stories about Nephi (large of stature, a builder
of ships, a king and warrior who wielded the Sword of Laban), Enos
(a hunter), Helaman (a captain) and the 2,000 Stripling Warriors, and
Captain Moroni (a Nephite general), I came to realize that one could
be religious and a strong man as well. I did look at all the pictures
throughout the Book of Mormon, and the Arnold Friberg paintings

of muscled prophets, generals, "ripped" stripling warriors, and the prophet-generals Mormon and Moroni contributed to this overall impression of masculine yet religious men in the Book of Mormon. [2]

These prophets wrote about Jesus and prophesied that he would come to visit their people. I wondered what Jesus would say and do when he came to them. That evening when I came home from work, at about ten o'clock, I was looking forward to reading more but—given my lack of sleep the previous night—was looking forward to sleeping even more. So, I decided I would get a good night's rest and finish reading the book the next day. But again I had a very strong feeling that I should read the book. So, I sat at my desk and began reading, thinking I would read for a little while then go to sleep.

I read on, through the night, feeling the same wonderful strange feelings of joy and excitement. As I read I had many questions: Could these things really be true? Could God really exist? Does God really know me? Could Jesus Christ really be the Son of God and the Savior of the world? Could I have my sins forgiven? Could I really experience the joy and peace and purpose that the people I was reading about felt?

My eyes were sore and my body ached all over. And again, many times during the night I wanted to put the book down and sleep, but each time I decided I really needed to get to sleep I felt strongly that I should keep reading. Though tired, my anticipation at the appearance of Jesus among the Nephites continued to grow.

Finally, I came to 3 Nephi Chapter 11. I read with great interest and was greatly impressed with all that Jesus said and did. He was not at all the "weak" Jesus I had remembered from my youth but rather,

2. The Arnold Friberg paintings that were in the Book of Mormon I read, are available at: deseretnews.com/top/704/0/Arnold-Fribergs-religious-paintings.html

to my 18-year-old athletically-oriented self, was a strong man filled with both love and power. Here was someone I could count a hero and strive to emulate. I felt great love for Jesus and wanted to be with him and become like him. And although I did not understand the theology of the Atonement, yet I had read repeatedly that he had suffered for me and that I could be forgiven of my sins by believing in Jesus.

With renewed vigor and purpose, I continued to read the Book of Mormon. At about 5:00 a.m. I was running out of energy, was extremely sore, and was starting to nod off as I read. I was about twenty pages from the end of the book and I decided that I would get some sleep and finish the book later that day. After I had made this decision, and started to get up, I felt an overwhelming feeling and very clear thought that I needed to "finish the book now." At the same time, I suddenly felt renewed energy. In fact, I felt as if I had just awoken from a good night's sleep. And the soreness of eyes, neck, back, and legs disappeared.

So, I stayed in the chair and continued reading until I came to some verses that Mrs. Leininger had marked. She had underlined Moroni 10:3–5 in red pen and highlighted them with a yellow highlighter, and had written in the margin in all caps, "VERY IMPORTANT VERSES. READ THESE CAREFULLY!" I carefully read these verses several times and tried to understand what they were suggesting I should do. I came to understand that I should ponder certain things. I pondered about how good the Lord had been to the peoples of the earth and to me personally.

Then it came to me that the verses were suggesting I should pray and ask God if the Book of Mormon was true. In the Episcopal church, whenever we prayed we knelt. So, I knew I should kneel to pray. I knelt at the side of my bed and, with faith in the Jesus Christ that I had read about in the Book of Mormon; I asked God to forgive my sins and asked if the Book of Mormon was true.

It is not possible for me even to begin to adequately express in words what then happened. But I must try. I felt the same type of wonderful feelings I had felt since I first began reading the Book of Mormon, but at such an intensified level of power and depth that I cannot describe. I had never felt such power and love before. It was as if a river of pure water rushed through me, washing away all my sins. It was also like a ¬raging fire purged away my old self. I felt completely clean and like an entirely new person.

And not only was there great power in what I experienced but the depth of love I felt was beyond description. I felt loved at the deepest levels of my soul. I felt that, although I did not know God, God knew me perfectly. And although God knew me perfectly—all my sinfulness, pride, vanity, selfishness—He still loved me in a way that I had never felt loved. And although I knew I did not know much about God—yet, somehow, I knew God in a way and at a depth that I cannot express.

Along with this came the certain knowledge that the Book of Mormon was true—was the word of God in every way. I knew with perfect certainty that this book was from God. The sure knowledge that the book I had just read was absolutely true in every way was seared in my mind, heart, and soul. No human or earthly power could possibly come close to changing what I felt. In fact, I had the thought that it would not matter if the Pope, Billy Graham, and all the religious people in the world tried to convince me that the Book of Mormon was not true. I knew, for myself, that it was the word of God.

I felt my heart and mind changed in a profound way. I no longer wanted to be what I was and do what I was doing. I only wanted to do what God wanted me to do. I did not know what that was but I was

filled with a joy and excitement that is beyond my ability to express.
I never wanted to do anything but love and serve as many people as
possible. I wanted to tell as many people as possible about Jesus Christ
and about the Book of Mormon.

I also felt that God had a purpose, a mission, for me. Somehow,
I knew my life would not be at all what, until then, I had thought
it would be like. I saw glimpses of myself teaching many people in
various situations about Jesus Christ and the Book of Mormon and
I knew that this would be my future. I was incredibly excited about
this new future. I did not know what to do to get there but somehow
I knew that God would guide me along the path to fulfill what He
had in store for me. For the first time in my life I openly wept tears of
gratitude, love, relief, and pure joy.

This experience lasted about thirty minutes. Finally, I arose from
my knees and climbed into my bed. I lay awake pondering what had
just happened. I was more wide-awake and excited than I had ever
been in my life. I could not wait to learn more about this book I had
read, about Joseph Smith who translated it, about Jesus whose sacrifice
had made possible what I had just experienced, and about the Church
that had this book.

As I lay there thinking and wondering what I should do next
I heard my mom downstairs in the kitchen getting ready for work.
Without thinking, I went downstairs and told her that I had read the
Book of Mormon and wanted to learn more about it. I said I had many
questions and asked her if she would ask Mrs. Leininger to call me.
She looked very surprised but said she would.

TENDER MERCIES & LESSONS LEARNED

As I look back, after forty years, on those incredible two nights and on my first prayer that early morning, I marvel at the goodness and kindness of my Heavenly Father. I did not deserve to receive the gospel. I was a sinful, proud, vain, arrogant, sarcastic, cocky, worldly teenager. I am eternally grateful to God the Eternal Father, to his Son Jesus Christ, my Savior, and to the Holy Ghost for the witness they provided me of their existence, their love, and their willingness to forgive me and to allow me to become part of The Church of Jesus Christ of Latter-day Saints—the kingdom of God on earth.

Over the decades since then I have felt the power and love of God more times than I can count. And I have had many other marvelous experiences that show God's tender mercies for me. Yet I have never forgotten what I experienced during those two days and nights nor cease to feel eternally blessed by the gift of a sure witness of God's existence, love, power, care, and willingness to forgive me of my sins.

Nor can I ever deny that I was given, by God, a sure witness of the truthfulness of the Book of Mormon. I have since read many books and articles and heard many talks and lessons about the Book of Mormon. They have helped increase my knowledge of the book, its doctrines, stories, and lessons, and have increased my intellectual understanding of the contents of the book. Yet all of that pales in comparison to the power of the witness I received from the Spirit that November morning in 1977.

Over the years, I have also read many things that question, challenge, or attack the truthfulness of the Book of Mormon. I understand that many people, for many reasons, have difficulty accepting the Book of Mormon, the visits of the Angel Moroni, the Gold Plates, and the use of Joseph's seer stones in the translation process. I understand that many people, for many reasons, cannot or will not bring themselves to honestly read and faithfully pray about the Book of Mormon. I have known others who at one point enjoyed a testimony of the reality of God, of the truthfulness of the restored gospel, and of the Book of Mormon but who, for one reason or another, have lost that sweet testimony.

Wherever you find yourself, my dear friend, I say to you, in love and humility: I know that God lives and answers sincere prayer. I know that Jesus is the Christ and only through faith in him and his atoning sacrifice can sin be washed and burned from the soul. I know that the Book of Mormon is the word of God and a true witness of the Lord Jesus Christ. I humbly echo the words of Moroni and invite you to pray in faith to God the Eternal Father, in the name of Jesus Christ, and receive your own witness of these truths so that you too might obtain the joy and peace that God, in His tender mercy, has in store for you.

CHAPTER 2

Family & Faith Background

To provide some context for my investigation of the LDS Church before I was baptized, and the first few years of my membership in the Church, some discussion of my family and religious background may be helpful. After this Chapter, I get back to what happened after I read the Book of Mormon.

My mother, Elizabeth Stenen, was married twice before she met my father, Melvin Dollahite. My mother's mother, Katherine, was a good Irish Catholic woman who, like many of her fellow Irish Catholic immigrants of that era, had a serious problem with alcohol. Elizabeth's father, Iver Stenen, a strong and quiet man who had left his home in Norway as a teenager and stowed away on a ship to gain passage to America, spent much time away working in the shipyards.

When she was under the influence of alcohol, my grandmother abused her daughter Elizabeth. My mother ran away from home in her late teens and got married. Her first marriage, from which she had my sister, Lana, ended in divorce. She married again but her second husband had a mental illness and her second marriage was annulled. To get away from her mother and to begin a new life, my mom moved from New Jersey to California in her early twenties with her daughter.

She obtained a job at a photo finishing store, taking the place of Mel Dollahite, who was a photographer in the Naval Reserves. He had been called to active duty and was in Italy. Her boss told Elizabeth that he would need to give Mel his job back when he returned from military service. She kept hearing what a wonderful man he was, but she only thought of him as the guy who was going to take her job away from her and deny her the ability to support her daughter. But after several months, when Mel returned, the boss did not lay her off after all and Mel and Elizabeth became friends. Elizabeth was two years older than Mel and at first rebuffed his attempts to court her.

Mel had been born and raised in Oklahoma but his parents moved to Marin County California during World War II so his father could work in the shipyards building Liberty Ships for the Navy. His father was killed by a drunk driver when Mel was fourteen. The local paper ran a story about the death, mentioning that L. C. Dollahite left a wife and five children behind. An Episcopal Priest, Father Todd Ewald, read about the accident and the family and went to the Dollahite home with food and clothing and spiritual consolation. Although the Dollahites had belonged to a small Baptist church in Larkspur, they did not attend often. Father Ewald and his wife gradually developed a strong relationship with the family to the point where a couple of the children began attending Holy Innocents' Episcopal Church. My father remembers attending on his own for a time as a teenager. When Mel's mother, Mabel, died a couple of years later, Father Ewald and his wife essentially adopted Mel and his four siblings. When he was twenty years old, Mel joined the Navy.

On returning from military duty in Italy, Mel was rehired at the photo shop. He took a friendly interest in this beautiful, intelligent, strong-willed, single parent, and a paternal interest in her adorable seven-year-old daughter, to whom he quickly became a father figure. Elizabeth had been hurt and disappointed by men before, but now that he was not going to steal her job, and seeing his persistent care for her and her daughter, she found herself gradually becoming attracted to this tall, handsome, caring, and easy going man. After several months of deepening friendship, Mel and Elizabeth were married by Father Ewald at Holy Innocents on January 11, 1958.

I was born a little less than a year later on December 17, 1958. A couple of weeks after my birth, I was baptized by Father Ewald at Holy Innocents. Before my baptism, my parents were asked by Father Ewald to designate who they would like to be my godparents—those who would be responsible to assist in my spiritual upbringing in the event something happened to my parents, or if they failed in their responsibility to raise me in the Christian faith. As my godfather, my parents chose my father's younger brother, Gene, who was the most devout of his brothers and who went on to become a Deacon in our parish and later an Episcopal Priest. Father Ewald was delighted with that choice.

When my mother informed Father Ewald that she wanted her friend, Ann, to be my godmother, Father Ewald asked about Ann. She had been my mother's dearest friend since childhood. When Father Ewald inquired about her religious background, my mother told him Ann was Jewish. Father Ewald said that she could not have a Jewish woman be her son's godmother for a Christian baptism. My mom told him that Ann promised she would see to my Christian upbringing. Father Ewald said that it just was not possible to have a Jewish godmother for a Christian baptism since a godparent must be a baptized Christian who has been confirmed. My mother, being quite a strong and stubborn woman, said that if he was unwilling to allow this then I would not be baptized. Father Ewald relented and allowed Ann to be my godmother. She has continued to watch out for me and we have sometimes exchanged Christmas and Hanukkah cards.

When my parents moved to the town of Fairfax, California, a couple of years later we began attending St. Augustine's Episcopal Church. At age nine, I was asked to serve as an acolyte (altar boy) to Father Wilmington at St. Augustine's. To enable me to do so, I had to be confirmed three years earlier than was the norm in those years

(typically age twelve). I took confirmation class for a few months
and was confirmed by the laying on of hands by the Bishop at Grace
Cathedral in San Francisco.

Another important and exciting religious event in my childhood
was serving as the acolyte in assisting Father Wilmington when he
baptized my little brother, Keith, who was born when I was nine.
After repeated invitations from Father Ewald to come back to Holy
Innocents' Church, my parents decided to return to attending Holy
Innocents again even though it meant making the thirty minute drive
each way.

I served Father Ewald as an acolyte at Holy Innocents for a couple
of years, performing a number of tasks. I lit all the candles throughout
the sanctuary before the service began. I carried the large cross at the
front of the Processional that includes the altar boys, the choir, the
Deacon(s) and the Priest and goes from the back of the church to the
altar at the beginning of the service. During the service, I sat near the
altar providing whatever assistance Father Ewald needed. I assisted
him in preparing and serving communion host (unleavened wafers)
and wine to the congregants. At the end of the service, I snuffed out
the candles using a bell-shaped silver extinguisher (or snuffer), and
carried the cross at the front of the Recessional out of the sanctuary.

My mother was in the Altar Guild, a women's service group in
the church, at one point serving as its president. The Altar Guild was
responsible for cleaning and preparing the sacred communion vessels
(silver chalice for wine and trays for the host or unleavened wafers);
insuring proper liturgical colors for all hangings on the altar and
lectern (from which the Bible was read); and caring for the priest's,
deacons' and acolyte's liturgical vestments (robes). My father was a lay
reader in the church which meant that, at a certain point in the service,
he went up to an ornate lectern and read selected passages from a large

Bible. I remember that each time he finished reading the few verses that were assigned for that day he said in a formal voice, "This is the word of the Lord."

Whereas St. Augustine's had more of a "low church" service, Holy Innocents had a "high church" or traditional approach to the weekly Eucharist (Communion) services. Thus, it had much of the formal religious pageantry of the traditional Catholic Latin mass including the use of incense, chanting in Latin, and so forth. Although the Eucharist service was very formal, Father Ewald liked to have the congregants applaud for a particularly well-done hymn sung by the choir, even though this was highly unusual and caused a little consternation among some of the more traditional older ladies. For me, the only less-than-positive things about the "high church" nature of the Eucharist service were (a) the great amount of smoke generated by the burning incense, (b) the chanting in Latin that I did not understand, (c) the long (to me) sermons that went over my head, and, to my little-boy mind, (d) the seemingly interminable time spent kneeling on the padded stools during the prayers.

SPORTS: THE RELIGION OF MY YOUTH

While family and church dominated my childhood, in my youth I began to spend increasing time in sports with friends. In fact, I was so devoted to excellence in athletics that you could say sports became my religion. My focus was on becoming the best athlete I could become. I played organized baseball, basketball, football, and tennis in addition to a number of other sports and games on an informal basis. I also spent many hours each day playing and hanging out with my close friends. To me, friendship was as important as sports. During my teen years, my focus was on becoming a professional tennis player. If things had gone the way I was imagining they would, I would have traveled the world playing tennis—and I would have wanted to have my friends with me.

Two additional aspects of my upbringing will help in better understanding my conversion to and membership in the Church of Jesus Christ of Latter-day Saints. One was the feeling I had of being an outsider looking in that came both from moving frequently and also from not being a member of the dominant faith in my community (Catholicism). The other was a sense of inferiority I developed from the socioeconomic status my family had in relation to the number of very wealthy families surrounding us.

Because our family moved seven times within the small town I was raised in, I was often the "new kid on the block" and found myself on the outside looking in. I tried to maintain my friendships with kids from "the old neighborhood" but that was often difficult and I had to make new friends. This was not always easy since the kids were not always welcoming toward me as the new kid and I sometimes felt like the proverbial "fifth wheel" in a group of friends. The fact that I was good at sports helped make these transitions somewhat easier as I made friends through the teams I played on.

Because I was raised an Episcopalian, while the majority of my friends and classmates were Catholic, I also felt like an outsider looking in. The Catholic kids had a sense of identity and a sense of community, not unlike what many LDS kids experience as members of the Church. This came from the lingo my friends used and the schools they attended (St. Rita Catholic school). This was never a major issue and no one was ever rude to me because I was not Catholic. It was just a sense of not being a full-fledged member of something important to many people around me. But I was invited to participate in Catholic

Youth Organization basketball by my friend Rob Guidi, and this
helped me feel more a part of things.

My sense of inferiority also came from the fact that our family
was merely middle class and Marin County was decidedly upper
crust. In fact, Marin was (and remains) one of the wealthiest counties
in the nation. As a young kid, we lived in a tiny house in downtown
Fairfax and I had the run of the downtown area which was wonderful.
Then, for several years during my elementary school years, we moved
into an apartment complex on the outskirts of the Oak Manor
development—one of the nicest neighborhoods in Fairfax. All my
friends lived in nice homes with yards and basketball hoops in their
driveways. Again, no one ever taunted me as a "poor kid" but we just
did not have what others had. My mother tried her best to provide
me with what the other kids had in the way of clothing and sports
equipment but it was clear that they had more and better things and
experiences.

Then, in high school, when I began taking tennis seriously, I
found myself in an entirely new and extremely wealthy environment.
In many ways, tennis is a sport for the rich. Equipment, lessons, club
memberships, travel, and clothing are very pricey. In order to develop
my skills, I needed to be able to play year-round which meant playing
on indoor courts. The only indoor courts around were in Larkspur at
the Mt. Tam Tennis Club. There was no way my family could afford
to buy a membership which cost thousands of dollars to join and
hundreds of dollars each month. But in high school, with the income
from my job at the movie theater, I was fortunate to be able to barely
afford a "junior membership" which was only $100 a month.

The first time I drove my 1970 Chevy Impala into the parking lot
at the Mt. Tam Tennis Club, I noticed that nearly every vehicle was a
foreign luxury car (I parked between a Mercedes 500SL and a Porsche

911 Targa). It quickly became apparent that I had entered a different world. People at "the Club" were very comfortable with their great wealth. Most were not really aware that I was from the other side of the economic tracks but just assumed I could easily afford all the things they could in the way of equipment, lessons, clothing, meals, travel, and so forth. A few folks were quite generous with me and only rarely did someone make an outright comment about my economic status, but the easy confidence that seems to come with wealth was palpable.

When I dated girls from the Club I found myself driving into neighborhoods in Belvedere and Tiburon that exhibited a degree of conspicuous consumption I could hardly believe. When I drove up in my late model Chevy and their parents found out I was from Fairfax (a little hippie town) and my father was a police officer and I was one of the "Junior Members" (a euphemism for the kids from families who could not afford to have a full membership), they were not impressed and some let me know that I did not really measure up.

In my early youth, religion quickly moved down my list of interests and priorities, until it disappeared completely from my life. And although I was never poor, I often felt like an outsider looking in on the life that the truly privileged people lived.

Since sports and friends came to dominate my life and outlook, I will try to convey a sense for how important athletics and friends became for me. I had always had a "best friend" growing up as well as other close friends. Probably because our family moved so often and because my sister was nine years older and my brother was nine years younger than me, I felt a strong need for close friendships. We lived in seven different homes in Fairfax, a town of only 7,000 people. Because of our frequent moves, I had four or five different best friends in my life until I joined the Church. I also had a close circle of other friends and associates from work, school, and sports. Like many of my friends, I also usually had a steady girlfriend.

Most of my friendships involved sports. The kind of bonding that occurs between guys who play with and against each other is not unlike the bonds that are forged in battle—the Band of Brothers idea that started out as a military metaphor but is now also an athletic one. Indeed, the toughest dilemmas of my youth revolved around conflicts between the deep desire to win in all competitions and the even deeper desire to maintain friendships with those I was competing against.

Every summer my friends and I played sports from morning till evening every day of the week. We played pick-up games of baseball, basketball, and football. We played tennis and ping-pong. We went bowling, swimming, fishing, and hunting. My best friend, Rob Guidi, and I played ping-pong all summer in his backyard. We set up the ping-pong table on the lawn and, dressed only in our cutoff shorts, we pounded balls and dove all over the place trying to get well-hit balls.

Rob and I also played "curb ball," where you throw a tennis ball against the curb trying to hit the top corner and thus ricochet the ball flying over the fence behind the thrower. I built a basketball backboard in shop and my dad and I put it up in the little, rocky area between our apartment building and the one next to ours. Rob built a backboard and his dad put it up in their garage where we would play H.O.R.S.E. all day, shooting baskets off the wall and over the rafters.

Life was sports and friends. Sports and friends were life.

When I was about ten, Rob invited me to play on his basketball team that was sponsored by the Catholic Youth Organization (CYO). I played CYO ball for St. Rita Catholic Church for a couple of years. I traveled with Rob and our other teammates to many Catholic churches in Marin County playing games in their "church gyms." Along with many of the boys, I wore a St. Christopher medal on a chain around my neck during games. St. Christopher is the patron saint of travel and protection. Although this was a Catholic thing, my parents got me a St. Christopher medal as well. Some of the more devout boys would kiss their medal for luck before shooting a free throw. Others would cross themselves (make the sign of the cross) before shooting their free throws.

The best player in the league, Hoss Parnow, had a particularly innovative free throw ritual. He would bounce the ball three times and then toss it up a few feet out in front of him with a great deal of backspin. While the ball was in the air he would cross himself and then catch the ball that had landed and bounced back to him. Then he would shoot. I thought it was the coolest of all pre-shot rituals. Because he almost never missed I thought there was serious power in Catholic athletic rituals!

Of the various sports I played, baseball was the one at which I was best. I began playing Little League when I was nine and played organized ball until just before beginning high school. I had a lot of success as a pitcher, one year having a record of thirteen wins and no losses. In one game, I struck out every batter I faced (fifteen batters in five innings). The coach of the opposing team prevented me from pitching a perfect game (striking out all eighteen batters in a six-inning game) when he refused to have his team bat in the sixth inning, claiming it was too dark although there was plenty of light. My coach, Joe Lordan, later told me he learned that the opposing coach's son held the Little League record for most strike outs in a game (seventeen) and he did not want me to break his son's record. Later, Coach Lordan told me he thought I could pitch in the majors (the highest professional baseball league) and this was a dream of mine for a few years until another sport, tennis, came along and captured my heart.

When I was about twelve, my mom decided that I should play tennis since it was a sport I could enjoy throughout my life while I would probably not play the other sports beyond high school. At first I thought tennis was a "sissy sport" since they wore little white shorts and said things like, "15–love" and "15–all." One day my mom gave me a tennis racket and some balls and told me to go play for two hours and not to come home until I had. I went to the tennis courts in downtown Fairfax and sat on the wooden bench fuming at my mom for making me play this "sissy sport."

As I sat there, I noticed a muscular, tanned guy teaching a bunch of women in short skirts how to play. They were all flirting with him saying things like, "Babe, could you show me how to hit my backhand?" and "Babe, is this how I should hit my serve?" Since I had just gotten to the age when I stopped thinking girls were stupid and was beginning to think they were pretty cute, I was impressed with this scene. It was obvious that "Babe" (I later learned his name was Babe Ramponi) was clearly not a sissy, and the ladies clearly thought he was worth paying a lot of attention to. I began thinking that maybe tennis was not such a bad sport after all.

Babe came over to me and asked me my name. I told him and he said, "Dave, if you will shag balls for me for a while I'll give you a lesson after I'm done with my group lesson." So, I picked up balls for Babe for the next half an hour or so (hearing a lot of "Babe, will you show me how to hold my racket?" kind of talk). Then Babe gave me my first tennis lesson and invited me to take lessons with him. Thus, my lifelong love of tennis began.

Not long after this I played my first tennis tournament. I got killed in my first match (6–0, 6–0). After I played, I watched the best player in the tournament, Jim Lowell, beat the kid he was playing pretty easily. Jim and I had played basketball and football against each other in Junior High. We went and got a Slurpee at 7-11 and I learned that his father was a great tennis player and coach and Jim was a member of a tennis club and had private lessons several times a week.

At about this age, I choked on piece of steak while sitting at our family dinner table one night. I tried to tell my parents I was choking but no sound came from my mouth. Finally, my mother saw my face turn red and screamed to my father that I was choking. He began pounding on my back (this was before the Heimlich maneuver was invented). He pounded for a couple minutes but the piece of meat did not become dislodged—in fact it seemed to get more lodged in my throat.

Then something extremely interesting happened. While my father continued to pound on my back and my mother screamed, everything became very quiet and every event in my entire short life literally passed before my eyes like a video on high-speed fast forward. I saw things that I knew I had experienced when I was very young but had forgotten. One event was riding a little red bicycle down the steep road from the Pavilion in Fairfax and having a bad fall where I skinned my knees badly. Finally, the piece of meat flew out of my mouth and I began coughing.

When I had recovered from this I told my parents about seeing my entire life pass before me and I asked if I had ever crashed a little red bike on the Pavilion hill. They said that yes, when I was only two or three years old I had a red bike with training wheels and had a bad crash on that hill. Because of this experience, all my life I have known that everything we do is "recorded" in our minds. When I hear the phrase "my life passed before me" or "passed before my eyes" I know that people are describing a literal experience, and when I read in the scriptures that we will be judged for all our actions and all our thoughts, I know that those are faithfully and accurately recorded by every person's mind.

In my freshman year of high school, I played basketball on the freshman basketball team with Jim Lowell and he and I became good friends. We also played doubles together on the tennis team, going undefeated and helping Sir Francis Drake High School win its first league championship ever. I continued to play baseball, basketball, and tennis until my sophomore year of high school when I decided to focus on tennis. I joined a tennis club with indoor courts that had less expensive "junior memberships" for kids whose parents could not afford to join "the Club." I had to work as many hours as possible at the Tamalpais Theatre to pay for this.

In my senior year, a bunch of guys with whom I had played basketball for many years talked me into trying out for the varsity basketball team. I had not played my sophomore and junior years so that I could focus on tennis year-round. They convinced me it would be fun to have one more year with all the guys. Basketball was "king" at Drake High and I doubted that I would make the team but I did try out and barely made the team. I spent most of the year "riding the pine" (sitting on the bench) and not playing except for "garbage minutes" at the end of the game.

In addition to playing basketball together our senior years, and playing on the tennis team, Jim and I often double dated, he with his girlfriend, Cheri, and me with my girlfriend, Anne—a devout Lutheran. Jim and I often talked about playing college tennis and traveling to Europe together to play professional tennis and then, at some point, opening up a tennis club together.

In my senior year, I developed a recurring staph infection in my foot that I periodically had to have lanced and drained and the doctor made me not play for weeks at a time. The doctor told me that because of my high arches and the pounding that competitive tennis demanded, if I continued to play so much tennis I would likely have this condition throughout my life. This recurring injury seriously hampered my ability to play at my best because I could not move well on the court and was rusty from not playing while my foot healed. I lost a couple close matches to highly ranked players that I may have beaten had I been healthy. Had I won those matches, I likely would have been offered scholarships to play tennis at college. But those offers went to other players.

In our junior year, I played number one singles and Jim played number two. The coach gave me the Most Valuable Player award. In our senior year, my foot injury plagued me throughout the season so Jim played number one and I played number two and three. We both thought Jim would be given the Most Valuable Player award, but the coach again gave it to me because I only lost one match and he said I had been a positive influence on the team.

In the summer after we both graduated from high school in 1977, Jim and I played each other in the finals of the Boys 18s in the same tournament in which I had played and lost my first match (the Marin Independent Journal Championships). Jim had been looking forward to wining the Boys 18s division of this prestigious tournament since he was a kid. In our regular practice sessions, Jim had beaten me about twenty times in a row that summer. But in the finals, I played well enough to beat him and win the championship. Jim was so upset that he went out and got drunk that night and stepped on a broken bottle and got a bad cut on his foot. The next day, Jim was hung-over and limping so much from his foot injury that we lost in the doubles final against a team that otherwise we likely would have beaten easily.

This turned out to be the last tournament that I played as a junior. A few weeks later Jim went off to play college tennis at the University of Oregon (eventually playing number one for them) and I went to a local junior college and did not play competitive tennis. I was quite upset by this since it seemed that all the years of hard work and dedication to my sport were going up in smoke. My dreams of playing college tennis, playing throughout Europe, making a bunch of money, and being a famous tennis player were dashed.

TENDER MERCIES & LESSONS LEARNED

The Lord blessed me with great parents who taught me the importance of being honest, working hard, and obeying the law. Both of my parents worked hard every day and provided me with the necessities of life and a number of niceties as well. Although we were never rich, or close to it, I never felt like I would not have enough for my needs and I always knew that my parents would do their best to provide me with as much as they could toward what I thought I really needed to succeed in sports.

They provided me with a moral and religious upbringing that laid the foundation for my future religious involvement and commitment. Although I chose to disassociate myself from the faith my parents raised me in, I am grateful my parents took the time and made the effort for our family to be involved in the Episcopal Church.

Although my mother was raised in a very difficult family situation with an alcoholic mother who became violent when drunk, my mother never abused substances and thus provided me with a stable and positive family environment. And although my father lost his parents when he was fairly young, he never turned to any number of addictions or negative behavior patterns that could easily have been possible. I am grateful that Father Ewald and his wife informally adopted my father and his siblings after the death of their parents since I am sure this provided them with much needed stability and direction.

Although their marriage was not perfect, my parents made a great partnership and provided me with a model of stable marriage and working out issues with remaining true to marital vows. My parents never beat me—although one time, when I said something especially rude to my mother, my father did slap me across the face. Since he never hit me otherwise, this served to impress on me how important it was to him that I respect my mother.

The Lord blessed me with great friends who meant a lot to me while growing up. My friends were not always a perfect example to me in what I should and should not do but they were great guys who I love and appreciate. In many ways, I had an idyllic childhood, full of fun and friends, and security. My friends and I were able to play from morning till bed time (except that pesky part about having to go to school) and I never had to experience the tragic loss of a dear friend.

The Lord also blessed me with some athletic skill that has brought me much enjoyment and given me some degree of confidence in life. I was also blessed with great coaches in all the sports I played. These men mentored me and taught me many useful lessons. Being involved in sports taught me how to work hard to improve, the ability to deal with challenges and setbacks, and the willingness and confidence to take chances in life.

One of the great joys in my life was when our championship Little League team, the Fairfax Shell (the Shell gas station that sponsored the team) team of 1972–73, got together for a 30-year reunion back in Marin County. We honored our three coaches, Joe Lordan, Tony Damato, and Manny Barretta, for the great example they were in our young lives. I made the trip from Utah for this reunion and enjoyed every minute of it. As a devout Mormon, I did not drink any of the abundant supply of alcohol provided. All the other guys were drinking from the bar during the mingling before the meal began. A number were already a bit tipsy when it was time to start the dinner. I was asked to offer the grace on the meal and there were some shouts of "Amen!" during the prayer. When I finished, the guys broke into applause, something I have not experienced before or since. I must admit that I was even more thrilled to hear Coach Lordan say he thought of all the young men he had coached over more than thirty-five years, he thought I had the best chance to make it as a big-league pitcher.

My recurring foot problems and the fact I was not offered scholarships to play college tennis turned out to be providential. Had I been off somewhere playing college tennis with the prospects of playing professionally in reach, I doubt that I would have read the Book of Mormon and been willing to make the kinds of dramatic life changes I soon made. The recurring staph infections in my foot, and the athletic setbacks they precipitated, allowed me to be prepared for the radical changes in lifestyle, friendships, and life goals that membership in the Church of Jesus Christ of Latter-day Saints would require.

Because we lived in several places in the town I grew up in, I learned to be comfortable moving around which has stood me in good stead since joining the Church. I have moved a number of times beginning with my move to BYU, then on to New England for my mission (which involved many moves), then back to BYU, then to the University of Minnesota for graduate school, then to North Carolina for my first university position, then to BYU to join the faculty there. Many of my high school friends have basically remained in the same area we grew up in and I am grateful I have been able to move to follow the promptings of the Holy Ghost without difficulty.

CHAPTER 3

"This is a great church!"

It was now Friday, the morning after I finished reading the Book of
Mormon. Having asked my mom to tell Mrs. Leininger that I had
read the Book of Mormon, I then had another very strange thought:
"I should go and get a haircut." My hair was the typical length for
a teenage male in 1977—way over my ears and as far down past my
collar as my mom would let me have it. As was the case for many other
kids in that era, throughout my teenage years my mom and I had had
many arguments about the length of my hair—her always wanting it
shorter and me always wanting it longer.

Thus, the idea that, on my own, I should get a haircut was
completely foreign to me. But I responded to the feeling and went to
my barber, Fran, and told him I would like "a real haircut." When
he asked me how short I wanted it I said I did not know but I would
let him know when to stop. Fran gave me a funny look and started
cutting. He cut my hair to just below my ears and asked if that was
good. I said no I wanted it shorter. He raised his eyebrows and said,
"Are you sure?" When I nodded, he cut it to about mid-ear. He asked
if that was short enough and I said I needed it shorter. He said, "What
has happened to you?"

I responded, "I really don't know. I read the Book of Mormon and
I just feel like I need to have shorter hair."

He said, "How short do you want it?"

I said, "Well, not like a military buzz. Ah, I know. Like a
businessman; yeah, like a businessman."

He said, "Do you mean above your ears and off your collar?"

I said, "Yes."

He said, "Are you sure?" I said I was. So, he continued cutting.

I had no idea why I felt a need to cut my hair. The only Mormon male I knew about was Donny Osmond (from the Donny & Marie show on TV) and his hair was fairly long—well over his ears. So, still not understanding why, I walked out of the barber shop with the shortest hair I had had in many years. It felt strange and yet, somehow, I just knew it was what I was supposed to do.

That night, about midnight, Mrs. Leininger called me. She said my mother had told her I had read the Book of Mormon and that she was happy to try to answer any questions I had. She apologized for calling so late, saying that she was in charge of a "youth conference" and had just gotten home from a day of meetings and activities.

I had many questions including: Why did Jesus have to suffer and die for our sins? Why was there evil in the world? What happens after death? My biggest question was what caused the feelings I had had while reading the Book of Mormon but I did not know how to describe the feelings or ask the question so I never asked. I knew it was from God but still had not made the connection that I had felt the Holy Ghost.

She happily answered all my questions and shared a number of ideas about the Book of Mormon and about Jesus. She seemed genuinely and enthusiastically happy to spend that time telling me of her faith. We talked for nearly three hours. I was stunned that a woman who was older than my mother was willing to talk with a teenager about religion for so long in the middle of the night.

More than once during the conversation she invited me to church the next day. I told her that I wanted to come to church soon but that I felt I needed to read the Book of Mormon several more times before then so I would be more likely to understand the priest's sermon. As a kid, I had never really understood the priest's sermons or the reading from the King James Version of the Bible that my father and other lay readers did.

So, when I thought of what the Mormon service would be like, I pictured men reading from a large copy of the Book of Mormon lying on an ornate lectern. I assumed that what the priest said would go way over my head and I wanted to understand what I would hear at the Mormon Church. She told me there were many Mormons who had never read the Book of Mormon all the way through and that I would have no problem understanding the talks at church. But I told her I just felt like I should read the Book of Mormon several times before coming to church.

Again, she urged me to come to church the next day, telling me it was a special meeting—a "youth conference" and there was a "special speaker" from Salt Lake City and that it would be a "fast and testimony meeting." Something about the word fast appealed to me. I remembered feeling like the church services I attended as a kid went on forever, so the idea of a "fast meeting" appealed to me. I finally accepted her invitation to attend church the next day. She said the meeting was at 9:00 a.m., described where the church building was (about a thirty minute drive), and gave me directions to get there.

After getting a few hours of sleep, I woke up on Saturday, November 26, 1977, and got dressed to go to church—it would be my first time in any church building in about six years. I had a blue corduroy suit that I had worn to our high school homecoming dance the year before which I had not put on since then. I borrowed one of my dad's white shirts and a tie and drove to the San Rafael Stake Center. [3]

I parked, got out of my car, and walked up to a side door of the church where I saw Mrs. Leininger waiting for me. She recognized me because a number of times I had gone to pick my mom up from work. I was usually in my tennis clothes which often included a headband to keep my hair out of my eyes. She looked very surprised at my appearance and said, "Dave! You look just like an Elder!" I asked what an "Elder" was and she said, "Oh, you'll see."

As we walked into the building I expected to see crucifixes, candles, statues, and all the other things I associated with a religious building. Mrs. Leininger brought me into a large room with a full-sized basketball court and a large stage that she called the "Cultural Hall." Many rows of folding chairs were facing the stage and on the stage was a podium with several people sitting in chairs. She led me to a seat near center court. I noticed that nearly all those in attendance were teenagers — and a number of them were attractive young ladies. Remembering that most of those who attended the church I was raised in were elderly women, I thought, "This is a great church!"

As I looked around I still did not see any of the things I associated with a religious building. No crosses, no altars, no candles, no statues, and no pews with the fold-down stools for kneeling. I looked for stained glass windows, but all I saw were two nice clean glass basketball backboards with brand new nets. This felt very familiar and comfortable for me since I had played basketball all my life. I thought again, "This is a great church!"

---

3. A Stake Center is the church building from which the Stake President (analogous to a Catholic Bishop) administers an LDS Stake (analogous to a Catholic diocese).

I was waiting for the organ to begin playing and the acolytes, priest, deacon, and choir to parade into the meeting dressed in robes. But instead a man in a suit simply stood up and began conducting the meeting. We sang, someone said a prayer, and then someone introduced a "Brother Brenton Yorgason" as the special speaker from Utah. He spoke for about an hour and told a number of wonderful and often humorous stories. There was a lot of laughing and to me this seemed unusual for church. The church I was raised in did not have much laughter in it. I even understood almost everything he said. I thought yet again, "This is a great church!"

So, I was feeling really good about my experience until suddenly it occurred to me that I had forgotten to bring money for the offering or collection. I knew that after the sermon they passed the collection plate to receive the monetary offering from the parishioners. As a kid, if I had forgotten to bring money I always felt awkward when the plate was passed to me and I had to just pass it to the next person. So, I turned to Mrs. Leininger and whispered, "I'm sorry, I feel really bad, but I forgot to bring money for the offering."

She said, "For the what?"

I said, "For the offering. You know, when they pass the plate around."

She said, "Oh, we don't do that."

I thought, "Wow, you get to sit in a gym with people your own age, and listen to funny stories, and you don't have to pay anything. This is a great church!"

But, more than any of these thoughts, what struck me again and again was that I was feeling the same wonderful and strange—though now more familiar—feeling I had had while reading the Book of Mormon and while praying. I did not understand what this feeling was but I knew it was from God.

After "Brother Yorgason" finished speaking, one by one a large number of the teenagers stood up and spoke about their spiritual feelings about Jesus, Joseph Smith, the Book of Mormon, and other religious ideas. Most began by saying something like, "I want to bear my testimony." I was impressed with the courage and commitment of these young people to stand up in front of so many other people their age and share their most deeply personal thoughts, feelings, and experiences.

Many of those who spoke seemed close to my age and included several very clean-cut guys and a number of the prettiest girls I had ever seen who glowed with a kind of light I had not seen before—except perhaps in my devoutly Lutheran girlfriend from high school. Many of the youth, including some athletic looking young men, wept openly without shame or apology. This—having males showing such emotion—was a completely new and wonderful experience for me. The only time I had ever "cried in public" was when I watched the movie Brian's Song on TV in our living room and I tried as hard as I could to not let my parents know about the lump in my throat and the tears welling up in my eyes. But since my experience the morning before, when I had wept openly for the first time, I felt that I knew what they were experiencing.

When all those who wanted to speak had done so we sang a song, someone prayed, and the meeting was over. We all stood up and Mrs. Leininger turned to me and said, "Well, Dave, what did you think?"

I heard myself say, "It was incredible! How do I join your church?"

She smiled widely and said, "Really?!" When I nodded enthusiastically she turned toward the corner of the hall and motioned for someone to come over. As I looked to where she was beckoning, I saw two young men in suits and ties with really short hair and some kind of name tags on their coats striding toward me with very big grins on their faces. It seemed like they had been waiting for this signal.

They came over and Mrs. Leininger introduced us; Elders Hawkes and Christensen each shook my hand very vigorously in the "adult way" (not how my friends and fellow athletes shook hands with other ball players). I had never seen guys with such short hair (about the length of mine I later realized). I thought they were the funniest looking guys I had ever seen. But something about them was extremely appealing to me.

At one point in our conversation, I asked them, "Do you guys actually go around dressed like that in public?"

They just smiled and said, "You bet!" and asked me if they could teach me about the Church. I said that would be great. We arranged for me to go to the Leininger's home and for the "Elders" to come and teach me. Before going to the Leininger's home I was invited to have lunch with Brother and Sister Yorgason. I guess the Leiningers had told Brother Yorgason about me and he and his wife were very kind and friendly to me. They told me they had several children back in Utah and they also had a six-week-old baby girl in a bassinet on the floor.

After lunch, I followed the Leiningers to their home in my car for my first gospel lesson from the missionaries.

TENDER MERCIES & LESSONS LEARNED

During these first couple of days of my experience with the Lord and His restored gospel, the Spirit whispered repeatedly and somewhat insistently to me. I had no known prior experience with things of the Spirit and the Lord was very kind and patient in helping me to recognize and heed the spiritual promptings He was providing to me. He was schooling me in the importance of listening to promptings, however unusual they might be.

It was indeed a tender mercy that the Lord sent LoDonna and Ray Leininger into my life at a time when I was willing and able to receive their wonderful influence. I do not believe the Lord has had more willing, dedicated, generous, and loving member missionaries than the Leiningers, and I was the grateful beneficiary of their goodness.

As I look back now on Sister Leininger's willingness to do member missionary work from midnight to 3:00 a.m. on that particular night, I am even more grateful. She must have had a long and stressful day dealing with hundreds of youth and all the arrangements for the conference. This must have followed weeks of planning the conference. And she was to begin another full day of the conference in just a few short hours. Yet not once during our conversation did I get the sense that she would rather be doing anything else than talking to me and answering my many questions. That Sister Leininger would be willing to spend three hours on the phone with the son of her coworker is a testament of her love of the Lord and His restored gospel.

I find it curious that the Lord would inspire me to get a haircut even before I attended any church meetings. At that point, I had never seen LDS missionaries and if I had I would have thought they were very funny looking. Indeed, when I saw them the next day that is exactly what I thought—even though by then I looked a lot like them and had a deep desire to go and do exactly what they were doing as soon as possible.

As I think about my background, experiences, and personality, I do not think I could have come to a better first meeting of the Church. I would like to believe that the power of the witness I was given by the Lord about the truthfulness of the Book of Mormon would have allowed me to weather a less-than-wonderful first church meeting. However, it was a tender mercy from the Lord that my first church meeting involved sitting on center court and hearing the gospel taught by someone, like Brother Yorgason, with deep spiritual insight and a wonderful ability to tell uplifting, edifying, and humorous stories and then to hear a number of wonderful youth bear testimonies.

A couple of years later, when I was a missionary, I found it interesting how often the first time our investigators came to church was a fast and testimony meeting. I used to hope and pray that members would bear testimony of simple truths and not get into the "mysteries" and I would get nervous when certain members would decide to bear their testimony and cringe when certain things were said. Although sometimes investigators said they thought the meeting was weird, I was surprised how often our investigators thought that testimony meeting was great.

Over the years, I have noted how often converts I have met or heard bear testimony have mentioned that their first church meeting was a testimony meeting. It seems the Lord often likes to have those of His children who are investigating the Church to hear testimony borne by the Saints. Even when unusual or potentially embarrassing things are said, the power of the Spirit carries pure testimony to the hearts of listeners.

Brenton Yorgason helped me get in contact with Wayne Pearce, the tennis coach at Brigham Young University (BYU), and arranged for me to go to Provo to work out with the team. Over the years, Brent and I became friends. In fact, he obtained his doctorate from the same department in which I obtained my bachelor's and master's degrees and in which I am now a professor (BYU School of Family Life). Brother Yorgason introduced me to Alan Osmond who has since become a friend as well.

The Yorgasons' daughter Jennifer, who was a six-week-old infant in the bassinet on the floor next to Sister Yorgason, grew up and attended BYU and for two years worked with me as a graduate student at BYU about twenty-seven years later. I was the chair of her master's thesis committee and we have published a scholarly article on religious conversations between parents and their adolescent children based on interviews I did with Christian, Jewish, and Muslim families in New England and Northern California.[4] It is a small world when you are a Latter-day Saint.

---

4. americanfamiliesoffaith.byu.edu/Content/pdf/Youth%20and%20
Religion/S_48%20Talking%20About%20Religion%20JAR%20article.pdf

CHAPTER 4

"What is this feeling?"

I sat on the sofa in the Leininger's beautiful home surrounded by
Mr. and Mrs. Leininger, Elder Hawkes, Elder Christensen, and a
couple of the Leiningers' adult children. There was a strong feeling of
expectation and enthusiasm in the room. I learned that Elder Hawkes
and Elder Christensen, who both grew up on potato farms in Idaho,
were spending two years of their lives, at their own expense, sharing
their faith with others. They told me they went around knocking on
doors trying to find people to talk to.

My only experience with door-to-door religious preaching was
when one day, a couple years before, a couple of Jehovah's Witnesses
came by our home. When they told me they wanted to talk about the
Bible with me, I got rid of them as quickly as I could. I do not think
I was particularly polite about it either. I thought if these two young
men had knocked on my front door before I had read the Book of
Mormon I would certainly have tried to quickly get rid of them as
well. They were the most unusual young men I had ever met. These
Idaho farm boys looked, spoke, and acted unlike anyone I knew. Yet
in the same way that I now wanted to become more like Jesus Christ, I
somehow wanted to become like these missionaries.

As the Elders taught me, one or another of the members of
the Leininger family would jump in and teach an idea or share an
experience or share their "testimony" of what was being taught. Each
person was on the edge of his or her seat and filled with enthusiasm for
what they were teaching. I was amazed that these successful, happy,
and kind people all seemed so excited to teach me about their faith. It

seemed to me like they would rather be doing what they were doing than anything else.

The missionaries were both very knowledgeable about the Bible and the Book of Mormon and were both humble and yet enthusiastic about their faith. They had ready answers for all of my questions — and I had many. And it seemed that everyone deferred to these two young men — even Mr. Leininger, who was a pediatrician and, from what Mrs. Leininger had told me, was a "Counselor in the Stake Presidency" (at the time I didn't know what that meant).

The missionaries had a bound set of pictures called a "flip-chart" that they used to illustrate what they were teaching me. They told me the story about how Joseph Smith had been searching for which church to join and had prayed to learn from God which church he should join. Everything I was being told was new and different from anything I had heard before but somehow it all made sense to me. But more interesting to me was that at various points during our conversation I felt the same strange yet wonderful feeling I had felt while reading the Book of Mormon, during my prayer, and when hearing Brother Yorgason and others speak at the youth conference. I somehow knew this feeling was from God, but I did not know what it was called or why I only felt it at certain times.

Then an incredible thing happened. I was wondering what the feeling could be when the missionary who was speaking stopped mid-sentence, closed his flip-chart, looked me in the eye and said, "Dave, what you are feeling right now is the Holy Ghost telling you that what we are teaching you is true. That is what you felt when you read the Book of Mormon and at church. The Lord wants you to be baptized into His Church. Will you be baptized two weeks from today?"

I was astounded! This guy I had just met, who was only a little older than me, had read my mind and, somehow, he knew that I was feeling something and had felt it before. There was no possible way he could have known that unless God had told him. To me this was a miracle.

I said, "Yes I will! And then can I go and do what you are doing?" Remember that when I finished reading the Book of Mormon, during my prayer, I had glimpses of myself teaching people about Jesus and the Book of Mormon; I knew I would be doing that and I wanted to get started with it as soon as possible.

The Elders looked extremely happy and very surprised at the same time. They said they were thrilled that I wanted to be baptized but explained that I would need to wait for at least a year before I could be a missionary. I said that I did not want to wait for a year but wanted to go right away. They told me I needed to be a member of the Church for a year so that I could learn the gospel and prepare to enter the temple before my mission.

I was very disappointed that I could not begin my mission immediately, but I accepted that I needed to learn more about the things I would be teaching. So, I said, "Okay. What should I do to prepare myself to be the best missionary possible?"

One of the Elders said, "You should go to BYU and take Book of Mormon, Bible, and missionary prep classes."

I said, "Okay. What is BYU?"

He said, "It is a Mormon university in Utah."

I said, "Okay. Where is Utah?"

He said, "It is in the Rocky Mountains."

I said, "Where are the Rocky Mountains?" I knew they were, like the rest of the country, somewhere east of California. But I really had no idea exactly where they were. Then I said, "Okay, I'll go to BYU to prepare for my mission. How do I get in?"

Mrs. Leininger said she would get me an application and Mr. Leininger said that perhaps I could get a tennis scholarship and said he would ask Brenton Yorgason to contact the tennis coach at BYU to arrange for me to try out with the team. He also said he would write a letter of recommendation for me to get into BYU. This was good because my high school GPA was only 2.2 and my first semester at College of Marin (a junior college) was a straight C average.

That day, the missionaries taught me another lesson or two, I had dinner with the Leiningers, and there was a "fireside" that evening (Brother Yorgason spoke again). President Leininger did speak with Brother Yorgason and he said he would make contact with the coach of the BYU tennis team to arrange for me to go to BYU and work out with the team to see if I could obtain a scholarship. The missionaries said they would teach me a lesson (there were six) every couple of days or so between now and my baptism. They also invited me to attend "Family Home Evening" with the young adults on Monday evening and they invited me to play basketball at the Stake Center that Thursday evening.

TENDER MERCIES & LESSONS LEARNED

The Lord was very kind to bless me with an outpouring of the Holy Ghost of such magnitude that I could not help but know it was from God. To receive this outpouring several times in the first few days of my involvement with the Restored Church was a great blessing. I have since learned that what I experienced is fairly rare. In the mission field, I worked with many people who were much more spiritual, righteous, and well-prepared for the gospel than I was, yet who did not receive spiritual manifestations nearly to the extent of those that I was blessed with.

To be able to hear the gospel in the home of an active LDS family like the Leiningers was a great blessing. On my mission, I learned that the most effective way to teach the gospel was in the home of an active, faithful LDS family. My own family has had the opportunity to have the missionaries into our home to teach the gospel to investigators. I wish every LDS family would pray mightily for the opportunity to teach someone in their home.

The Lord also blessed me with superb missionaries. Elder Hawkes and Elder Christensen were both humble, spiritual, obedient missionaries who knew the gospel and the scriptures extremely well. Since they were the only missionaries I knew, I naturally assumed that all missionaries were that way. It was not until my own mission that I learned there is great variety of the levels of preparation, dedication, and commitment to obedience among missionaries. From the moment I met these two great young men I worked as hard as I could to become as much like them as possible before my mission.

CHAPTER 5

Efforts to Talk Me Out of Baptism

I drove home full of excitement about what I had learned and experienced and committed to do. I was going to be baptized in two weeks, was going to BYU to work out with the tennis team, I was going to go to BYU in the fall, and I was going to go on a mission a year after I was baptized.

I arrived home at about 10 p.m. and found my parents watching television. My mom asked me, "Where have you been all day?"

I said, "At church!"

She said, "What? You've been gone since morning and it's after 10!" I explained about the various meetings and meals and missionary lessons and fireside. My mom sighed and asked, "So, what did you think?"

I said, "It was incredible! I loved it! I'm going to be baptized in two weeks!"

"What! You certainly are not."

"Yes, I am." I said.

"No, you are not joining that church in two weeks. You don't know anything about that religion, much less your own religion, or any other religion. So here is what you are going to do. You are going to take a year and study the Episcopal Church, the Mormon Church, and other churches. And then if, at the end of the year, you still want to be baptized, then you may do so."

And I said with passion, "No, that is not what I'm going to do! This is what I'm going to do: I'm going to be baptized in two weeks, and then I'm going to go to BYU in the fall. And in a year I'm going to go on a mission for the Church!"

My mom said, "There is no way you are going to join that church in two weeks. You don't have any idea what that church demands of its members. It is a way of life. You are not mature enough to make that kind of decision on so little information. You are just being immature and impetuous."

I said, "I realize I don't know much about it but I know the Lord wants me to be baptized and go on a mission and I'm 18 and I can make my own decisions." My parents were extremely upset with me and I was upset with them. Didn't they realize how wonderful this was for me, and how excited I was, and how much I knew this was right?

The next few days were very difficult as my parents made it clear they thought I was being ridiculous about this. But I continued to investigate the Church. What with missionary lessons, Family Home Evening, and church basketball I was spending a lot of time with church activities. They continued to express great disappointment and even anger that I was moving ahead with my decision.

I thought and prayed about this over the next few days. In order to let my parents know that I understood their concerns, but also how serious I was about this, I told them that I had decided that I would wait until six weeks after my initial baptism date to be baptized. During that time, since I would be on Christmas break, I would spend every waking minute studying about the Mormon Church, the Episcopal Church, and other religions too. They really wanted me to take more time but they could see that I was trying to respond to their concerns so they said they appreciated that. By this time, it was clear to them that I was completely serious about joining the Church.

When I told the missionaries that I had decided to delay my baptism by six weeks they were not at all happy. I explained that I wanted to be baptized as soon as possible — in large part because I wanted to become a missionary as soon as possible. But I explained that I felt that it was important to honor my parents' strong desires for me not to make such a major life decision without being informed.

I told the Elders that I intended to spend all my time studying the faith as well as honoring my parents' desire to learn of other faiths. They tried to discourage me from delaying my baptism, even having me read a passage from the Book of Mormon that I should not "procrastinate the day of your repentance" (Alma 34:33). I think perhaps they worried that delay might lead to a different decision. I tried to assure them that I had already made up my mind to be baptized but felt that I could be a better missionary to my family if I honored them in this. They very reluctantly went along with my decision.

So, for the next 7 weeks I read religious books from morning to night, every waking moment I was not at work or at church functions. I borrowed many church books from the Leiningers. I read the New Testament, the Doctrine & Covenants, The Pearl of Great Price, *A Marvelous Work and a Wonder, Jesus the Christ, The Articles of Faith, Teachings of the Prophet Joseph Smith*, and many other books on the LDS faith. I also read about the history, teachings, and practices of the Episcopal Church and about several other religions.

My parents asked my Uncle Gene, who was now a full-fledged Episcopal Priest who had changed his name to Father Damian, to come over to our home and try to talk me out of being baptized. As my Godfather, he felt responsible to keep me true to the faith in which I was baptized and raised. He talked with me for quite a while, explaining about and all the reasons I should not join the LDS Church. He told me that the Mormon Church was not Christian. I told him I had read the Book of Mormon and it talked about Christ all through it, that every prayer I had heard was said in the name of Jesus Christ, and that the missionaries talked about Christ all the time. He told me the LDS Church was a cult and I was being led astray. I told him I knew that God, through his Holy Spirit, had told me the Book of Mormon was the word of God and that I should join the Church. I assured him that I was going to be baptized and become a missionary for the Church. He was quite upset and told me he and Father Ewald were disappointed in my decision.

One of my high school acquaintances, a Jehovah's Witness, heard that I was studying to become a Latter-day Saint. She came to my house with her mom and spent a couple hours using Bible verses trying to convince me the Mormon Church was false. They were obviously skilled at this kind of debate for they had a Bible verse for every point I raised and they said a number of unkind things about the LDS Church and seemed very upset that I was not seeing the superior logic of their beliefs. I was surprised at the level of negative emotion they expressed I said that I did not know enough about the Bible to refute their arguments but that I knew the Book of Mormon was true because the Lord had manifest that to me by the Holy Spirit. They suggested I should not rely on emotions for religious truth; only the Bible was the word of God. I asked them why they thought it was that while I read the Bible I felt exactly the same feelings that I had experienced while reading the Book of Mormon. They did not have a good answer for me.

Sometime after I read the Book of Mormon I had a troubling conversation with my dad. I was sharing with him some biblical passages that foretold of the coming forth of the Book of Mormon (Isaiah 29:9-24; Ezekiel 37:15-22). After listening to my explanation my father said, "But, Dave, you are assuming that I believe the Bible is the word of God."

I said, "Well, yes. Don't you?"

He said, "No, I believe it is a collection of myths and inspiring moral stories."

I said, "But when you were a Lay Reader in the Episcopal Church you always ended your reading by saying, 'This is the word of the Lord.' Didn't you believe that?"

"No. But that is what you were supposed to say. So, I said it."

I was stunned to learn that after all these years of assuming my father believed that the Bible was God's word, he really did not. But then he said something even more troubling to me. He said that if he could see the Gold Plates he might believe in the Book of Mormon. This seemed to me like seeking for a sign and when I told him that Joseph Smith was told to deliver the plates back to the Angel Moroni. He said, "How convenient" or something like that. I came to learn later that my father did not really believe in God but only in science.

TENDER MERCIES & LESSONS LEARNED

The Lord was very kind to help me stand firm against the arguments and strong negative emotions of my parents, uncle, and friends. I was a tender plant and could easily have been scorched and uprooted by this searing opposition to my new faith. The Lord put truth into my mind and strength into my heart to allow me to come through this opposition more strongly committed to being baptized than I was before.

Part of the reason my family was so upset was that Reverend Sun Yung Moon's Unification Church (Moonies) was very active in California and many young people were joining that church (called a cult by most people) and cutting off all contact with their families and former friends. My parents knew at some level that the Mormons were not like the Moonies, but there were some of the same "strange beliefs" and significant lifestyle changes and so they were worried about me.

I have since learned that whenever the Lord tries to bring someone from darkness to light that person nearly always faces opposition of some nature. The opposition I faced was mild compared to what I have seen in some cases. I was never threatened with being disowned by my family, nor was my life, safety, or livelihood threatened. Many others have faced much stiffer opposition than I did. Even so, I am grateful to the Lord for helping me to weather these initial storms and stay true to what had been revealed to me.

CHAPTER 6

Questions & Commandments:
The Missionary Discussions

During the weeks I was taking "The Discussions" (as the missionaries called them), I learned the basic teachings and practices of the church I knew I was going to join. Because the Lord had blessed me with such an outpouring of the Spirit while I read the Book of Mormon and when I prayed about its truthfulness, I accepted everything the Elders taught me without question. In fact, as the discussions progressed I realized that, previous even to my reading the Book of Mormon, the Lord had been preparing me to accept certain commandments.

On the second discussion, the missionaries told me they were going to explain to me the purpose of life—what they called "The Plan of Salvation." I thought my life was about having fun, being a good athlete, and trying to make a lot of money playing and teaching tennis. They said they were going to answer the three most important questions in life. These were: "Where did I come from?" "Why am I here on earth?" and "Where am I going after this life is over?" Before I read the Book of Mormon and had my experience in prayer, I had not given much, if any, thought to these questions. But now I could see that they were important questions to have answers for.

To answer these questions, the Elders took out a piece of paper and drew a diagram that summarized the Plan of Salvation. The diagram

showed (a) the pre-existence[5] where we lived as spirits, (b) mortal
birth with a "veil of forgetfulness" making it such that we have no
recollection of the pre-existence, (c) the earth life which involved living
by faith, learning to overcome opposition, being tested to see if we
will keep the commandments, (d) physical death where our spirits are
separated from our bodies, (e) the spirit world which includes Paradise
(for the righteous and repentant) and Prison (for the wicked or
unrepentant), (f) resurrection and judgment, and finally (g) the three
degrees of glory (Celestial, Terrestrial, Telestial) in the heavens. Again,
I felt the Spirit witness to me that what they were saying was true, not
just logical—which, to me, it was—but absolutely true.

After the missionaries finished drawing the chart and explaining
the Plan of Salvation and showing me how the Lord had revealed the
answers to the three big questions, I thought that I now understood
"What life was all about" and I felt incredible joy and excitement. For
the first time, I realized that I was here on earth for a sacred purpose
and that from now on everything I did would focus on fulfilling the
divine plan that the Lord had revealed through his prophet Joseph
Smith. I was now even more excited about becoming a missionary and
explaining to everyone I could what the purpose of their life was and
how they could fulfill the Lord's purposes for them.

Near the end of the six discussions, the missionaries taught me
about the commandments that Latter-day Saints were expected
to observe. They taught me about the Law of Chastity, the Law of
Tithing, keeping the Sabbath day holy, the Word of Wisdom, and

---

5. In those days Mormons tended to use the phrase "pre-existence" but now tend to
use the phrase "pre-mortal existence" since that term better communicates the fact
that all people existed in the pre-mortal life before being born.

other commandments. Because of the power of the witness I had received, I think I would have agreed to live whatever commandments they taught me.

When the missionaries explained the Law of Chastity to me I accepted it immediately, even though this was counter to the beliefs and standards of my surrounding culture and what my friends believed. I could see there was something very different about the LDS young women I had met, and now I understood at least part of the reason why.

When the Elders explained the Law of Tithing, I remembered my reaction at the first LDS meeting I attended on learning that Mormons do not "pass the plate" in their meetings: the idea of a religion that did not ask you for money was extremely appealing to me. But, as the missionaries explained the principle of giving one tenth of all that the Lord blesses us with back to the Lord, it made perfect sense to me and I agreed to live the law. They also explained about fasting and fast offerings and although I had never heard of fasting, much less thought of doing it myself, this seemed like a great way to help the poor. And though I was surrounded by wealth in the place I grew up, during my prayer after reading the Book of Mormon I had felt great love for all of God's children. So, fasting to help them made perfect sense.

Despite my long pattern of devoting Sundays to playing and watching sports and working at various jobs, I also immediately accepted the principle of keeping the Sabbath day holy. Although I had hoped to play professional tennis and then teach tennis for a living (and each of these would require me to work on Sundays), I committed that I would not play tennis again on Sundays even if this meant that I could not do what I had planned to do as a career. Although at that time I had no idea what I would do to earn a living, I knew the Lord would provide for me. I have never regretted this decision.

Although I did not realize it at the time, the Lord had sent someone to help prepare me to accept the Word of Wisdom without hesitation. A few weeks before I read the Book of Mormon I had an interesting conversation with our new assistant manager at the theater where I worked. He only worked at the theater for a few weeks and I do not remember his name. I will call him Martin. Martin began working at the theater and introduced a stricter approach than our manager who was an alcoholic and spent most of his time upstairs "counting money" (which we knew meant he was drinking).

Martin was a few years older than the group of us high school kids who had been working together at the theater for a few years and who over the years had become great friends. He was not what you would call a cool guy—in fact he was what we called a nerd—and I thought he was also a bit uptight and bossy. Really, he was just trying to run a tight ship as he had been trained to do.

One evening, soon after Martin became our assistant manager, I saw him at a party I had attended. I was surprised to see him there since I did not take him for a "party guy" and, sure enough, I noticed that he was not ingesting alcohol, tobacco or any of the other substances that were available. Yet he seemed to be having a good time and was friendly with a number of people there.

The next night at work I asked him why he did not take any of the stuff that was at the party. He told me he was a devout Lutheran and that he never wanted to do things just because "everyone was doing it." I asked him why he bothered to come to such parties if he was not going to do what everyone else was doing. He said he enjoyed spending time with his friends but never wanted to let peer pressure dictate what he himself did.

When Martin said this, something very unusual happened within me. Even though he was not the kind of "cool" guy I would normally have looked up to and wanted to emulate, I was deeply impressed by his character and inner strength to resist the strong peer pressure that I knew was brought to bear against anyone who did not drink and smoke and take drugs. I suddenly had a strong desire to be like that, and I made a personal decision that I would no longer allow what others thought or did to influence me. In fact, I decided that I would be like Martin in his avoidance of the things available at the parties I attended. For the next several days I felt a surge of inner strength, independence, and maturity. I fully intended to follow his example at the next party I attended.

Thus, a few weeks later, when the missionaries explained the Word of Wisdom to me (no alcohol, tobacco, drugs, coffee, tea, or caffeinated drinks), I immediately accepted it and committed to live the Word of Wisdom from then on. Coffee, tea, and caffeinated drinks were not on the list of things that I had previously decided to avoid, but I committed to avoid them as well. The Elders explained that although drugs and other addictive substances (like caffeine) were not specifically mentioned in the revelation known as the Word of Wisdom (see D&C section 89), they were understood to be part of what was proscribed. I could see the logic and wisdom of that.

In fact, in my new-convert zeal to fully live this new faith the Lord had led me to, I became a bit of a Word of Wisdom fanatic for a time—at least in one area. As I spent more and more time with my new LDS friends over the next several weeks, I noticed that they seemed to eat a great deal of chocolate and some drank a lot of hot chocolate (it was winter time). It seemed like whenever Mormons got together they had treats of some kind—which was fine with me as I really enjoyed this aspect of my new religion. But I wondered about hot chocolate. I knew that chocolate had a lot of caffeine. And I reasoned that since hot chocolate was a "hot drink" and the Lord specifically stated that "hot drinks are not for the body or belly" (D&C 89:9), hot chocolate should also be proscribed based on two of the principles the Elders had taught me (no hot drinks and no caffeinated beverages). So, I decided to avoid hot chocolate as well.

I explained my decision to Tina, a wonderful LDS young woman I had begun to date on the day I was baptized. Tina was a rock-solid, well-grounded, and very religious young lady who lived the gospel with exactness. I saw this manifest when, after we had been dating for a couple of weeks, we were driving along in the car and I reached over and put my hand on Tina's knee. She took my hand off her knee and put it back on mine. I looked at her and said, "Really?"

She smiled, while nodding, and said in a firm voice, "Really."

I said, "Okay!"

Tina liked to have hot chocolate and homemade fudge on Sunday evenings. I enjoyed this as well and over the first few weeks after my baptism, it became a bit of a Sunday evening ritual with Tina and me. But when I explained to Tina that I had decided not to drink hot chocolate because of the Word of Wisdom, I was surprised that she did not immediately accept my position and join me in "full obedience" to this "commandment." She said she agreed with my reasoning but that no one had ever asserted that there was a problem with hot chocolate and so she thought it was fine.

Over the next few weeks I continued to assert my position and she continued to disagree with me, having talked with a number of her fellow Latter-day Saints. She patiently tried to bring me around to the position of the Church while indicating that she respected my desire to live the gospel fully as I understood it. I was so adamant and stubborn that we actually had a couple of mildly heated discussions about the issue. When Tina left for a week to attend "Girls Camp" on Mount Shasta I did a lot of thinking about this issue.

While she was gone, I was brought to see that I was being excessive in my application of the principles I had learned. Here is how it happened: I was with a group of LDS friends at a Young Adult Family Home Evening and hot chocolate was being served. I asked why they were drinking something that must surely be disallowed by the Word of Wisdom. They said that hot chocolate was fine to drink. I explained my reasoning and why I would not drink it. Most concurred that my reasoning was sound, but said that it was still fine to drink hot chocolate. Being an arrogant and argumentative teenager who had what I thought was an ironclad rationale for my position, I held my ground and said I thought they were violating the Word of Wisdom.

At one point in this conversation—which was becoming a bit of an argument—someone said, in a way meant to settle the matter once and for all, "Well, the Stake President drinks hot chocolate!" In my zeal I said, "Well, then the Stake President needs to repent!"

By the facial expressions and verbal response of my new friends, it became immediately clear to me that I had crossed some kind of line. Ron Wilmore, a newly returned missionary, passionately stated, "No Dave, YOU need to repent! You are on the high road to apostasy!"

Although the logic by which I had reached my position still seemed sound to me, I felt a spiritual witness that Ron was right and I was wrong. I realized that I was not in harmony with the Church, its leaders, or its members on this issue. I accepted on faith and the witness of the Spirit that I was in the wrong, not they. This was not easy for me since my mother had drilled logic and sound argument into me from an early age and I still did not feel like a logical reason had been offered not to include hot chocolate in the list of proscribed beverages. But I accepted that I needed to change my position and stop being a "Word of Wisdom fanatic." So, I "repented" by joining my fellow Mormons in partaking of some hot chocolate.

After I had been brought to my new understanding, I was excited to tell Tina of my change of mind and heart. When she returned from Girls Camp she called me and said she was really looking forward to seeing me. So, I went over to her house. She was very excited about her experience at camp and said I would be so proud of her. She burst out in a rush of excitement and said that she had been doing a lot of thinking about my position on hot chocolate and decided that I was right after all and so every night at Girls Camp when everyone else was drinking hot chocolate around the campfire to stay warm (she said it was freezing every night) she just drank water or milk!

Tina looked at me with excited anticipation at how happy I would be that she had come to "see the light" and how proud I would be of her strength and discipline. I said, "Wow, I am really proud of you! But actually, while you were gone, I realized that you were right and I was being fanatical about hot chocolate and so, actually, I've been drinking hot chocolate."

She said, "What! You mean I spent several days in the freezing mountains not drinking hot chocolate and you've been down here drinking it?!" I said I was really sorry but I had been convinced by the Young Adults—and the Spirit—that I was wrong. I know that in time she forgave me and we later laughed about this episode but, for a few minutes there, it is possible that Tina did not have entirely Christian feelings toward me. And I could not blame her.

TENDER MERCIES & LESSONS LEARNED

Having now been involved in missionary work with hundreds of people over the last forty years (including a full-time mission and service as a stake missionary and stake mission president), I have learned how difficult it is for many people to change their lives in the ways the gospel requires. I have seen many people refuse to or at least struggle with the idea and practice of obeying any number of the many commandments the Lord asks the Saints to live. So, looking back I am surprised at the way I accepted quite a demanding set of commandments that was to dramatically change the way I lived my life. None of my long-time friends were doing any of the things I was asked to do and it turned out that Mom was right: when I committed to be baptized a couple of weeks before, I really "had no idea what I was getting into" with the uniquely demanding LDS lifestyle.

I can only thank the Lord for His great kindness in blessing me with a witness that was strong enough and deep enough to change my heart and allow me to accept the commandments without hesitation. While I have made my share of mistakes and certainly have not always lived the commandments to my fullest ability to do so, I have always remained committed to striving to live the commandments and have taken great joy in the process of teaching my children to do likewise. I know it is in their earthly and eternal well-being to do so.

After being a member for a couple of months I had a small crisis in relation to the Sabbath day. One Sunday morning after Sacrament Meeting, Sister Leininger asked me if I would be willing to do her a big favor. I said, "Sure!" She then handed me her car keys and some money and asked me if I would fill her car with gas. She said that she had spent all day Saturday driving around our very large stake doing church work (she was a stake officer), and had to do additional driving for church assignments the rest of Sunday.

I had committed to keep the Sabbath day holy, which included not making purchases on Sunday except in emergencies, and so I was surprised that Sister Leininger would ask me to do this. But I loved and respected her so much and I knew that the empty tank was not a result of pleasure driving but from doing the Lord's work on Saturday. This seemed to be one of those "ox in the mire" situations mentioned in the Bible. However, while driving their car to the gas station I still felt divided loyalties — on the one hand I felt loyalty to the Lord and His commandments about the Sabbath. On the other hand, I felt loyalty to the Leiningers for all they had done for me in bringing the gospel into my life. This was one of those experiences I have had in the Church where I needed to weigh obedience to a particular gospel principle, as I understood it, with the immediate responsibility to meet someone's legitimate need.

CHAPTER 7

Church Ball &
My First Trip to Utah

Just a few days after my first church meeting, I played my first game of "church ball." My first experience with Mormon church basketball was memorable on several accounts. Throughout my life, I had played a lot of basketball—both organized church ball with my Catholic friends during elementary school (Catholic Youth Organization), and on the basketball teams in junior high and high school, along with countless pick-up games in all kinds of settings with all kinds of people. During all those games, I had heard every conceivable swear word, seen all levels of competitiveness, and helped break up arguments and fights of all kinds. But none of this really prepared me for my first basketball game with my new LDS friends.

I had been invited to play with the Young Adults at the Stake Center—on the same floor where I had felt the Spirit so strongly on attending my first LDS meeting a few days before. The game opened with a prayer which I thought was really cool since I did not remember ever starting a ballgame with a prayer that asked for protection from injury and help in being good sports. The fact that the game was in a gym inside a church building, the fact that I had met the guys in our Young Adult Family Home Evening and found them to be very nice guys, and the fact the game began with a prayer suggested to me that the game would be really good natured and fun with none of the anger and poor sportsmanship I had seen in other sports events. For the most part this was true, although I was surprised at the level of intensity.

The first surprise I received was after I took my first shot just a couple of minutes into the game. When I missed the shot, I yelled out what I usually yelled out when I missed a shot in basketball or tennis: "Oh, God!" This was a phrase I heard at least a hundred times a day from my family and friends and it meant no more to me than if I had said, "Oh, shoot!" or, "Oh, man!" But it quickly became very clear that my new Mormon friends and associates had a very different view of this phrase. Instantly after I yelled this out, all the players simply stopped playing and turned and looked at me. The cultural hall suddenly became deathly quiet and everyone on the stage watching the game stopped their conversations and stared at me as well.

One of the guys came over to me and said, "Dave, you can't do that in here."

I said, "Do what?"

"Swear."

I said, "I didn't swear." I had heard and said a wide variety of swear words and, to me, "God" was definitely not one of them.

"Yes, you did."

"What do you mean? I didn't swear."

"Yes, you did. You took the Lord's name in vain. That is the worst kind of swearing."

"So, I can't say, 'Oh, God'?"

"No!" several of the guys said while cringing.

"Oh. Sorry. I didn't know that was swearing."

I then noticed some people saying to each other, "He's a non-member," and those who heard nodded their heads as if that explained and, to some extent, excused why I would have said what I did.

But when the game got going again, I learned that although Mormons might not use the same swear words I was familiar with, they certainly did say certain words in a way that seemed an awfully lot like swearing to me. Throughout the rest of the game when someone missed a shot I heard a number of strange words like "Gad" and "Flip" and "Fetch" and "Judas Priest" said with exactly the same kind of anger and intensity as I had ever heard various swear words being said. So, I learned that while you could not say certain words, you could substitute letters such as an a for an o so that "God" was not okay but "Gad" was.

I learned two other lessons during the "High Priests" game that followed ours. After our game ended, I sat on the stage and watched the next game. It was older men who played with even more intensity and less skill than the younger guys I had played with.

There was one player who kept aggressively fouling other players. Each time he was called for a foul he screamed, "NO! I didn't foul him!" He became more upset each time he was called for a foul until after the fourth or fifth foul within a ten-minute span of the game he snapped and completely lost it. After being called for this last foul, this man screamed in crazed agony while running around the court waving his arms and crying, "No! No! No! I didn't touch him! I swear I didn't touch him!" It was clear to me that he had suffered some kind of serious mental breakdown. Some other players escorted him off the court and out of the cultural hall, him still screaming like a mad man.

I turned to the woman sitting next me and asked, "Who is that?" She said, "That is Brother McMurphy*, he's on the High Council."[6] I thought to myself that whatever the "High Council" was, I did not want to be on it since it must make you go crazy.

---

6. When I use a pseudonym to protect someone's privacy, I indicate it with an asterisk.

The game went on and a few minutes later those same men came
back into the cultural hall with Brother McMurphy. And while just
a few minutes before he had been completely out of his mind, he
now was calm and went around apologizing to everyone. I had never
seen such a sudden and complete transformation in my life. Then I
heard people whispering that "they gave him a blessing" and I asked
what that was. The woman sitting next to me explained that brothers
holding "the priesthood" had laid their hands on his head and blessed
him by the power of the priesthood to recover. Thus, the third thing I
learned in my first experience with Church basketball was that there is
serious power in priesthood blessings.

* * *

A few weeks after beginning to investigate the Church, my friend and
coworker at the theater John Lathrop and I took off in my 1970 Chevy
Impala to cross the desert to visit Utah and BYU. Brother Yorgason
had contacted Wayne Pearce, head coach of the BYU Men's Tennis
team and arranged for me to visit BYU and work out with the tennis
team. When John learned that I was going to Utah he asked if he
could come along since he was a serious skier and had heard that Utah
had great snow. I was happy to have him along for the company and to
help drive.

It was fun to drive through the Sierra Nevada range and then
across the Nevada and Utah deserts. I must admit that across the Salt
Flats we got the car well up over 100 miles per hour. I guess it was
good I got this out of my system before I was baptized! Like most
teenage males, I drove way too fast. Sometimes when I was heading
out the door my mom would say, "Dave, drive carefully!"

I would reply, "Mom, when you're going 100 miles an hour you have to drive carefully!"

And my mom would shoot back with, "Don't even joke about that!"

To which, under my breath, I would say, "Who's joking?"

On the way to Utah, John told me that he was a direct descendant of the John Lathrop who was on the Mayflower. He said he had read that the Mormon prophet (Joseph Smith) was also a descendant of John Lathrop (I later checked this out and it is true). During the week we were there, John planned to ski at as many resorts as possible whereas I planned to spend as much time as possible at Temple Square and BYU. I also brought along several books to keep up on my reading of LDS Church material. John did go to many ski resorts during that week. It turned out that I only went skiing with John at Sundance in Provo and at Snowbird in Salt Lake City. John and I rode the tram to the top of the mountain at Snowbird and in the time it took me to get down the hill John went up and down several times. I have never been skiing since!

My first visit to BYU was an amazing experience. I had never seen a place so clean and filled with so many clean-cut, modestly-dressed, happy people. Everyone smiled and was so friendly and helpful to me as I walked around campus. And I had never seen so many square acres of space without beer bottles and cans, cigarette butts, and other kinds of trash. I felt a wonderful spirit about the place and wanted to be a BYU student as soon as possible.

I went to the indoor tennis courts and met Coach Wayne Pearce and some guys from the team. Coach Pearce asked me to hit with the number-six player for an hour or so. I had hardly played in the last several weeks since I was so focused on my intense study of the Church. But I played as well as could be expected given that I was so rusty and given that Provo is at 4,500 feet altitude (tennis balls tend to fly long in high altitudes).

After we finished playing, Coach Pearce told me that he had already awarded the scholarships he had available to him but that I was good enough to play on the team and invited me to be on the team. I thanked him and told him I would think and pray about whether to play or not since my main reason for coming to BYU was to prepare for my mission.

The next few days, while John was at the various ski resorts, I spent each day and evening at Temple Square seeing every exhibit and every film more than once. A couple of senior missionaries assigned to Temple Square had seen me there all day and asked if they could teach me a discussion and I was happy to be taught by missionaries as well as by the amazing educational resources and media available in the visitor's center.

That evening, when I came out of seeing the First Vision film for the second or third time, Carrie, a pretty young lady of Laurel age (17–18), introduced herself to me and we chatted for some time. Carrie was at Temple Square on a Young Women's activity. She seemed excited to be able to do some missionary work with a non-member guy from California. When it was time for her to leave, she asked her leaders if it was okay if I drove her home and they said that was alright. On the ride home, she said something about seeing her mother's "garments" in the laundry basket.

I said, "Her what?"

She said, "Her garments."

I said, "What are garments?"

In a nervous voice she said, "Whoops! Never mind."

I said, "What do you mean, 'never mind'? What are garments?"

"Um . . . nothing. Never mind," she said.

I said, "No way! What are garments?"

Very reluctantly, she explained that they were sacred undergarments worn by Latter-day Saints who have been through the temple and she described them.

I said, "Well, I'm not going to wear those."

She said, "Yes, you will. If you want to go on a mission you have to go through the temple and you will have to wear them after that."

I said, "Well, I'm definitely going to the temple and I am definitely going on a mission, but I'm definitely not going to wear what you are describing."

Carrie became emotional and said I was the first non-Mormon she had met and she felt so bad that she had brought it up and seemed worried that what she had said would influence my decision to be baptized. I told her not to worry and that I was absolutely going to be baptized. She said that I should ask the missionaries when I got back home about them. I did. As I sat down with the Elders after returning from Utah they asked, "So how was your trip?"

I said, "It was wonderful. I loved every minute of it. But what is this about garments?" The Elders gave each other a look and stumbled through an explanation that satisfied me although I still had some level of discomfort about the idea. On the day I was baptized a few weeks later, while Elder Hawkes and I changed back into dry clothing after he baptized me, I saw LDS temple garments for the first time. Suddenly, in a way I did not understand, not only did I accept the concept of wearing sacred garments but I had placed within me a yearning for the time I would be able to wear them myself. Indeed, from then on whenever I saw the telltale signs of LDS garments under a man's white dress shirt, I had a sense of "holy envy" or a strong desire to wear garments as soon as possible.

TENDER MERCIES & LESSONS LEARNED

In the years I have been a member of the Church I have played a lot of church ball and have watched a lot of church ball games. But I have never played in nor seen a game as memorable as the one I experienced that first evening. And in the more than twenty-five years I have been playing tennis on the BYU tennis courts I have heard every conceivable kind of substitute swear word yelled out by faithful but frustrated Latter-day Saints. One guy I played with—at the time serving as a bishop—yelled "Sugar!" One guy yells at himself in Portuguese (he swears he is not swearing). Another guy sometimes yells "Chicken lips!" and "Chicken liver!" To which I shoot back, "Hey, this is BYU! No more of that fowl language!"

I have seen a lot of otherwise grown and good men become extremely upset and angry when they get on a cultural hall basketball court after a prayer has been said. One Latino man in my ward's Elders Quorum was playing a church ball game when a player from another ward flung an ethnic slur his way during the game. Our ward member became so angry he walked out of the cultural hall and stopped coming to church because he was so upset and offended. I spent nearly five years as a young men's president and watched many church ball games among the youth and have never seen anything like the bad behavior that I have seen among the adults. The young men (and even more so the young women) have a much better attitude and approach to the game than the Elders and High Priests. I guess church ball is another one of those things where the adults in the Church can learn from the youth.

It was a tender mercy for the Lord to allow me to see BYU even before I joined the Church. I had only been investigating the Church for a couple of weeks when I went to Utah. Seeing the BYU campus provided a clear and tangible witness to everything I was being taught about the LDS lifestyle. BYU was so different from anything I had ever seen and I felt the Spirit just being on the campus. Seeing so many hundreds of modestly dressed young women and clean-cut young men was very inspiring to me as I compared that with what I was raised with.

When we graduated from high school, a number of my high school friends went off to Chico State which was known as the biggest party school in California. They tried to talk me into attending there as well. I am not sure why I did not go but looking back I see this as another tender mercy of the Lord. Many who went there spent most of their college years drinking and doing drugs. Some of them became so addicted to alcohol and drugs that they are still suffering the consequences including addiction, disease, divorce, and death.

If I had been offered a scholarship to play tennis at BYU, I probably would have decided to play since neither my parents or I had money to pay for college. But without the financial incentive of a scholarship, I thought it would just mean several hours a day that I would be playing tennis instead of preparing for my mission. In some ways, I now wish I had decided to play, just to have had the experience of playing college tennis. But I am grateful that the Leiningers were so generous in helping me afford to attend my first year at BYU so that I did not have to work to support myself. I was able to spend all my time preparing for my mission, studying enough to make passing grades (and thus remain enrolled), and teaching the gospel to my roommate (quite a story in itself that I share in Chapter 12).

The time I spent at Temple Square allowed me to immerse myself in Church doctrine and history in a way I could not have in California. Seeing the Salt Lake Temple—where I would be married five-and-a-half years later—was a testament in stone to the faith and devotion

of the Mormon Pioneers and helped me better appreciate what they
went through. Seeing the *Christus* statue, the Seagull Monument,
the Tabernacle, and the various films and displays allowed me to get
a crash-course in LDS history and doctrine. I came home from Utah
even more excited about this new gospel and church I was learning
about.

My introduction to temple garments, although not the ideal
way for someone to learn about these sacred symbols of devotion to
eternal covenants, in some way forced me to continue to live on faith.
I certainly was being introduced to a number of new, different, and
somewhat unusual beliefs and practices. But the Lord poured out His
Spirit on me so that I was able to accept these things on faith.

CHAPTER 8

Baptism & Confirmation: A Great & Terrible Day

I continued to take the missionary discussions and study everything I could get my hands on about the restored gospel and other faiths as well. After two months of investigation, on Saturday, January 28, 1978, I was baptized and confirmed a member of the Church of Jesus Christ of Latter-day Saints. The baptism took place in the Stake Center where I had first attended church. In addition to a large number of ward members, in attendance were my parents, my older sister, Lana, my younger brother, Keith, my uncle Gene (dressed in his Episcopal priestly robes), and his wife, Loni. My family members, especially my parents and uncle, were very unhappy that I was being baptized into another church. They felt that I was leaving the Christian faith for a non-Christian sect. I think they also felt that I was, to some extent, betraying the religious legacy of my family.

I was extremely excited to finally be baptized for the remission of sins and to receive the Gift of the Holy Ghost. Because I had spent the previous eight weeks in deep study of the restored gospel of Jesus Christ, I now felt that I had an intellectual testimony of the gospel as well as a spiritual testimony. I felt that I was entering the kingdom of God with a much better sense of what I was doing and why it was going to be one of the most important days of my life to that point (second only to the day eight weeks before when I had received my witness of Christ and the Book of Mormon in prayer).

I felt the Spirit strongly in the baptismal service and I knew this was what my Heavenly Father wanted me to be doing. After being baptized by Elder Hawkes I came up from the water filled with joy and peace and a sense of complete newness. I was sad that Elder Christensen had been transferred and was not able to come back for my baptism.

I was filled with joy and excitement and after changing into dry clothes I came back into the room where the service was being held. I was filled with the spirit of joy and peace as I walked through the door into the room where everyone was gathered.

Immediately, I noticed a very different feeling in the room and everyone's head was facing down. I wondered what had happened. My mom looked up at me and the expression on her face was one of anger and disgust and then she shook her head and looked down. I was confused about what was happening.

I sat down on the front row and noticed a cassette tape player on the table and realized an audio cassette tape was playing. As I listened to what was being said, my confusion and then horror grew. The man speaking on the tape was using a mocking tone to belittle the beliefs and practices of other churches—especially the Episcopal Church. As he continued ridiculing the church that my parents had raised me in and still belonged to and in which my uncle was a priest, I could not believe that someone had thought that playing this tape was a good thing to do at my baptism.

The feeling in the room grew more oppressive and I could almost feel the anger emanating from the back of the room where my family was sitting. Finally, President Leininger stood and turned off the tape and sincerely apologized to my family. But the damage was done. I learned just how angry my family was and how much damage had been done after my baptism.

The talk on the Holy Ghost helped to bring the Spirit back into the room — at least for me — but my family was so angry that I could still feel the tension from them. Then it was time for me to be confirmed. President Leininger placed his hands on my head and said, "David Curtis Dollahite, by the authority of the holy Melchizedek priesthood and in the name of Jesus Christ, I confirm you a member of The Church of Jesus Christ of Latter-day Saints, and say unto you: receive the Holy Ghost." When he spoke the words "receive the Holy Ghost," I felt a powerful rush of the exact same spiritual love and light that was now becoming more and more familiar to me. President Leininger then gave me a marvelous blessing, promising many wonderful opportunities to serve and share the gospel.

After the baptism, my mother pulled me into a room away from the other people, pointed her finger in my face, and said to me with barely controlled rage, "I cannot believe how incredibly rude your church is to invite us here and then ridicule our beliefs. I have never been so insulted in my life. Now, I want you to listen very carefully. I don't ever want to hear another word from you about your religion. You are not to say one word, not one word to me or anyone in our family about your church. Is that clear?"

Thus, my first meeting as a member of The Church of Jesus Christ was the most bitter-sweet church meeting I have ever attended. It was a great day for me because I became a member of Christ's restored church and kingdom and received the incomparable Gift of the Holy Ghost. But it was also a terrible day for my family in terms of their feelings about this new church and their resulting complete lack of interest in — indeed their total rejection of anything to do with — the church I had joined and committed my life to.

I was so excited about the gospel that from the beginning of my association with it I began sharing it with anyone and everyone who would listen to me. And, until after my baptism, when my mom told me I could not talk with them about the Church, I had shared as much of what I was learning as I could with my parents.

Another serious issue arose when my parents and I got home. My parents knew that Mormons were married in a temple that non-Mormons were not allowed to enter. When we got home from the brunch hosted by Sister Leininger after my baptism, the first thing my mom said to me was, "So does this mean that we will not be able to come to your wedding?" She looked extremely sad. I was not sure what to say to this since I did not know what the Church's policy was about family members. I said that, yes, I was going to be married in the temple but that I hoped she would be able to attend.

Tina had given me a journal as a baptismal gift. The day following my baptism I wrote the following:

> *This was my first Sabbath Day as a member of the Church of Jesus Christ of Latter-day Saints. I know this church is true, that it is the true restored Church of Jesus Christ, the Savior. My baptism was yesterday and it was a very nice, spiritual experience. I hope the Spirit touched my family and softened their hearts that they might someday investigate the church as I did and find the love and truth of the gospel. My life has truly changed for the better since joining the Church or should I say since being introduced to the gospel and the wonderful truths it contains. I hope my Heavenly Father helps me to grow stronger in faith and knowledge. I must study the scriptures and pray and always work toward a goal in my life, whatever that goal may be. (Personal Journal, page 1)*

TENDER MERCIES & LESSONS LEARNED

Despite the very negative fallout from the tape that was played at my baptism, I was extremely excited to be a brand-new member of the Church of Jesus Christ. I later learned that the new missionary who took Elder Christensen's place had thought it would be a good idea to play this tape, thinking it would convince my family their church was not true and lead them to want to investigate the LDS Church for themselves. As it turned out, he could not have been more wrong about the results of that tape being played at my baptism. On my own LDS mission, I said and did some pretty dumb things and many of the young men and women who serve as LDS missionaries are not always as mature, sensitive, and perceptive as their parents and fellow Saints might wish.

I was so grateful to the Lord for bringing me into His fold. As I look back on the way the Lord brought me into the Church, I feel deep gratitude for His many tender mercies during this time. He brought me out from a wicked culture in a way that was just right for me. I almost certainly would not have listened to missionaries had they come by our house; I had rudely sent the Jehovah's Witnesses away when they came by and laughingly told my friends how weird they were. And although I had not seen Mormon missionaries before my first day at church, they looked even stranger to me with their suits and short haircuts, so I am sure they would have received the same kind of rejection from me.

I doubt I would have responded to an LDS young lady trying to share the gospel with me. My devoutly religious high school girlfriend, Anne, had tried to interest me in her Lutheran church but my effort was to try to influence her away from her faith rather than for me to move toward hers. Since Mormonism had a lot more strictures than

Lutheranism, I likely would have only tried to encourage a Mormon girl to lower her standards to become more like me.

Given my personality, attitudes, and experiences with religion, I needed to have my own witness directly from the Lord. And it needed to be on my own, not under the influence of another person. The Lord knew me and tailored how I was introduced to the Church. I also consider it an incredibly generous tender mercy for the Lord to have blessed me with an unshakable spiritual witness to serve as a foundation for a lifetime of spiritual and religious commitment and service.

Over the years that I have been in the Church, despite the many efforts of atheists, anti-Mormons, former Mormons, and "intellectual" Mormons to challenge my beliefs or even influence me away from the Church, I have always been able to rely on the powerful witness I received directly from the Lord about the truthfulness of God and His gospel. I know for myself, independent of any other person, that God lives, that faith in the Atonement of Jesus Christ brings complete forgiveness of sins and a literal purging of the soul of sin, that the Book of Mormon is the word of God, and that God answers faithful fervent prayer. Thus, despite any arguments brought to bear on me by others, I have never wavered from my testimony.

The thing I have spent a good deal of time pondering about is why I was picked out to receive the gospel, and to receive such a strong, clear witness, when I knew many people who were much more religious and much better people than I was that were not so blessed. I have often felt that if almost any other person had received the kind of witness that I received they would surely have reacted just as I did and come into the Church and remained fully committed to it. I know that, compared to the kind of life I was living in relation to the many others I knew, I did not deserve to receive the witness I received.

The only thing I can say in my defense is that I did follow the promptings to read and pray and I did immediately choose to change in whatever way I was taught to change by the Lord's servants. And, despite my many weaknesses and foibles, I have tried to remain faithful to the gospel throughout my life. So, I guess the Lord knew me well enough to know that such an outpouring of His Spirit would not be "wasted" on me.

To this day, I continue to feel that I did not deserve to receive the gospel; that it was a tender mercy of God to provide a young man such as I was with a sure witness of the restored gospel of Jesus Christ. And I continuously feel deep gratitude for His tender mercies toward me. When I first heard our oldest daughter, Rachel, as an eight-year-old girl, stand before a congregation and bear her sweet testimony of the gospel, I wept with joy that my child had a testimony of the things I knew to be true. And as I have been able to baptize each of my seven children and many others who I have been privileged to teach, I always think of the Lord's gracious love for all His children.

CHAPTER 9

Memorable Meetings Following Baptism

I attended three particularly memorable meetings and had a memorable home teaching visit in the months after my baptism before I left to attend BYU. The first meeting was when I gave my first Sacrament Meeting talk, the second was a fast and testimony meeting where someone gave an anti-Book of Mormon "testimony" and asked to have his name removed from the records of the Church, and the third was a stake conference with a surprising person in attendance. The home teaching visit was with a descendant of Jedidiah Parley* who was not active in the Church.

The first Sunday after my baptism I went up to the bishop and asked if I could speak in Sacrament Meeting and tell about how I gained my testimony. He said that in his years as bishop he had never had anyone actually ask him if they could speak in church. He said that he was delighted to have me speak and asked if I could I give a ten-minute talk in a couple of weeks. I said that I could do it any time, the sooner the better, and I asked if it was okay if had more time, perhaps twenty minutes or so. He said he had never had anyone ask for more time for a talk, but that, yes, that was fine.

A couple of Sundays later I stood before my new brothers and sisters and told them about how the Lord had blessed my life by inspiring me to read the Book of Mormon and by pouring out His Spirit in great abundance on me while I read and when I prayed to know of its truthfulness. I told about how my study of the gospel and of other faiths had given me a firm testimony of the doctrines of the restored gospel. I spoke of how I felt when I was baptized and confirmed and told them that I planned to do everything in my power at BYU to prepare myself to be the best missionary I could be for the Lord. While I spoke, I felt the Holy Ghost with me, guiding my words and bearing witness to me that what I was saying was true. It was the first of many times that I felt the inspiration of the Spirit while addressing a gathering of Saints.

* * *

On the first Sunday of each month, Latter-day Saint wards (congregations) hold "fast and testimony meetings." After the Sacrament of the Lord's Supper (a.k.a., Communion, Eucharist) is administered to the congregation, members are invited to share their testimonies by expressing their thoughts, feelings, and experiences about their religious beliefs. Members typically include statements including phrases such as "I know the Church is true" or "I testify that Jesus is the Christ" or "I know the Book of Mormon is the word of God."

The first LDS meeting I had attended included testimonies from dozens of faithful youth, and was a spiritual feast. While I was investigating the Church, the two testimony meetings I had attended in the ward were also wonderful. I enjoyed testimony meetings since so many different people were able to share their experiences and convictions; and the spirit was strong when anyone bore pure testimony of Christ and his gospel. Thus, I assumed that every testimony meeting was as wonderful as the first ones I had attended.

Soon after I was baptized, I attended a fast and testimony meeting that turned out to be one of the most interesting, intense, and spiritually important meetings I have ever attended. In this meeting, I learned that the Gift of the Holy Ghost that I had recently received would help me to discern clearly between good and evil influences and between truth and falsehood.

After the member of the bishopric who was conducting bore his testimony and sat down, a brother whom I had met once or twice but did not know well stood at the pulpit before the congregation. Brother Claude Heater[7] seemed very sad and quite anxious. He began by saying that he had been doing a lot of intense study of the Book of Mormon and had come to the conclusion that it was not the word of God. He said he had found certain internal inconsistencies and that he no longer had a testimony of it. He said he had then done more studies about Joseph Smith and had decided that he was not a prophet of God. He went on to say that he wanted to have his name removed from the records of the Church. He then sat down.

Of course, I was surprised and saddened by what this brother had said. It seemed to me that he had taken an overly intellectual approach to his studies. But even with my fairly limited knowledge of the doctrines and history of the Church, I noted what I considered problems with his facts and his reasoning. He seemed devoid of the Spirit of the Lord but seemed filled with the pride of his own intellect. Indeed, I did not feel the sweet spirit of the Holy Ghost at all during the time he spoke. There was actually a kind of dark feeling that pervaded the small chapel. While I felt like he was a good and honorable man who had made a tragic mistake and felt sorry for him, I also felt deeply that he was very wrong about his attitude, his approach,

---

7. I use Claude Heater's actual name because he has publicly shared these same ideas and was a public figure in the sense that he was a well-known opera singer and played the part of Jesus in the 1959 film *Ben Hur.*

and his conclusions—and that he was wrong to take time in an LDS testimony meeting to say what he said.

After Brother Heater sat down, a sister stood in the congregation and the deacon[8] passing the microphone around handed it to her. She expressed her love for Brother Heater and said she would continue to love and support him. This was followed by a few other similar expressions of love and concern for Brother Heater.

During these expressions, I felt a better spirit in the room and felt the darkness begin to diminish. But during the time these other sisters and brothers were expressing their love and support for Brother Heater, I noticed that Ron Wilmore, a newly returned missionary who was sitting in a pew a few rows in front of me, was visibly agitated. I had played basketball with Ron a few times and had had a number of gospel discussions with him. I knew that he was a very intense guy with a strong knowledge and testimony of the gospel.

Finally, as the deacon came up the middle aisle Ron jumped to his feet and took the microphone from him. Ron spoke clearly in a strong and somewhat perturbed voice, "Since this is a fast and testimony meeting, I'd like to bear my testimony! I know that God lives. I know that Jesus is the Christ. I know that Joseph Smith was a prophet of God. I know that the Book of Mormon is the word of God! In the name of Jesus Christ, Amen!"

And then Ron handed the microphone back to the deacon and sat down. As Ron bore his testimony I felt a powerful rush of the Spirit

---

8. In the LDS Church, deacons typically are 12 or 13 years old boys. In most LDS testimony meetings people go to the pulpit but in this ward, at that time, they decided to have a deacon pass the microphone around so older people would not need to make their way up to the pulpit.

each time he stated what he knew. I knew that what he said was true. I felt like I was on fire and the full light and warmth and power of the Spirit returned to the room as if someone had turned on the lights.

* * *

On February 2, 1978, I was ordained a priest in the Aaronic Priesthood and soon after received a home teaching assignment. My very first home teaching appointment was to visit the Parley* family. My home teaching companion said he had been the Parleys' home teacher for some time and that they had been completely "inactive" for a couple years. I asked what being inactive meant. He explained that this meant they did not attend church or participate in any way.

This made no sense to me. Until then I had only met active, faithful Latter-day Saints and the idea that there could be people who had the truth and did not live it was incomprehensible to me. How could someone have the fullness of the gospel and all its blessings and not be fully involved in the Church? Having myself just been privileged to come from darkness into the light, I did not see how someone who had the light would choose to live in the dark. Then I remembered Brother Heater and wondered if the Parleys had similar issues.

We were invited in and sat down with Brother Parley, Sister Parley, and their children. My companion explained to the Parley family that I had just joined the Church and this was my first home teaching visit. Given that this was my first home teaching visit, and my first official duty as a newly ordained priest, I tried to listen and learn.

However, it seemed to me like the discussion proceeded on a fairly superficial level and did not really address issues of deep import. At some point the discussion turned to the Parleys' activity level in the

Church. I really wanted to understand why a member of the Church could be "inactive." So I asked Brother Parley why he was not active in the Church. He said: "Your bishop offended me and I won't ever come back as long as that man is bishop." I asked what had happened.

He said he had gone in to see our bishop for assistance in his role as a professional. On the wall of the bishop's professional office, Brother Parley noticed a painting of a prominent early Church leader and asked if the bishop was a descendant of that person. When the bishop said that he was, Brother Parley mentioned that he was a descendant of Jedidiah Parley and the bishop then said something about how interesting it was that most of the descendants of his (the bishop's) ancestor (a famous early LDS Church leader) were faithful Church members, but that most of Jedidiah Parley's descendants were "a bunch of apostates." Brother Parley told me, "Well, I walked out of his office and I'll never set foot in the Church again as long as that man is the bishop."

I was too new in the Church to know anything about the accuracy of the bishop's statement, but even a naïve and insensitive nineteen-year-old like I was could appreciate to some degree that what the bishop had said was insensitive. I wondered whether he was just joking with Brother Parley. But, regardless, the bishop's words obviously had deeply offended Brother Parley. I was too young and inexperienced in the Church to realize that insensitive things said by Church leaders can have a crushing effect on those whose faith was grounded on anything other than a firm testimony borne of the Holy Spirit.

So, I asked Brother Parley why he would let an insensitive comment separate him and his family from the blessings of the restored gospel of Jesus Christ. He looked at me like I had a lot of nerve to say such a thing. Then he went on about how the bishop should not have said such a thing and how great Jedidiah Parley was and how the bishop had no right to insult his family and so forth.

I said to Brother Parley that I was so grateful for the tremendous blessings of the gospel that had just come into my life, and could not imagine letting what someone else said or did take those blessings from me. I wish I could say that Brother Parley and his family took my words to heart and decided to return to activity. But during the rest of my several months in the ward, before heading off to BYU, he did not.

* * *

A few months after I was baptized, I was sitting in the chapel of the Stake Center at the end of my first stake conference having enjoyed a spiritual feast. After the closing prayer, I stood and was watching the large congregation of my fellow Saints filing from the meeting. Several rows in front of me I saw a tall athletic young man stand and turn around. He looked just like a guy from my high school named Warren Pino. Warren was a couple years older than me and I had played basketball and baseball with him now and then. Given our age difference, we were not really friends, but from my own observation and from his reputation, Warren was one of the nicest guys I knew. He was nice to everyone—even the younger guys and the kids who were not "cool." Therefore, I admired him.

Well, this guy looked just like Warren—except that he had a missionary haircut, was dressed in a suit, and was in an LDS stake conference. Thus, I thought it could not be my buddy Warren. While Warren was a great guy he did not seem like a religious person—much less a Mormon. This guy was looking at me with the same curious and surprised look I must have been looking at him with. We stared for several seconds and then slowly made our way toward each other with me asking "Warren Pino?" and him asking "Dave Dollahite?" at about the same time. We each nodded and smiled at each other's question and shook hands enthusiastically.

He asked, "What are you doing here?"

I said, "I just joined the Church!"

He looked stunned and said, "No way! I can't believe it!"

I assured him it was true and then I asked, "What are you doing here?"

He said, "I'm getting ready to go on my mission to New England, Portuguese speaking!" He told me he had not been active in the Church in high school but had recently become active again and was leaving on his mission soon. I told him I was preparing for my mission by going to BYU in the fall. He was as stunned and as thrilled as I was to learn someone else from Sir Francis Drake High School was LDS.

TENDER MERCIES & LESSONS LEARNED

It was a tender mercy to feel the Spirit of the Lord guiding my thoughts and words when I gave my first talk in a Sacrament Meeting. Although I had never done any public speaking, I somehow felt completely comfortable doing this. In my prayer after reading the Book of Mormon, I had seen myself teaching people about Jesus and the Book of Mormon and since then I have tried to be a witness of God and what He did for me as often as possible.

The experience of being in the meeting where Brother Heater bore an "anti-testimony" taught me that the Gift of the Holy Ghost I had received at baptism allowed me to discern clearly between light and dark, truth and error, goodness and wickedness—between human kindness and support, as nice as that is, and the divine power and influence of God. I am very grateful for this lesson as I have had many other experiences in life when I have heard or read about others who have lost their way or who are adversarial toward the Restored Church of Jesus Christ. The Spirit has helped me to discern the truth and thus avoid falling into the pits and traps set to ensnare the unwary or the unwise people, or those who will not humble themselves and patiently wait on the Lord.

I later came to learn that Claude Heater was an accomplished opera singer and played the role of Christ in the 1959 movie Ben Hur (you mainly see his hands). This may help explain why some of the LDS members of the Greenbrae Ward seemed to treat him with such respect. He has gone on to create and maintain a blog in which he criticizes the Book of Mormon and other LDS Church teachings.

In the months and years following my first home teaching visit with Brother Parley, I came to learn that there were many wonderful people who, for one reason or another, had times when they were less active in the Church. I learned that frequently the reason was at least partly to do with some kind of offense that had been given or received. I learned that I should try not to offend or be offended. I learned that my job was to strengthen my brothers and sisters—not judge them about their level of activity.

My experience in meeting Warren Pino at the Stake Center turned out to be providential in an important way for Warren and me. I was very excited when, about a year later, I received my call to serve in the same mission Warren had been called to. I was thrilled to learn I would be laboring in New England with a fellow Drake High Pirate. When I got to New England, I learned that Elder Pino had been transferred to a Portuguese-speaking mission in South Africa. So although I was not able to actually work with Elder Pino, providentially I was able to be of assistance to him near the end of my own mission to New England. During the last four months of my mission, I served as an Assistant to the President and thus lived in the mission home in Cambridge, Massachusetts.[9] Because the heating bills for this stately but massive building were more than a thousand dollars a month during the winter, the mission president received direction from Church headquarters to sell the mission home. I was asked to help move hundreds of boxes of old "Letters to the President" from the basement to the dump. These letters were written by each missionary each week and read by the president and his assistants. I was told that until just one year before (just before I came on my mission) the letters were not returned to the missionary at the conclusion of his mission.

When I saw boxes full of letters from thousands of missionaries who had labored in the mission over many decades, I asked the mission president if there was some way to get these letters to the missionaries who wrote them. He said that would be impossible and we would just need to throw them out. I was sick at heart at the prospect of all those letters being thrown away. Then I remembered that Warren Pino had been in this mission for a year before being transferred to South Africa and I felt prompted to ask President Tempest if it was okay for me to see if I could find Warren's letters and send them to him. He said that would be fine. So, I prayerfully searched among the unorganized boxes and was led quite quickly to the box where Elder Pino's letters were. I took the fifty or so letters out and mailed them to his home address.

---

9. The mission home is where the mission president, his family, and two missionaries called to be Assistants to the President lived. Additionally, missionaries who are just arriving in the mission field and those who are heading home after their service stay there for a few days at the beginning and end of their missions. The Massachusetts Boston in Cambridge, was a large, old, stately mansion.

I later received a letter from Warren expressing deep gratitude for the letters. He said he had not kept a journal during the first year of his mission and those letters served as the only record of his missionary experiences. This was another witness to me that the Lord knows all about the details of every one of His children — especially His servants — and watches over them and seeks to bless them in whatever way He can.

CHAPTER 10

Changes & Challenges of a New Mormon

Joining the Church of Jesus Christ of Latter-day Saints when I was barely nineteen years old was a wonderful blessing in many ways. It meant that I was young enough to attend BYU, serve a mission, and marry in the temple. It meant that I had not developed the life habits and family patterns that an older person would have. I could essentially start my LDS life as a young and energetic person with my future before me.

But there were also changes and challenges that were not always easy. Long-held relationships with family and friends changed, and, sadly, some ended. New friendships needed to be formed. Patterns of life, goals for the future, and a number of other things needed to be changed in dramatic ways. It also meant learning a new culture because Latter-day Saints have a distinct set of terms, values, assumptions, ways of interacting, and so forth. Looking back, I see that the Lord blessed me in many ways to make these changes easier and to help me overcome these challenges.

When I joined the Church, my values, standards, and lifestyle changed so dramatically that I had a difficult time maintaining the friendships that had been so important to me throughout my childhood and youth. I tried to share the gospel with my friends, assuming they would quickly come to discover the truthfulness and joys of this wonderful new faith as I had.

But it became apparent that none of my friends were quickly—or perhaps ever—going to follow me into membership in the Church. This was very difficult for me to understand. I often wondered how I, who had no Mormon friends and was not a religious person, could have had such a clear and overpowering witness from the Lord about the truthfulness of the gospel; and yet my friends, who now had an LDS friend who was telling them how wonderful it was, showed such a lack of interest. But I could not blame them since the previous efforts of my religious friends and family members had not made me seriously investigate their faiths either.

I called one of my best friends, Jim Lowell, who was away at the University of Oregon on a tennis scholarship. Jim was very bright and a very moral person. So I expected him to be receptive to the gospel. When I called and told him I had joined the Mormon Church and was extremely happy, he was incredulous. For several minutes, he refused to believe I had become a Mormon and was sure I was just pulling his leg. He seemed to know something about the Church—at least what Mormons were not allowed to do—and he could not believe that I had voluntarily become a member of such a restrictive religious group. When I assured him I had indeed converted to the LDS faith, and was extremely happy, he wished me well but said he had no interest in hearing about it.

I talked to another good friend, Rob, the one who had been mugged and become a Born-again Christian and called to attempt to convert me several months before. He said he was no longer religious and was not interested in hearing about what I had discovered.

I thought that certainly my old girlfriend, Anne, who I had gone steady with in high school, and who was a devout Lutheran, would be interested. She also said she was happy for me but was happy in her faith and not interested in investigating the LDS Church. I spoke with her another time or two and she remained uninterested.

So, as much as I would have loved to see my friends obtain the joy and peace I had received through the restored gospel, they simply were not interested. Because of my abrupt and dramatic change, I no longer felt comfortable with some of my friends and the activities they typically participated in. One experience captured this more starkly than any other I remember.

A few months after I joined the Church some of my friends invited me to play in a softball game at a local ball field. I went, looking forward to seeing a bunch of folks I had not seen for some time as well as some others I had been in closer contact with. When I arrived, there was a great deal of alcohol lying around. There were two or three kegs of beer, and dozens of six-packs of beer, including a six-pack at every base so that those who got on base could imbibe and not have to wait until they could get to the beer on the sidelines. I thought about leaving but decided it would be better to remain and be a good example rather than reject my friends solely because they drank alcohol.

As the game progressed so did the state of inebriation of everyone else there. And with their progressing drunkenness came a corresponding diminishment in their ability to do anything resembling throwing, catching, hitting a ball, or even standing upright much less running. Each time I got up to bat it really did not matter where I hit the ball since people were falling down drunk and unable to do anything to prevent my casual jaunt around the bases with the ball being thrown into left field or to the base behind me or over the fence. When I did eventually leave, there were some people moaning, groaning, and throwing up in the bushes or wherever they happened to be when the urge hit them.

I had only about two months to speak with my parents about the gospel before the fiasco at my baptism which led to their insisting that I not discuss my new faith with them. But there still were little opportunities that emerged. In April, I brought home a video tape of General Conference and watched it. I was so excited to finally hear the prophet and apostles. At one point, my mother came into the living room and watched for a few minutes while President Kimball was speaking. I felt the power of his words and testimony and said to my mother, "Can you tell that he is a prophet of God?"

She replied, "No, he just seems like a nice old man to me." This was difficult for me because I felt the Spirit as he spoke and I strongly believed he was a living prophet. I could not see how my mom did not recognize this as well. It was five months later at a BYU devotional that I first heard the prophet speak in person and that was an incredibly important experience for me (one I will share in detail later), but as a convert of just a few months, seeing and hearing President Kimball for the first time on video tape was very meaningful for me. Unfortunately, I could not share my joy with any of my family or friends from before my conversion.

Having to develop a whole new set of friends after having such close friendships with people over much of my life was not easy. But it was necessary. The Lord blessed me with some wonderful friends in the Greenbrae Ward and San Rafael Stake. Tina Storey, Ron Wilmore, and Debbie and Doug Leininger were some of the most important, but there were others as well. Tina invited me to attend early morning seminary; I went once and found it interesting although many of those kids were years younger than me and I was no longer in high school.

I cherished the Young Adult Family Home Evening program that, each Monday night, allowed me to receive fellowship and friendship.

My regular attendance there was a real blessing but also led to a difficult encounter with my parents. One Monday night as I was leaving our house after dinner my mom asked where I was going. I said, "To Family Home Evening."

She then said, with thick irony, some sarcasm, and perhaps with pain in her voice, "Can you explain to me why you leave your own family and your own home and go miles away to spend the evening with others at what you call 'Family Home Evening'? Shouldn't you have 'Family Home Evening' at home with your own family?"

I said, "I would love to have Family Home Evening with you and dad here at home. That would be great! We could have a song and a prayer, and I could teach a lesson or we could read the scriptures, and we could play some kind of game, and then have refreshments! That would be wonderful!"

My mom said, "Well, Dad and I are just going to watch TV, but you could stay home and watch TV with us and call that Family Home Evening."

I said, "But that is what you do every night and that is not Family Home Evening. That is just watching TV."

Mom said with a little anger and a little hurt, "Well, we are your family and that is what we do."

I really did not know what to say to that. I said something about really wanting to be with my friends and that we could watch TV on another evening and I left. Looking back, I wish I would have stayed home and watched TV with my parents that night. What I did not fully realize then was that my parents were afraid they were losing me to the Church. I was spending increasing amounts of time in church activities and study and had decided not to attend classes at the local junior college (College of Marin) in order to work full-time to earn money for BYU. They knew I was leaving for BYU and then going on

a mission and then going back to BYU and so they could see the time
with me slipping away.

On a different occasion, I was heading off to another Church
activity and my mom said to me, "You have been a member of that
church for a few months now and going to all these church things and
I don't see what you get from it. You were always a good kid, and you
are still a good kid, and I don't see why you spend so much time there."

I said, "Mom, it has changed my life in so many ways I can't even
begin to tell you. I'm a completely different person."

She said, "You are the same good person you were before."

I said, "Don't you realize all the things I used to do that I don't do
anymore?"

I was about to begin listing those things — nothing terrible but just
the typical "juvenile delinquent" and high school things that the kids I
hung around with did — when my dad said, "Dave, don't!"

I think he was protecting my mom. She was disappointed in some
choices that my older sister had made after being caught up in the
hippie movement of the 1960s. I think that he knew Mom felt like
she had raised me well and did not want to learn that I was not as
good a kid as she thought, and it was the Mormon Church that had
"reformed" me.

In fact, the most important things that I felt had changed for the
better in me had less to do with the substances I no longer partook
of than with how I treated others and my life goals. Before my
conversion, I was often sarcastic and used my sense of humor to tear
others down rather than build them up. When I was younger, I had
too often been a mean — and sometimes even cruel — tease to guys
who I perceived as not being cool. I now felt terribly about this. Since
my conversion, I had become a much kinder person and strived to

build others up. But my mother had no way to really know the many and deep ways I had changed.

One of the challenges I faced as a new convert was changing my patterns of media viewing. Since I worked at a movie theater for most of my high school years and because my parents had cable TV in our home, I had seen many films and programs with inappropriate content. In my efforts to change these viewing habits after joining the Church I was much more careful about what I watched. However, there were times when I was watching a program and an inappropriate scene came on. I was not always as quick as I should have been to change the channel or turn off the TV.

One time when I was struggling with this issue, I was reading the Book of Mormon and came across a verse where Nephi asked the Lord to "make me that I may shake at the appearance of sin" (2 Nephi 4:31). I was greatly impressed at this request by Nephi. I thought it might serve as a kind of early warning for me to avoid things I should not see or hear. I felt prompted to ask the Lord to grant me with the same blessing Nephi had asked for—that I would shake at the appearance of sin.

Several days later I was watching cable TV one evening and was flipping through channels with the remote. I began watching a certain program and after several minutes I suddenly began to shake. I thought there might be a draft in the room because the shaking became stronger. Then I realized that this was an answer to my prayer (that I would shake at the appearance of sin) and I realized that something I should not see was about to appear on the show I was watching. The shaking became even stronger. But I did not do what I should have done—immediately turn off the TV. I kept watching and, sure enough, an immoral scene came on and the shaking ceased.

I then realized that the Lord had answered my prayer in a very direct and powerful way and I had not heeded the spiritual warning the Lord was kind enough to send me. I felt very badly and asked for forgiveness. I also asked for a second chance in obtaining spiritual warnings of impending evil. However, this specific blessing (literally shaking before sin, evil, or temptation appeared) was not immediately bestowed. This makes sense to me since I had treated lightly the Lord's mercy when he granted me this warning. Over the years since then, the Lord has occasionally blessed me with this type of clear manifestation of coming spiritual danger even though I do not deserve it and have often struggled with this issue.

TENDER MERCIES & LESSONS LEARNED

The Lord was most gracious and merciful to me in my early months in the LDS Church. He blessed me with good LDS friends, with powerful spiritual manifestations and answers to prayers, and with the opportunity to share my newfound faith with many friends. I felt I was not a very good missionary since none of my friends joined the Church. But I learned that each person has moral agency and various barriers that prevent them from an honest and thorough investigation of the Church. And I realized that the Lord had blessed me with an extraordinary conversion experience that allowed me to be willing to make dramatic changes.

For me the softball game was an object lesson in what addictive substances do to people. As I was the only one in full possession of my faculties, I could observe this spectacle with clarity and see that the jokes or behaviors that seemed so hilarious to those under the influence of alcohol were actually not that funny. For a time, everyone was sure they were having a "great time" but that soon progressed to illness.

I am very sad that over the years a number these people, and other friends and acquaintances of mine from the years before I converted, continued to drink, smoke, snort, and pop various addictive substances into their bodies. Each time over the years when I have learned about another divorce, wasted life, suicide, or death resulting from such abuse, I have felt both great sadness for my former friend or acquaintance and tremendous gratitude to the Lord for His tender mercy in saving me from what would likely have been my fate as well.

In the forty years since my conversion I have had the great blessing to work with a number of wonderful people who have also had marvelous spiritual experiences and who have made significant life changes in the face of challenging circumstances. I cannot possibly ever fully express the gratitude I feel every day for the Lord's tender mercies to me in bringing me from darkness into light, from ignorance into truth and from bondage into the wonderful freedom of the restored gospel of Jesus Christ.

I am ashamed to say that, because of pride and embarrassment, I have not always told the story about my asking to "shake at the appearance of sin" with complete accuracy and honesty. I have sometimes suggested that I heeded the spiritual prompting and changed the channel. This was brought to my memory when I attended a gathering of former members of the Greenbrae Ward held in Salt Lake City in the spring of 2017. As the gathering was concluding, I was chatting with a person who I had known back in the Greenbrae Ward when I was a new convert. This person happened to mention that I had shared this experience and that they still remembered it (after nearly forty years). I was stunned that someone would remember such a thing so long after it was shared, and I was embarrassed that this must have been someone to whom I gave an inaccurate, and dishonest, account of my experience.

I am deeply troubled by my willingness to not provide the full and honest account of what I did. I hope and pray that this person, and anyone else who heard me share the partially inaccurate account of this story, will forgive me and learn from my weaknesses—both my weakness in not responding to a clear spiritual prompting, and my weakness in not honestly telling what happened. I guess you could say it thusly: If you are not going to tell the truth when sharing a sacred experience, then don't tell it at all. I am happy to say this is the only example of my providing a knowingly misleading account of one of my sacred experiences.

CHAPTER II

Revelation on the Temple & Priesthood Ban

As I continued to grow in my understanding of the gospel through attendance at various kinds of Church meetings and through reading all the LDS books I could find, the spring and early summer flew by. Of course, given how few books I had read voluntarily before reading the Book of Mormon, all this reading was a new experience for me. All the Church meetings and all the Church books were a delight for me as I felt like a giant dry sponge soaking up the living waters of gospel knowledge.

I was continuing to become more familiar and comfortable with LDS culture. There were a couple of things I thought were curious.

Latter-day Saints often prayed for "moisture" and thanked God for sending "moisture" whenever it rained. I thought it was strange to pray for and be grateful for rain. I hated rain. Rain meant I could not play tennis or other outdoor sports. Never once in my life was I grateful when it rained. And since the only kind of "moisture" I was familiar with was rain (and occasionally sleet), I wondered why they did not just say rain. Not until I later moved to Utah did I realize that many Latter-day Saints grew up on farms in a desert environment and depended on all kinds of "moisture" for survival.

The other thing I thought was unusual was the way a number of LDS families prayed. The only times my family prayed when I was growing up was on Christmas and Easter when my uncle Gene (the Episcopal priest) came to our home for dinner. My mom would ask

Gene to "say grace" before we began eating and he always asked us to join hands while he said grace. As a teenager, I was not religious nor did I feel especially close to my family members. But something about holding hands always felt good to me, even if it was a little unusual. I noticed that all LDS individuals folded their arms when they prayed and in a number of families everyone turned away from each other and leaned on chairs and sofas and couches while kneeling. I decided that when I had a family I hoped we would face each other and hold hands when we prayed.

From early in the process of my conversion, my whole focus was preparing myself to be the best missionary I could be. Since I had been told that the best way to do that was to go to BYU and take religion classes there, I was awaiting word from BYU about whether my application would be accepted. I acted on faith that even with my paltry 2.2 high school GPA and 22 on the ACT, I would be accepted. I decided not to attend college at home but to work full-time to save money for BYU and for my mission. My parents were not happy with this decision, but I just felt like it would all work out.

When I received the letter from BYU that I had been admitted as a student for the fall of 1978, I was very happy. My parents had mixed feelings. On the one hand, they were proud that I had been admitted to a real university—not just the little junior college I had been attending (which admitted everyone). On the other hand, I would be moving out of state. They knew that, following one year at BYU, I intended to go on a two-year mission (with no coming home for weekends or summers). So, for them this new church I had joined was taking me even further away from home and family.

Although my mother dropped out of high school to get married, she always highly valued education and so she was excited her son, who had previously focused entirely on athletics, was now going to focus on academics (she thought). For me, the fact that I was now going to attend BYU had nothing to do with academics but everything to do with preparing for my mission. BYU was simply nine months' worth of mission preparation before I entered the MTC (Missionary Training Center). I had now been around the missionaries enough to know that I had a great deal to learn if I was to be an effective missionary for the Lord. The Lord blessed me with two great missionaries who had a very solid gospel knowledge and this inspired me to learn all I could in the short time period I had before I would be called to serve.

One day when I was talking with my parents about going to BYU my mom said, almost casually, "Well, if you are going to Provo, Utah, you will be able to meet your great aunt Ethel Frisbee Dollahite." When I asked who this person I had never heard of was, she said, "She is a Mormon lady who is always trying to get me to help her do genealogy."

I was stunned. There was another Mormon named Dollahite who lived in Provo, Utah! I said, "I have an aunt who is a Mormon?!"

My mom said, "Well, a great aunt by marriage. She was married to your grandfather's brother for a while. She does a lot of genealogy. She has written me a number of letters over the years trying to get me to give her information about the Dollahite family. She will be happy to know another Dollahite has become Mormon."

This news stunned and thrilled me. Although I did not think that I was going to BYU to meet long-lost Mormon relatives, it turned out to be among the most exciting and spiritually surprising parts of my first year there.

In the meantime, I continued to work to earn money. I got a full-time job at a pharmacy delivering medications to hospitals, nursing homes, and private homes. When my boss learned that I had joined the LDS Church, he told me that his wife was African-American and forcefully and repeatedly told me how racist my church was for denying the priesthood to blacks. I asked the missionaries about this and they told me that there were those in the pre-existence who were "fence-sitters" in that they did not enthusiastically accept the Father's plan but did not go along with Satan's plan either. They said these spirits were born as blacks.

This was the only thing that the Elders ever taught me that did not feel right to me. It did not make sense to me given my experience with the black kids I knew. They were as likely to be passionate about what they believed and to be committed to causes as any white kids—often even more so. And they seemed to be even more religious. It was not just that what the Elders said did not square with my experience; it just did not feel right to me.

I then had many discussions with the Elders and with other Church members about this issue. The only rationale I heard that made any sense to me was that we really did not know why this policy was enacted and we hoped the time would come when the priesthood would be extended to all worthy males. Even though I did not personally like the policy, I accepted on faith that this was not a reason to doubt the truthfulness of all I had been taught. I joined my faith and prayers with other Latter-day Saints that the priesthood would soon be extended to all deserving Latter-day Saint men.

Despite my misgivings about this issue, my testimony of the gospel continued to grow. On June 4, 1978, I wrote the following in my journal:

> My testimony of the truthfulness of the restored Gospel grows
> stronger every day. I know that Jesus is the Christ, that Joseph
> Smith was a true prophet of God, and that Spencer W. Kimball
> is a prophet. I know that the Book of Mormon as well as the

Bible is the word of God, and that if we follow its teachings we will have eternal life. . . . I must become much more humble and prayerful if I am to become a spiritual man. I truly want to marry in the Temple with an active, loving, spiritual L.D.S. girl. I can't wait to fulfill a mission and have a family and have the gospel of Jesus Christ a part of that family.

The Mormon attitude on family and the importance of it are very important to me. It is my hope and sincere prayer that I will develop into the kind of man that my Father in Heaven wants me to become and be able to be a righteous leader of my family. I must become more prayerful and faithful if I am to achieve this goal. I must bear my testimony to anyone who might read this: I know that the Church of Jesus Christ of Latter-day Saints is the true restored Church of Jesus Christ. I would exhort any one to read the Book of Mormon and then ponder it and ask God if it is true. I did and I received an answer and I am eternally grateful to my Father in Heaven for allowing me to do so. (Personal Journal, page 3)

One day in mid-June, I came back from my deliveries and walked into the pharmacy. My boss said to me, "Well, Dave, it just said on the radio that your church has finally done the right thing and decided to give the priesthood to black men." As the week went on I heard more about this historic change and there was much discussion about how President Kimball was a living prophet and that this change would have a great impact for good throughout the world. Like other Latter-day Saints, I happily sustained the new policy when it was read in Sacrament Meeting. In the testimony meeting a couple of weeks following this announcement, many Saints said they had been praying for years that the priesthood would be extended to all worthy members and there were many tears of joy shed.

As the summer quickly passed, I continued to read all the LDS books I could get my hands on, to attend all the LDS meetings I could attend, to have as many gospel conversations with my LDS friends as I could have, and to share the gospel with as many of my friends as would listen.

About this time, I had a wonderful dream that strengthened my testimony of Christ and of his Latter-day work that I had joined myself to. In the dream, I was standing with many other people who were facing the rising sun. The sky was clear and there were no buildings or trees between us and the horizon far away in the distance. Then very gradually, and a great way off, small clouds began to form. These clouds grew in size and definition and beauty and began coming closer to us. It seemed like the clouds were emerging from another sphere or dimension and soon the entire sky east of us was filled with huge rolling clouds coming toward us.

As they gradually got closer we could see that there were thousands of majestic beings in the clouds and in the midst of all of them was the most majestic person of all, dressed in deep yet bright crimson robes. I knew it was the Savior and I knew that this was his great Second Coming. The power and love that he radiated was beyond anything I had ever seen, but I had the same spiritual feelings I had come to know so well. Then he descended to the ground.

He came to the large group of us who were gathered and I was so happy to see him and to be there when he came to reign on the earth. He looked at me and spoke to me briefly and I will never forget the feelings of joy and gratitude I felt. I then awoke with a powerful rush of the Spirit and was weeping tears of joy. It took a moment to realize this was only a dream and not an actual event. It felt so real. From time to time throughout my life, I have been blessed with a few other dreams of great spiritual power and meaning to me. I consider these dreams among the choicest tender mercies the Lord has granted me.

Later, when I thought about this, I was surprised that in my dream Jesus wore red robes. In the paintings that I had seen of the second coming, Jesus was dressed in white robes. When I told a couple of returned missionaries about this dream, one of them said that he thought there was a scripture in the Doctrine and Covenants about Christ being "red in his apparel" when he came again. He later found the reference for me (D&C 133:46–48). I did not remember having read those passages in my one reading of the Doctrine and Covenants although it is possible that I had. Regardless, I thought it was a tender mercy to have some kind of experience—even though just in a dream—of the marvelous events yet to come when Christ descends in the clouds to rule and reign on earth for a thousand years.

TENDER MERCIES & LESSONS LEARNED

Only decades of studying Church history has allowed me to understand that a revelation of such broad implication, like the one given to President Kimball in 1978, only comes now and then. Of course, the Lord's prophets, seers, and revelators receive revelation daily to administer the Church. But revelations that change long-standing Church policy do not occur that often. I am extremely grateful to the Lord for His tender mercy in allowing me to be able to sustain one such revelation only months after I joined the Church.

Learning that I had LDS relatives was both extremely surprising to me and deeply comforting. I thought I was alone in the Church and now I knew I had an LDS aunt and perhaps cousins. I looked forward to meeting my Mormon relatives in Utah.

Being admitted to attend BYU right after my conversion and before my mission was an incredible tender mercy from the Lord. My faith and knowledge of the gospel was greatly strengthened during the nine months I spent in Provo and I met many wonderful people who helped me learn better how to live the gospel. I felt sure that the experience of being away from home for a year—even if only in the safe and convenient confines of BYU—would help prepare me for being away from home for two years on a mission. And I was about to learn that persistent, faithful prayer was answered—sometimes in amazing ways. ✺

PART II

Brigham Young University & Mission Preparation

CHAPTER 12

Persistent Prayers & Missionary Miracles

During the summer I was preparing to go to BYU, I began thinking that although taking BYU classes in the Book of Mormon, Bible, Doctrine and Covenants, and Missionary Preparation would be very helpful for me, what I really needed was to have a non-Mormon roommate. Then I could actually have the chance to share my conversion experience with someone, bear my testimony to him, and teach him the gospel with the missionaries at BYU. This seemed like just the right thing to best help me prepare to be the best missionary I could be. I began praying almost every day that I would have a non-LDS roommate.

I knew that BYU was a Mormon university but I did not realize that it was 98% LDS and the chances of having a non-LDS roommate were extremely low. But that did not matter to me since the Lord had answered my prayers thus far and I was being taught that the Lord always answered sincere prayers offered in faith. I prayed almost every day for this with new-convert childlike faith.

In late August I loaded up my 1970 Chevy Impala and drove across the desert to Provo, Utah. As I drove through the Salt Flats it seemed that both actually and metaphorically the road ahead was wide open and the horizon was limitless. I was driving into the unknown but with faith and optimism that all would work out well for me. I was thinking about what my time at BYU would be like and looking forward to meeting my great aunt Ethel—a Mormon relative.

I had decided not to try to play on the tennis team so that I could focus on preparing for my mission. I reasoned that the three to four hours a day I would have to spend at tennis practice would take away from time I could spend studying the gospel in preparation for my mission. Although my preference would have been to take nothing but religion classes, I was told that I could only take two per semester. But in order to stay in school to take the religion classes, I knew I had to pass the other classes (e.g., English, physical science, and biology). I had no real interest or intention to study for those classes except just enough to get passing grades. Again, I thought about how wonderful it would be to have a non-LDS roommate to be able to teach the gospel to.

I drove into the parking lot of the dorms I would be staying at—a place called Deseret Towers. I found Q-Hall, the building I would be living in, and went inside. I went to the window where the Hall office was, said hello to the woman working there, told her my name, and asked her who my roommate was. She told me the name of my roommate and told me which room I was in. I said thanks and then asked, "By the way, is my roommate Mormon?"

She looked at me a little funny and said, "Well, I assume he is."

I asked, "Would you please check for me?" She looked at me like I was a little strange and went back to a file drawer, and looked in a file.

She turned around and said, "Yes, your roommate is Mormon."

I said, "I'm really sorry, but there has been some kind of mistake. My roommate is not supposed to be a Mormon. Could you please just check one more time?" Now she looked at me like I was not just strange but rude as well.

She pulled out the file out and while looking at it walked back over to the window where I was standing. She then pulled out a piece of paper and said, "Hmm, that's interesting. Your roommate is a member of the Church. But it says here that he just had an appendicitis attack, is in the hospital having an emergency appendectomy, and will not be arriving for a couple of days. So, I guess you'll be alone in your room for a few days." I thanked her and took my two suitcases up to the room.

When I got into my room, I put my suitcases down, closed the door, knelt by one of the beds, and prayed, "Heavenly Father, I thank thee for helping me arrive here safely. You know that I am here to prepare to serve you as a missionary and that I would really, really like to have a non-Mormon roommate. If it be thy will, may I please have a non-Mormon roommate?"

I arose from my knees, opened the door, looked down the hallway, and saw a guy getting a drink from the water fountain at the other end of it. I walked down the hall, and when he was finished getting his drink, I said, "Hi, I'm Dave Dollahite."

He said, "Hi, I'm Bob Day."

"Hi Bob. Where are you from?"

"Washington, DC," he said.

"Cool, the nation's capital. How many stakes are there in Washington, DC?"

"What's a stake?" he asked.

"Oh, you're not LDS?"

"No. I'm Catholic," he said.

"Cool. I was raised Episcopalian, that's really close to Catholic. So, what brought you to BYU?"

"Well, I'm not really sure. I'm into music and I had a Mormon friend in high school who told me BYU had a good music program. So here I am."

"Great! So, which room are you in?" I asked.

"Well, I'm actually not even in this building. I'm in the one next to this one. But a fire broke out in my room right before I arrived. They have no idea how it started since no one was even in the room. But there was smoke damage so while they are replacing the carpet and drapes they told me to come over here for a couple of days." He pointed to a room and I could see he was beginning to unpack.

"Do you have a roommate?" I asked.

"No, I'm on my own," he said.

I said, "Hey, my roommate is in the hospital and is not coming for a couple of days. Would you like to stay in my room until your room is ready?"

"Sure. That sounds great!" Bob said. He grabbed his bags and brought them down to my room. We hit it off wonderfully. That night I told him about my conversion to the Church and he was very interested. He was a devout Catholic but found my story interesting. We became fast friends. After a couple of days, we went down to the Hall office and told the head resident that we would like to be roommates if possible. We asked her if she could switch our roommates to have my roommate become Bob's. She said that would be fine. Thus, Bob and I became official roommates.

Bob came to church the first Sunday and after a couple of weeks the missionaries began coming over to our room to teach Bob the discussions. I was able to teach with them over the couple of months that Bob investigated the Church. His parents were not happy with his desire to be baptized and worked hard on him to get him not to join the Church. He had a lot of questions and issues he had to resolve since his family would call or write with issues they wanted him to consider. The similar experience I had with my parents allowed me to both understand and support Bob in his conversion process. Bob was baptized on October 28 (nine months to the day from my own baptism). He asked his friend from Washington, DC, to baptize him. It was one of the most wonderful days in my life.

TENDER MERCIES & LESSONS LEARNED

When I have told others about this experience with Bob Day, I have been asked what I think really happened. Did God cause my roommate to have an appendicitis attack? Did God cause the fire to break out in Bob's room? I have no idea how all those things are worked out. I really doubt the Lord "caused" the appendix to rupture right at that time just to answer my prayers, and I hope that is not what happened. Perhaps the fire was going to break out anyway and the Lord (or perhaps an angel over housing at BYU?) had Bob assigned to that room so he could end up in my Hall for a couple of days.

I do not know how the Lord or His angels work out all the details to answer such prayers in such ways. I only know that He answers prayers; even ones that require the Lord to "move heaven and earth" to answer them. Over the four decades of my active prayer life, the Lord has shown His tender mercies to me thousands of times in many ways. I just try to exercise faith and remain grateful each time He does.

The Lord's tender kindness in responding to my specific, if unusual, prayer reinforced for me the power of persistent prayer with complete faith. This confirmed the rightness of my coming to BYU to prepare for my mission. I loved teaching the gospel to a willing listener. Until then, all my efforts to share the gospel with people were met with indifference, resistance, or downright hostility. Being "on the other side of the flip chart" allowed me to see how the missionaries taught the discussions, used scriptures, personal examples, and metaphors, and how they responded to questions. Because of my experience in helping teach Bob the discussions and seeing him convert and be baptized, I was even more excited to get on my mission and spend every hour of every day teaching the gospel.

I had been a member about seven months when this prayer was answered. Over the years, I have reflected a great deal on this singular experience in my early church life. At the time, I assumed that all Latter-day Saints had these types of miraculous experiences all the time. You prayed in faith for something and the Lord did what it took to answer your prayer. I did not really understand then that many faithful Saints prayed in faith and did not always have the same kind of clear and immediate answers.

It was not until I wrote this Chapter that I realized another tender mercy of the Lord in allowing me to teach Bob. During the time I was teaching Bob, I had no idea that I would be called to the Massachusetts Boston Mission, a mission where most of those I met and taught would be Catholic. Because of the questions that Bob and his family members had, I worked with the missionaries to resolve a great number of concerns and issues that many Catholics would have. Thus, the nearly two months that I spent teaching Bob with the missionaries (plus the entire nine months I roomed with Bob and we talked about religious things) prepared me well for teaching many good Catholics during my two years in New England.

When I think of the fact that it took me decades to recognize that particular tender mercy, it illustrates how slow I sometimes am to recognize all the details of the hand of the Lord in my life. It also is another of a multitude of witnesses I have received that support Jacob's statement that "great and marvelous are the works of the Lord. How unsearchable are the depths of the mysteries of him; and it is impossible that man should find out all his ways" (Jacob 4:8).

CHAPTER 13

Meeting the Mormon Relatives & Seeing the Lord's Prophet

One of the first things I did when I got settled in Provo was to find a phone book and look up my great aunt Ethel Frisbee Dollahite. It was strange to look in a Provo, Utah, phone book and see the name Dollahite. I called Aunt Ethel and introduced myself. I told her I was Elizabeth and Mel's son and that I had joined the Church and was attending BYU. To say she sounded joyfully surprised would be an understatement. I did not know it was possible for someone as old as she was to exude such enthusiasm. She invited me over and said she would have her daughter come over as well.

A few days later I drove up State Street in Orem and found her small home. Ethel, who was in her seventies, and her daughter, Dorothy, greeted me most warmly. They asked about my family and invited me to tell them how I came to join the Church. After I told them all I knew about my extended family and my conversion story, they told me that Ethel, a Mormon girl from Utah, had met DeWitt Dollahite (who was the brother of my grandfather L. C. Dollahite) at a dance when he passed through Utah on his way to California during World War II. They fell in love and were married. After having children, they later divorced. Aunt Ethel told me that I had LDS cousins including Elaine Dollahite, who was about my age and was thinking of serving a mission.

It soon became clear that Aunt Ethel's great passion in life was genealogy and family history. She had pedigree sheets lying everywhere and had a massive copy machine that she had leased to copy the great number of papers and records she had collected. Aunt Ethel told me a strange and wonderful story about my ancestors. She was still trying to piece together all the facts and so she was not certain about everything but this is the gist of what she told me:

After Aunt Ethel and my great uncle DeWitt married, Ethel tried to gather genealogical information from DeWitt's father, Daniel Webster Dollahite Jr. But he was not only unwilling to provide any such information, he made it clear he was extremely hostile to the Mormons. This was partly explained by the fact that he was a Church of God minister and that church was passionately anti-Mormon. But even this did not seem to fully explain his great animosity toward Mormonism and toward genealogy in particular.

Aunt Ethel said that she later discovered why her father-in-law was so unwilling to give her any information that would allow her to baptize his ancestors. It turned out that DeWitt's grandmother (my great-great-grandmother), Elizabeth Keith, joined the LDS Church along with her parents and sisters. It seems that this caused a great division between Elizabeth and her husband, Daniel Webster Dollahite Sr.

Aunt Ethel said she thought that Elizabeth, after unsuccessfully trying to convert her husband, had actually left Daniel Sr. and baby Daniel Jr. and had gone to Utah to gather with the Saints. She said that although she was not sure about this she thought that this explained why her father-in-law was so upset at the Mormons—in his mind they stole his mother from him. This story was at once extremely thrilling and deeply troubling to me.

It was thrilling because it meant that I too had pioneer ancestors who made incredible sacrifices for the restored gospel. But it was deeply troubling to me because the idea that a mother would leave her husband with a newborn baby seemed wrong and not in keeping with what the gospel taught. So, I was glad when I later learned that subsequent research done by other Dollahite family historians has not confirmed her theory. It seems that while Elizabeth did join the Church with other family members, she did not abandon her husband and child.

Aunt Ethel told me about others of my ancestors, most of whom lived in the Southern states, including Daniel Webster Sr.'s father, Thomas Jefferson Dollahite. With these names I figured that if my father's family had not moved from the Southern states to California I probably would have been named something like Stonewall Jackson Dollahite. She told me our ancestors probably came from Ireland and the first of my ancestors to come to America was Francis Delahyde who came to Maryland in the early 1600s and was both high sheriff of Baltimore county and a member of the Maryland legislature.

It was wonderful to learn about my ancestors. But another major spiritual event for me occurred on September 12, 1978, when I first heard the living prophet, President Spencer W. Kimball, speak in person. Along with 22,000 other BYU students, I waited with great anticipation for the prophet's visit to BYU to give a campus devotional. I arrived early and sat with my friends waiting for him to come into the Marriott Center.

Suddenly, everyone rose to their feet and I looked down and saw President Kimball coming onto the main floor of the building. As I saw him, I felt a rush of the Spirit confirming powerfully that this was indeed the prophet of the Lord. As he spoke with his highly distinctive voice—a raspy whisper that invited careful listening—I knew that he was God's mouthpiece on earth and that I should give great heed to everything he said. He gave a great talk, "On My Honor," about how important it was to be faithful in keeping the standards of the BYU honor code.

TENDER MERCIES & LESSONS LEARNED

As a new convert, I had experienced some amount of distress once I had spent time with and observed so many strong and faithful LDS families. Although I loved my parents dearly and had been raised in a good home with good values, part of me wished I had been raised in the Church in a strong LDS family. I sometimes felt inadequate and inferior since I did not have ancestors that converted to the Church and crossed the plains, or because I was not raised in a family where religious devotion was the pattern. I also felt like I was part of a small, disconnected family whereas many of the Mormons I had met had these huge extended families who they felt connected to and with whom they had regular family reunions.

Once, when I mentioned this to another Church member, I was surprised and encouraged when he said sometimes he wished he was a convert. He said that converts often had such a strong testimony and such enthusiasm for the gospel. While the idea that a wonderful Latter-day Saint who was raised in a great family might sometimes wish he was a convert was thought-provoking, nevertheless, it seemed to me that so many Latter-day Saints were so much better than I could ever hope to be. And sometimes this caused sadness and longing. These feelings of spiritual and familial inferiority were to emerge as a major issue on my mission where I was surrounded by so many incredible young men and women.

Also, another source of feeling inferior among Latter-day Saints for me was that many of them knew a great deal about their faithful ancestors, including inspiring stories of courage and heroism.

Conversely, I knew almost nothing about my father's parents who died before I was born or about my mother's mother who I never met and who died when I was three. The only one of my grandparents I knew was my mother's father, Iver Stenen, who spent several weeks with us each summer and whom I loved and looked up to for his great courage and physical strength.

Thus, since I knew so little about them, I was thrilled to learn more about my ancestors. In a way that I could not really understand or express, meeting these Mormon Dollahite relatives and learning that I too had ancestors who converted to the Church, caused me to feel that some deep reservoirs of family connection were beginning to fill up.

President Kimball was the first prophet I knew and was to be "my prophet" for the first seven years of my Church membership. I developed a profoundly deep love and respect for him and for Sister Kimball. He proved a source of spiritual truth and inspiration for me in all I did to prepare for and serve an honorable mission for the Lord.

The Lord's tender mercy was manifest to me in great abundance that wonderful day as I basked in the presence of the Lord's prophet. And I could have had no way of knowing that my future wife, Mary Kimball—a granddaughter of President Kimball—was also there at the devotional and that this was the first time we were in the same place together.

CHAPTER 14

Death & Dream of Grandpa Iver

One January evening near the beginning of the winter semester, my mom called to tell me that her father, my beloved grandfather, Iver Stenen had died. She told me he was supposed to go to the doctor but instead hopped on his moped and drove down the highway to go bowling. There he suffered a heart attack and died. Mom said that he had directed that he be cremated and his ashes strewn at sea. She said she had not wanted to interrupt my studies and so she had already gone to Boca Raton, Florida, where he had lived, and rented a boat to take his ashes out to sea where she said a prayer and cast the ashes over the water.

I felt numb and powerless as she told me all this. The man who was the hero of my childhood, and the most generous grandfather anyone could have, was gone. I would not be able to go to his funeral and hear those who knew him best tell stories of his incredibly exciting life. And I would not even be able to go to visit his grave. He was gone—utterly and completely gone. This seemed impossible and unreal to me.

After my mom and I finished our phone conversation, I sat and thought about my grandfather. I remembered all the stories he had told me of times when he had "cheated death" through luck, skill, or guile. He had run away from his home on a farm in Norway at age seventeen and made his way to Southampton, England, to work as a merchant marine. He missed being on the Titanic by only weeks. He stowed away on a ship headed to America. While working in the shipyards in New Jersey, he had been knocked off a tow barge by two tankers squeezing and toppling the barge and he had swum under one of the tankers and climbed up the ladder, coming up behind those who were looking over the side assuming he was dead. He had survived motorcycle crashes, logging accidents, and the toppling of an electric tower he was working on. He also survived a fire set by his "crazy mother-in-law" (who set her home on fire to collect the insurance money) by climbing out a second story bedroom window into a tree with his young wife.

Every time he told me one of these kinds of stories I would say, "Grandpa, you could have died!" He would always smile and say with his Norwegian accent, "Naw, ven it's your time to go, you vill go!"

My amazing grandpa Iver had even survived being pierced in the side of his head with a brand-new metal-pointed dart—one I threw myself when I was about ten years old. I had received a new set of darts and was in our backyard looking for something to throw them into when I saw a window with six panes leaning against the house. One of the panes had been broken and my dad had replaced the broken window with a new one. I asked my father if I could throw my new darts and break the other panes of the broken window. I was both surprised and thrilled when he gave me permission to do this and then put a blanket behind and below the window to catch the broken glass.

I imagined myself as a pitcher in the World Series as I wound up and threw the darts into each of the panes. I had a pretty strong arm and the crash of the glass breaking was music to my ears. I backed up with each new pitch until I was at the other end of our small yard, ready to throw the last dart. I wound up and threw as hard as I could to break the last pane of glass. After I threw the dart I waited for the glorious sound of glass breaking, but heard instead a loud and pained voice from inside my house crying, "Oooowwwww!"

I ran into the house through the open back door and through my bedroom into the kitchen where I knew Grandpa was playing Solitaire (he loved to play cards). My dart was sticking out of his temple and there was a line of blood dripping down from the dart. As I got there, Grandpa pulled the dart out of his head and looked at it. I had seen enough Westerns on TV to know that if someone was shot in the temple, they were a goner so I cried out, "Grandpa! Grandpa! Are you going to die?!"

He wiped the blood off and said to me, "Naw, zis is nothing. But David, I do not think you should tell your mother about this. She vould kill you!" I was extremely glad he had given me permission not to tell my mom about what I had done, since she was extremely protective of her father and I think death would have been the least of my worries if she had seen or known what happened. In fact, I never did tell her this story until long after my grandfather had died. And, even then, she became quite upset at me.

When I remembered all the wonderful times with my grandpa I could not believe he was really dead. I guess I thought he would live forever. This was the first death of a family member that I had experienced. It was also the first death I had experienced since I had been taught about gospel doctrines such as the spirit world, resurrection, and eternal families. I believed all these teachings and had a testimony of them since I received a witness of the Plan of Salvation. So I believed that my grandfather's spirit still lived even though the remains of his body had been dissolved in the Atlantic Ocean. I believed that I would see him again at some point in the far distant future—either when I died or after the resurrection. But that seemed like such a long time.

That night I drifted off to sleep thinking about my grandpa and wishing I could see him again. The next thing I knew, I was walking toward a large mountain with a kind of cave opening at the bottom of it. As I walked closer, I saw a man emerging from the darkness of the opening. As he came into the light, I saw that it was my grandfather. I ran and embraced him and asked him where he had been. He said he had died and was now in the spirit world. He told me that everything I had been taught about the Plan of Salvation was true. He said he was still alive and that I would be with him again. He told me he was glad I had accepted the gospel since now I could help him on his journey. After this he said goodbye and sort of floated back into the cave.

I awoke feeling a powerful rush of the spirit. I knew that the Lord had given me this dream or vision or whatever it was. It was still dark in my room and I knew that this was more than just a dream. I was not sure exactly what kind of experience it was, but I knew it was sent by the Lord to help me deal with my deep sense of loss.

As I lay there pondering about this wonderful blessing sent by a loving and merciful God, I knew that I would not have these kinds of experiences every day but that the Lord was aware of my deepest needs and desires and would send such blessings according to my faith. I learned that believing something in principle or even having a spiritual witness of it did not take away the pain of loss. But I also learned for myself that divine consolation is real.

TENDER MERCIES & LESSONS LEARNED

As I think back on this tender mercy sent by a most gracious Heavenly Father, I am in awe of His constant attention to my spiritual progress and needs. He knew that in those early years I sometimes felt terribly inadequate as a Latter-day Saint. He knew that I deeply longed for the kinds of family connections that I constantly heard about from my new LDS friends, but did not then enjoy. He knew that I loved Him and would do anything I could to become a better person, a better disciple, and a better missionary for Him. And, in His own due time and in His own wonderful way, he drew me close to Him and His eternal truths and blessings. I look forward to seeing my wonderful grandfather Iver again and to meeting my other three grandparents whom I never knew in this life.

CHAPTER 15

Freshman Year & Automotive Miracles

Among the papers that BYU had sent me during the summer before I left for campus was a form asking me, among other things, what I planned to major in. In high school, I had never given any thought to what I might major in at college. My plan was to play as much tennis as possible, take whatever fluff classes I had to take to maintain my athletic eligibility, and then leave college and travel around the world playing tennis for a living for a while. Then I planned to open a big, lucrative tennis club where I would make a boatload of money teaching rich people how to hit forehands and backhands.

But in the spirit of at least pretending that I was going to BYU for something other than to prepare for my mission, I did some thinking about what I should declare as my major. One day before going to BYU, I was talking with my mom about this while we were watching a John Wayne Western on TV. While discussing the merits of a major in business or in coaching, I made an off-hand comment about John Wayne and how easy acting would be and how you could make a lot of money doing something that did not take any real skill. My mom said, "Actually, good acting is very difficult."

I said, "Look at John Wayne. He is just standing around saying his lines. It doesn't look very hard."

Mom then said, "Well, why don't you major in theater at BYU?"

I said, "Well, maybe I will." So, having never been in any plays, and having never even been to a play of any kind, and having always thought of the theater people at my high school as being weird or nerdy and definitely not the kind of kids I wanted to be like or hang around with, I declared myself a theater major and sent off the form to BYU.

So, I registered for an acting class at BYU and began to learn about this thing I thought was so easy. At first I thought my mom was wrong as it seemed to me that I was about as good as the other acting students. But it turned out my mom was right. The first play I tried out for had only four parts for males. Only five guys auditioned for the play. I was the only one who did not get a part. So, I rededicated myself to working hard at acting. Over the next two semesters I tried out for four other plays and two films, and was selected for all of them. I was blessed to be selected to play Galileo's son in a major production called Lamp at Midnight in the Pardoe Theatre, BYU's largest theater.

I had a lot of fun hanging around theater people. Rehearsing for and performing in plays gave me confidence in public speaking that I sorely lacked. While I had always been a gregarious person and was fairly confident in expressing my views in a classroom setting or in personal conversations, I had never had any training in speaking before larger groups of people. So, while I did not choose to major in theater to help me prepare for my mission, it actually turned out to be helpful to me in the thing I was really at BYU to do—prepare to talk to groups of people in many settings about the gospel.

I loved nearly everything about BYU (I did not really enjoy the cold and the snow). But my biggest issue was with my English class. While I did not enjoy the amount of red ink that marked up my feeble attempts to write decent papers, the real issue was that, to me, the professor seemed to criticize the Church quite often. I often wondered how he was allowed to teach at BYU. I later got to know him better and it turned out this good man was a wonderful Latter-day Saint with a strong testimony. But to my new convert soul he was a little too similar to the approach of Brother Heater—too much of an intellectual and skeptical approach to the Church and its doctrine and practice.

And I did not enjoy Physical Science 100 at all. I saw every minute spent studying the elements of the periodic table or the laws of gravity as time I was not studying the scriptures in preparation for my mission. My approach was to study as little as I possibly could for this class, and use that time instead for scripture study. Then, before every exam, I prayed fervently that the Lord would help me pass the test so I could stay at BYU preparing for my mission. I also took this approach with my American Heritage class, praying myself to a score high enough to opt out of taking the class but receiving the credit. I was blessed with solid C grades when I am quite sure I did not merit such marks from my own study.

Somehow, I knew that the time would come when I could not ask for such indulgences from the Lord. Looking back, I realize that I cheated myself out of important learning opportunities. When I returned from my mission I applied myself to serious study of my subjects. At that time, however, I was very grateful to the Lord for helping this ex-jock, budding missionary, and not-yet-ready-for-primetime university student through that first challenging year at BYU.

Except for those few things, I really did love everything about BYU. Every day I felt grateful for the chance to be at a place where everyone loved the Lord and tried to serve Him. I liked the guys on my floor. They were great guys. There was a group from Mesa, Arizona, led by Elmer Heap who were a lot of fun and were great examples to me. Each floor had a "floor chaplain" who was supposed to call everyone together for evening prayer and devotional and try to set good example. The guys on my floor elected me for this responsibility.

I took it seriously. I would go around the floor knocking on dorm doors to invite the guys to come to "floor prayer."

At about midnight on December 17, my twentieth birthday, I was lying in bed dozing off to sleep when I heard voices, intense whispers, and stifled laughter, outside my door. Before I knew what hit me a bunch of guys burst into my room and pulled me out of bed, carried me down the hall to the bathroom with everyone singing "Happy Birthday to You," and proceeded to dump me into a bathtub filled with ice cold water made from several wastebaskets full of snow and cold water. After I was thus rudely awakened, and after I had showered, the guys apologetically showed me a broken bottle that was in the bathtub that must have been scooped up accidentally when they were getting the buckets full of snow. Fortunately, I was not cut.

I was called as the chair of the Ward Activity Committee so I spent that year organizing activities for my ward. Our bishop, David Paulsen, was a philosophy professor at BYU and a wonderful spiritual leader. He interviewed me to receive my patriarchal blessing and ordained me an elder on March 4, 1979. That day I wrote in my journal:

> *I was ordained to the Melchizedek Priesthood today. It was a special experience. Bishop David L. Paulsen ordained me. I now have the privilege and honor of holding the Priesthood of God. I love the Lord and my Father in Heaven. I love the Gospel of Jesus Christ and I know it is true. I am so grateful for the scriptures and especially the Book of Mormon. I am so happy to have the friends I do. They are so neat and they strengthen me so much! Bob Day, my roommate is really coming along in the Gospel. His testimony is growing and he is looking to the Lord's church for help more and more. . . .*

*I can't wait to go on a mission! I want to teach the Gospel
of Jesus Christ to thousands. I want to baptize thousands and
I know I can with the Lord on my side. I want to marry in the
temple and raise a good LDS family. (Personal Journal, page 10)*

Holding the priesthood meant a lot to me and less than a month
later I had the chance to exercise my priesthood and administer to the
sick.

In the winter semester, I had a mission prep class that was
incredibly inspiring for me and only served to get me even more excited
about my mission. Receiving my patriarchal blessing was a wonderful
experience and confirmed to me that the Lord desired that I serve a
mission. Among other missionary-oriented messages it stated, "The
Lord knows of your desire to serve Him. . . . You shall be privileged
to go forth as an ambassador of the Kingdom of God to proclaim the
name of the Lord Jesus Christ. . . . There are many precious children
upon the earth who the Lord loves and your mission shall be to seek
them out." My blessing served to confirm and even increase the very
strong desire I already had to serve the Lord on a full-time mission.

Of course, BYU was filled with beautiful, bright, and spiritual
women. I dated about as much as other guys. One especially
memorable date was with a bright and spiritual young lady named
Cara who was also a convert to the Church. We went in my car to eat
at Marie Callender's restaurant in Orem. After we finished eating we
went back out to my car. When I reached into my pocket to get my car
keys they were not there. The doors were locked but we could see that
my keys were still in the ignition.

We had to hurry to get to a play at BYU. We were able to get a
coat hanger from someone and bent and maneuvered it in such a way
that we could almost get the lock to come up. The problem was that I

had the tall narrow kind of lock without the little knob at the top to prevent a thief doing exactly what we were trying to do. So, we were unable to get the locks to come up.

After a few minutes of this, when I was about to give up and call a friend to come and get us, I looked over the roof of my car and saw that Cara's head was bowed. I watched a moment in silence, not wanting to disturb her prayer. She looked up and said, "Okay, try the door handle." I pulled the handle and the door opened. Cara and I got in the car and she said, "I prayed it would open," in a simple, matter-of-fact way that indicated that she also had been used to the Lord answering her prayers. We made it to the play just in time. That was the first of many "automotive miracles" I have been blessed with since I joined the Church.

Even though a number of my buddies going on missions had girlfriends that had promised to write them throughout their mission, I had decided that I did not want to have a girlfriend when I left on my mission. I thought it would be better not to be distracted. However, as the time approached to depart from BYU and head back to California to earn as much money for my mission as possible, I developed this inexplicably strong desire to have someone write to me on my mission. I guess I thought that unless I had a girlfriend no one would write to me, even though three or four gals said they would.

Near the end of the winter semester I got in touch with the bishop in my home ward, Bishop Teare, and asked him how much money I needed to earn to pay for my mission. He said that there were people in the ward who wanted to help me pay for my mission, and so I would only need to earn enough for half the expenses. I said, "Bishop, that's very nice, but I really want to pay for my entire mission. That is what others do and I don't want any special treatment. I'll work as long as it takes to pay for my entire mission."

Bishop Teare said, "Dave, we want you to be able to be back at BYU in the fall semester [of 1981], so we want you to be able to leave by early August, and there are people who really want to help pay for your mission. Would you deny those good people the blessings they will receive by helping support a missionary?" What could I say to that? I told the bishop I would not want to deny anyone any blessings and so I would be happy to let them help support me. I asked how much I would need to pay for half my mission and Bishop Teare suggested an amount ($4,000).

So, I figured out how many hours I would be able to work from the time I got home in late April, taking a couple weeks to find a job, and being able to work until late July or early August. I figured out how much an hour I would need to make to earn $5,000 by then (deducting tithing, taxes, plus some extra for clothing and other things I might need). It came to $11.50 an hour. I had never earned more than $4.50 an hour and I had no skills that would allow me to be paid such an income. But I had faith the Lord would provide.

I also decided that I needed a job where I would be able to study the scriptures and memorize "the discussions" (the materials that missionaries memorized to teach from). My goal was to have all of the missionary discussions memorized before I entered the MTC. And I also thought that it would be good to have a job where I could teach the gospel in some way.

I began praying on a regular basis that the Lord would bless me with a job that would allow me to earn at least $11.50 an hour, allow me to study the gospel, and allow me to do missionary work. The fact that I could not conceive of any kind of job that anyone would pay me good money to study my scriptures and teach the missionary lessons to my coworkers did not deter me from praying for this with faith.

The semester ended and my friend Laura Grow and I packed up my car, said goodbye to our friends, and headed for home. Laura was in my ward and we had become good friends. I was to drop Laura off at her home in Modesto and then head to my home in Marin County. We were in the middle of the desert cruising along the freeway in my Chevy Impala up a very long hill. When we crested the hill, and began coming down the other side, my car suddenly died. Laura and I looked at each other and I just coasted down the long hill in the right lane. We both offered up silent prayers for some kind of assistance.

Near the bottom of the hill was an exit, so I coasted off the freeway and came around a long circular exit ramp. When the car had nearly stopped, I pulled off the road into the gravel parking lot of a small service station. We got out of the car and went into the station. The owner asked what he could do for us and I told him what had happened. He said, "Let's take a look at it." He grabbed a tool box and went out to the car. He opened the hood and played around for a couple minutes, tried to start the car, and then said, "Well, it looks like your starter is bad."

I asked, "Do you happen to have a starter that would fit my car?"

He smiled and said, "Well, it's your lucky day." He pointed to an old beat up Chevy over by the fence and said, "Just yesterday, I put a brand-new starter in that car over there and then it threw a rod right after I put it in. So, the owner brought it over here and told me I could sell it or use it for spare parts. The starter I put in it is exactly what you need." He went over to the other car and in about five minutes came back with the starter which he then put in my car in just a few minutes. Then he said, "Okay, you're all set."

I said, grabbing my wallet, "Wow! That is wonderful. Thank you! How much do I owe you?"

He said, "Nothing. The other guy paid for the starter."

I said, "Okay. Thanks! What about your time?"

He said, "It only took me a few minutes and I hardly even got dirty."

I said, "Well, that is really nice of you, but I really want to pay you something."

He said, "No thanks. I won't take your money. I'm happy to help. Why don't you just fill your tank with gas and we'll call it good."

So, we filled the car with gas, thanked our "automotive angel" profusely, and headed on back down the road to California. We had no other car problems. I dropped Laura off at her home in Modesto and headed to my home to begin job hunting.

TENDER MERCIES & LESSONS LEARNED

The Lord blessed me with many tender mercies during my first year at BYU: I had an incredible roommate; my prayers were answered and I was able to teach the gospel to a humble, open investigator; I was given a marvelous patriarchal blessing that gave me hope and great promises; I was ordained to the Melchizedek priesthood; I was able to meet and come to know many wonderful people; I was able to participate in a number of great plays and develop confidence speaking in front of groups — even large groups — of people; I dated some wonderful young ladies, a few of whom wrote to me on my mission even though we were not "boyfriend and girlfriend"; I had wonderful religion classes, particularly the mission prep class; and I had a chance to have a lot of fun with a bunch of really classy kids. I also experienced a couple of automotive miracles that paved the way for many others in my life.

Now I was ready to go and get that really good job to pay for my mission.

CHAPTER 16

An Incredible Job & an Inspired Call

My parents were happy to have me home safely from the long drive across the desert. They were happy that I had obtained passing grades in my first year away at school, but my mom could tell that my heart was not really into the academic aspects of college. She had hoped I might get serious about my education but my 2.0 GPA (higher grades in my religion classes and lower grades in the others) was an indication to her that I did not really "apply myself" to my school work. She was concerned that I would be called to some remote mission in Africa or the jungles of South America so that there would be two more years where I would not be exposed to "culture and civilization" as she had always wanted for me.

I continued to pray for the kind of job I needed to earn enough money for half my mission by early August. And I began my job hunt. But for the first couple of weeks I was not successful in finding employment that paid enough — much less that would allow me to study the scriptures and missionary lessons. I continued to pray in faith and work to find a job. After about three weeks I was becoming worried that time was flying by and I would now need a job that paid me closer to $12.00 an hour.

One evening some good friends of my parents, Don and Jill Guppy, who were from England, came over for dinner. On hearing I was looking for a job, Don said he would check with someone he knew who owned a construction company and who was always looking for laborers — skilled and unskilled — to work for him. The next day I got a call from Don who gave me the name and phone number of his friend. I called and he offered me a job paying $11.90 an hour—the union wage for unskilled laborers. I was thrilled, although I did not see how I would be able to study the gospel while doing construction work. But I felt this was the right job for me so I accepted it and continued to pray.

I showed up at the place I was told to go and was assigned to work on a crew of roofers who were going to be replacing the roofs on several cell blocks at San Quentin prison (the maximum-security prison in California). The other three men on the crew were all black guys from Oakland who had worked together on many roofing jobs. Two of them were roofers and one was a skilled laborer. I was clearly the odd man out in terms of my ability to provide anything more than grunt labor. But I was happy to work hard for almost $12.00 an hour.

We drove out to the San Quentin prison and were escorted through the cell blocks and through the yard where hundreds of prisoners were hanging around, lifting weights, playing handball, smoking, talking, and watching us. Most of these guys looked like the hardened criminals they were. I was glad to have an armed guard to escort us to our work site. We spent the first week taking off the old roof. There were many bullet holes in the roof where guards attempting to quell riots had shot their guns into the air. My coworkers and I joked that we hoped there were no riots while we were working on the roofs. Once we did find bullet holes through the place we had just replaced a couple of days before.

After a week of hard physical labor, I was happy with the money but still prayed that I would be able to study and teach the gospel. In the second week, the time came to put the new tar roof on the cell block, which was about the size of a football field. There was a huge kettle that melted blocks of hard tar into a sticky liquid that would then be pumped up onto the roof, a good fifty feet up.

By California law, someone had to be with the kettle at all times (because it was hundreds of degrees hot). That person would both chop up the blocks of tar to keep the kettle filled and turn on the pump when the guys on the roof pulled a cord with a bell on it. Since I was the least experienced of the four of us, they said I would be the guy on the ground tending the kettle.

On the first day of this new arrangement I only did about an hour of work and the rest of the time I stood or sat around with nothing to do. I had a conversation with one of the inmates through a fence. He was in for armed robbery and murder. I also picked through a pile of refuse near where the kettle was and found a porcelain toilet seat with a knife-shaped hole cut from it. When I asked a security guard about this the next day he said that inmates spent years making weapons just to kill someone who had wronged them. The inmate had used a series of razor blades to cut out the porcelain knife they called a shank.

When I described my day to the crew chief and asked what I should do the other seven hours a day he said, "Well, bring a book."

I said, "Really?"

He said, "Well, there is nothing else for you to do, so why not read?"

So, I brought my Bible and my discussions (the "Rainbow Discussions," so-called for the fact that each of the six lessons was printed on a different color of paper). I was able to spend seven hours every day studying the gospel, including during lunch. During the first week, I had eaten lunch with my coworkers. But they spent the time telling each other and me about their wild nightly exploits with many dirty jokes and swear words sprinkled in. So, I told them I needed to read my Bible and lessons to prepare for my mission. They thought this was fine and dubbed me "The Preacher." Since my three coworkers swore with such frequency and enthusiasm, I dubbed them "The Three Cusskateers."

At the end of the second week, they said to me, "Hey, Dave, we like to hear good preaching and you are studying to be a preacher. So why don't you preach to us every day during the lunch hour?" Of course, I was thrilled with this invitation, so from then on for the next couple of months I studied during most of the day and gave them the missionary lessons during the lunch hour.

For such "crusty" guys, my friends from the big city actually showed a lot of spiritual insight and asked a lot of good questions. I would like to say that they joined the Church, but as far as I know, none of them did. But we sure had interesting conversations each day and I was able to practice what I would be teaching on my mission. So, for the rest of the ten weeks (we reroofed several cell blocks), I got paid almost twelve bucks an hour to study the scriptures and teach the discussions to willing listeners. And by all indications they actually enjoyed our little "preaching sessions."

In May, I put in my mission papers and waited anxiously for my call. I was happy to serve wherever I was called, but I did hope that it might be an English-speaking mission. I felt that because I was so new in the Church, if I had to explain the gospel and try to tell my conversion experience in another language I would not be as effective a missionary. But I did think it would be cool to go to another country. I hoped I would be called to serve in some place like England, Ireland, or Australia.

Our neighbor Bob Hammond was excited that I was going to be a missionary. He had traveled the world with the Marines and been in many exotic locations. Every time he saw me he would say something like, "Maybe you'll go to Africa," or, "Maybe you'll teach the natives in the Amazon rain forests," or, "It would be cool to go to China." I remembered that a couple of months after I joined the Church, the Leiningers' son Doug had returned from his mission to Taiwan. I was surprised that a few times during his homecoming talk in Sacrament Meeting Doug had trouble remembering basic words in English and had to turn around and ask the bishopric what the word was for this or that everyday thing (e.g., chair, book).

Then one day the big white envelope from Salt Lake City finally arrived and I opened my mission call. I did not know that I was supposed to gather a bunch of people together and open my call with them, so I just ripped it open myself. I read that the prophet, President Spencer W. Kimball, had called me to serve in the Massachusetts Boston Mission and that I would begin my two-year mission on August 9, 1979. I was incredibly excited and accepted on faith that Boston was where the Lord wanted me to serve.

When I told my mom about where I had been called, she looked relieved and happy. She told me she had hoped that I would go somewhere where there were universities and that I would catch the spirit of education. She knew something I did not: there are over twenty universities in the Boston area. (I ended up being assigned to work in the University Ward there, which meant I spent a great deal of time on the campuses of Harvard, MIT, Tufts, Boston College, University of Massachusetts, and other schools.)

Then I went over to tell my neighbor Bob. With excitement in my voice I told him I would be serving in Boston. He said, "What! Boston?! No way! You write them and say you are not going to Boston. Tell them to send you to China or Africa or South America or some other exotic place."

I said, "Well, the call came from a prophet of God, so I'm sure that is where the Lord wants me to serve." Bob just shook his head and looked very disappointed.

From then until I left on my mission, I continued to work hard on studying the scriptures and the discussions, got a lot of practice teaching the concepts in the discussions, and asked all the returned missionaries in my ward and stake (including Warren Pino who was back from South Africa) for their advice about missionary work. I became more and more excited as the time to leave drew near. I had been preparing to serve the Lord as a full-time missionary for more than eighteen months—from the day I had my first missionary lesson.

When it was time for me to go buy some clothes for my mission, my mom insisted that she purchase them for me. While I would have bought the least expensive clothes that looked good enough for a representative of the Lord and His Church, my mom insisted on getting me the nicest clothes she could afford—much better than what I would otherwise have got. But, more than once, Mom made a point to say that she was not supporting my mission, but just supporting me as her son.

On May 29, 1979, I went to the Oakland Temple to receive my endowment. The beauty of the temple and the sacredness of the holy ordinances I participated in were overwhelming to me. The nature of the temple ordinances was very different from the Sunday worship I had become used to in the Church. But I was surprised how familiar it felt from my early years in the Episcopal Church. Not that the exact kinds of things occurred, but rather that the more liturgical (formal) nature of the temple rites were more like the high church services I had known as a child.

When I was investigating the Church the missionaries told me that the more liturgical type of service that many other churches had (they mentioned Catholicism) was "vain repetition" and not the true form of worship that Latter-day Saints had which was to be simple and "led by the Spirit." They said that the only written prayers in the Church were the Sacrament and Baptismal prayers. Because I trusted their teaching, and because I did not enjoy all aspects of the liturgy I had experienced in my childhood, I rejected the possibility that there was any value in a highly liturgical form of worship. Thus, I was surprised to find that in the most holy place on earth—the temple—the most sacred form of worship that Latter-day Saints participate in would be much more familiar to people from more liturgical faiths (like a Catholic or Episcopalian) than to a Baptist or a Pentecostal Christian or even to a Mormon who had not yet been to the temple.

TENDER MERCIES & LESSONS LEARNED

With the job I was blessed to get, the Lord had, once again, answered my prayers for seemingly impossible things with exactly what I had prayed for—and more. I came to refer to my job that summer as "preaching to the spirits in prison."

My parents were still not happy that I would be away from home (and not in college) for two solid years but at least I would be in a major center of higher education as opposed to the jungles of South America, India, or Africa. Indeed, the Lord also showed a tender mercy to my mom by calling me to a place that she could at least feel might influence me for good in the way she valued. Little did Mom or I know that the fire for knowledge and education that would be lit on my mission would impel me to not only obtain a university degree—the first in my family—but to also obtain a masters degree and a doctorate as well.

In fact, the three things my mother valued most—family, education, and faith—were greatly enhanced by my involvement in the restored gospel. My family thought that I had rejected my family when I joined the Church and that the Church "took me away" from them. In fact, the heavy emphasis the LDS Church places on family relationships has caused me to be far more focused on maintaining good family connections with my parents, siblings, and extended family than I would ever have maintained if I had not joined the Church. And, had I not joined the Church, I am positive that I would not have completed college, much less become a university professor. I am certain that I would not have made religion such an important part of my life had I remained an Episcopalian. I doubt I would have been in the least bit religious.

But all those things were in the future. For now, my whole focus was getting on my mission. That began with nearly four wonderful and eventful weeks in the Missionary Training Center. 🌺

PART III

My Full-time Mission

CHAPTER 17

Missionary Training Center &
Arrival in New England

When I was set apart for my mission I was given a missionary journal by the Leiningers. On the first page of this journal I wrote about being set apart on August 7, 1979:

> *I love the Lord dearly and I want to serve him with all of my heart, might, mind, and strength. I know beyond all doubt that God lives, that Jesus is the Christ and that the Church of Jesus Christ of Latter-day Saints is TRUE! I thank my Father in Heaven that I have this sacred testimony. (Mission Journal, page 1)*

On the first Sunday in the Missionary Training Center (MTC), among other things I wrote: "I know that my call is divine and I know that I am truly doing the work of the Lord. I believe all the commandments and I can't wait to tell as many people as I can about Jesus Christ" (p. 7).

When I entered the MTC I felt like I had gone to mission prep heaven since every person there was focused on helping prepare missionaries and every minute of every day was spent in the Lord's work. I was in heaven! However, I quickly learned that not all missionaries were there for the best reasons or were fully committed to doing the work.

As it turned out, my MTC companion was such an Elder. He proudly displayed an 8x10 photo of his girlfriend and made it clear to us he was only there because she would not marry him unless he

went on a mission. To let us all know how cool he was and all the fun
he left behind to serve, he used a marijuana leaf as a bookmark for
his scriptures. He was not really interested in getting up on time, in
studying the discussions, or in keeping mission rules.

I did my best to encourage him and motivate him but he made it
clear he really did not want to be where he was or be doing what he
was doing. But I also learned that even though not all missionaries
came out for the best of reasons, those who applied themselves to the
work often soon caught the spirit of what we had been called to do.
Sometimes it took a "Dear John" letter or a spiritual experience or the
joy of seeing someone's life change for the better.

One week into my MTC experience I was called to be a counselor
in our Branch Presidency for President Black. This gave me a chance to
learn about leadership in the mission field and gave me a greater sense
of concern for all the Elders and Sisters in our branch.[1] I was asked to
give priesthood blessings to an Elder and then a Sister. Exercising my
priesthood in this way was very gratifying for me. Each time I laid my
hands on someone's head and blessed them in the name of the Lord, I
felt the power of the priesthood and the Spirit flowing through me and
I heard myself saying words I would not have known to say or been
brave enough to say.

There was one experience in the MTC that I am hesitant to write
about. Before recording this, I counseled with my bishop about it
and, based on his counsel, I feel that I should include this. One night,
while drifting off to sleep after a long, hard day of productive work, I

---

1. A branch is a smaller congregation than a ward and is presided over by a branch
president (a ward is presided over by a bishop).

suddenly felt a powerful, dark, cold, and terrifying power take hold of me.

I felt pure evil gathered around me. I was more frightened than I had ever been. I knew what it was and began to pray with great desperation. But, no matter how hard I tried, I could not get any words out. I felt my tongue cleaving to the roof of my extremely dry mouth and felt I could not speak. I knew that I needed to vocally rebuke Satan in the name of Christ and command him to leave. So, I prayed silently with even more effort. But—for what seemed like hours but was actually only a couple of minutes—I was unable to speak out loud. I was now quite terrified at this power of such destructive malevolence that I knew I had no power to control on my own. I continued to pray with great effort until I was finally able to speak aloud, with great difficulty, the words, "In the name of Jesus Christ, and by the power of the Melchizedek priesthood, I command you to depart NOW!"

Immediately I felt the evil presence leave. I felt tremendous relief at being saved from terrifying power—a destructive power I had only read about before but now knew was extremely real and extremely strong. As I pondered on what had just happened, I was very confused. I thought that I would be protected from Satan's influence since I was a set apart missionary at the MTC. I know that I had not consciously done anything to invite such evil influence into my life. I was on a high spiritual plane at finally being on my mission and was really looking forward to teaching the people of New England about the restored gospel. I must admit that I wondered why the Lord would allow this influence to attack me while under the protection of the mantle of a mission call in a dedicated building. I suppose it is possible that the Lord allowed this to occur so that I would have a clear testimony of the power of the forces that are arrayed against the Lord and His servants. I hope to never have such an encounter again.

One day I had a special treat. About four months previous, before I left BYU to return to California, my great aunt by marriage, Ethel Frisbee Dollahite, had told me that her granddaughter, my second cousin, Elaine Dollahite was going on a mission and might be in the MTC at the same time I was. But I was so focused and busy in learning the discussions and how to teach and focusing on my leadership of the branch and dealing with a less-than-fully-engaged companion that I forgot to seek my cousin out.

But one day at lunch I sat down with the Elders in my district, and was diving into my meal, when I noticed a group of missionaries sitting down at the table across from me. When they were seated, I looked up from my plate at the person sitting directly across from us and saw "Sister Dollahite" on the name tag. I cried out, "Sister Dollahite!" and she looked at me then my name tag and squealed, "Elder Dollahite!" We had the chance to chat throughout lunch and a couple of other times before I left for New England. Sister Dollahite served in Montreal, Canada. We wrote to each other a few times on our missions.

On the two flights it took to get from Salt Lake City to Boston, I shared the gospel with a couple of my fellow passengers and gave away two copies of the Book of Mormon. On arriving in Boston, we were picked up by the Assistants to the President and taken by subway to the mission home in Cambridge. We shared the gospel with those we sat near on the subway and I was excited to do so. Then we went "street contacting" in Harvard Square, a famous landmark near Harvard University.

We got to the mission home and met President Richard Tempest and his wife Sister Ruth Tempest. President Tempest had been the mission president since July so we were only his second set of new missionaries. In the evening, we newly-arrived missionaries had a testimony meeting with the Tempests and the Assistants to the President—a couple of truly amazing Elders who were an inspiration to me. I expressed my gratitude to finally be in the mission field, my enthusiasm for the work, and my desire to share the gospel with as many people as possible. We also had our first interview with President Tempest. I learned that he was a strong and matter-of-fact leader and I looked forward to learning from him.

I was extremely excited to finally be in the mission field in which I would labor for two years. And I was very optimistic about every aspect of the experience. I was young (three months shy of twenty-one), energetic, and full of faith about the work. Based on my experience in gaining a sure witness upon praying for it, and on my experience in teaching my roommate Bob Day at BYU, and on my experience with the way everything worked out for me with my summer job, I was predisposed to assume that most people I spoke with would be very interested in investigating and then joining the Church. For example, after my first day in the mission field, I wrote:

> *I met some interesting people [and] I was able to speak to a couple of young men who were very interested in the gospel. One of them, a Jewish man, was a great man. He was very interested in our message and his friend seemed interested also. (Mission Journal, page 9)*

President Tempest assigned me to work with Elder Buhler in Fitchburg, Massachusetts. He said that Elder Buhler had only been out for two months and normally they did not allow new missionaries to train brand new missionaries ("greenies") until they had been out for at least five months, but told me that he felt this was where I was supposed to be. He said Elder Buhler was an obedient, hard-working Elder and that he trusted him to train me well.

The next day I was put on a bus for Fitchburg, a couple-hours bus ride outside Boston. When I arrived in Fitchburg I was met by my new companion, Elder Wayne Buhler, and one of our Zone Leaders.[2] As soon as we got off the bus, we loaded my two suitcases in the car and went tracting (going door-to-door with religious pamphlets or tracts) in a neighborhood. At the first home where someone let us in we sat down to share a message with a little old lady who was very kind and willing to listen.

I was so excited to finally be in someone's home, teaching the gospel, that I practically gave this kind, patient woman all six discussions! My companion and Zone Leader tried to help teach but I was not to be deterred from teaching and challenging this woman to be baptized. When the Elders finally extracted me from this home, they told me they liked my enthusiasm, but that I needed to try not to teach people everything all in the first lesson. Although part of me could see the logic of what they said, and over the next few months I tried to do a better job at presenting the gospel in smaller chunks, my natural talkativeness along with my pent-up desire to teach the gospel made it extremely hard for me to follow this good counsel.

When Elder Buhler and I got to our apartment, Elder Buhler said that while I was unpacking he would cook up some potatoes—he said he was raised on an Idaho potato farm and knew a lot of ways to prepare potatoes. I was predisposed to like missionaries from Idaho

---

2. Zone Leaders are experienced missionaries called by the Mission President to train and encourage missionaries in their area or "zone"—typically 10–20 missionaries.

since Elders Hawkes and Christensen, the two who taught me ("my missionaries"), also were raised on Idaho potato farms.

When I finished unpacking I came into the kitchen and asked Elder Buhler if I could help. He handed me a can of green beans, opened a small drawer, and said I could open the can. I rummaged through the drawer for a couple minutes but did not see anything that, to me, looked like a can opener. He came over and grabbed this little metal contraption, the likes of which I had never seen before, but which I assumed was a can opener. In my home, we had an electric can opener mounted under the counter, and I had not been a Boy Scout or done much camping, so I had no experience with this type of can opener.

I fumbled with the contraption for a couple minutes trying to find the part of it that you inserted into the can but could not figure it out. When Elder Buhler noticed this, he gave me a look that said, "You have got to be kidding," and said, "You don't know how to use that?" I said I had not ever seen such a can opener and he, I am sure exerting all his effort not to roll his eyes and burst out in mocking laughter, gave me another look that said, "Oh boy, this is going to be interesting." I learned later that what he was thinking was, "City kids."

The good news is that despite my complete ignorance of almost all things mechanical and Elder Buhler's farm-boy familiarity and confidence with such things, we got along great. I learned that Elder Buhler had not been active in the Church as a teen and had not intended to serve a mission until about a year before. But he was very excited to be on his mission and had faith that we would have much success in the tiny Gardner Branch we were assigned to. I was to spend the first five months of my mission in this area and came to love many people here.

TENDER MERCIES & LESSONS LEARNED

The Lord blessed me with a wonderful opportunity to begin to learn leadership by working with President Black in the MTC. While I suppose it would have been nice to have had a companion in the MTC who was more excited to be on his mission, I learned to love my MTC companion and was happy he remained on his mission and did some good work.

I had no idea that meeting my cousin in the MTC would affect me so strongly. I did not spend a great deal of time feeling sorry for myself about the fact that I was the only member of my family who was a member of the Church, or that I was leaving family and friends for two years without my parents or lifelong friends understanding or supporting me. I am naturally an optimistic, positive, and idealistic person and so I rarely think about less-than-positive things.

However, in the MTC and later on my mission, there were certainly times when I felt alone or sad. This happened mostly when other missionaries would get a lot of mail or care packages from home and I did not. Or if they told me about their fathers or older brothers giving them great advice in letters based on their experience on their missions. The Leiningers and three great gals who wrote me somewhat consistently were very kind and supportive and sent mail as often as they could. But something about seeing Sister Dollahite—another member of my family, however distant—there in the MTC was a powerful moment for me. It was tender mercy that I thank the Lord for.

My patriarchal blessing stated that on my mission I would be "protected from evil" and so I was very surprised that I experienced the presence of an evil spirit in the MTC. I still do not understand why that happened—was allowed to happen. However, from that experience I have never doubted the power of evil and of Satan's malevolent intent toward the servants of the Lord. Near the end of my time at the MTC, I had a very strong feeling that, when I returned from my mission, I would be a teacher at the MTC. In fact, I later taught there for three years — including a year teaching in the Jewish Culture program. It was while teaching at the MTC about two years after my mission ended that I had the strong spiritual impression that I should seek to meet the woman who became my wife. That turned out to be one of the greatest of all the Lord's tender mercies toward me. I'll say more about that in Chapter 26.

When I reached the mission field, the Lord blessed me with a wonderful first companion, great leadership in the tiny branch we were in, humble and faithful members to work with, and a number of wonderful people to teach. For these reasons, after exercising much faith, working hard for long hours, and with what Elder Buhler called "miracle after miracle" we experienced marvelous and nearly immediate success and great joy in the work. But it took several months to discover that, no matter how hard I worked and how much faith I exercised, I would be baptizing only dozens — rather than thousands — of New Englanders.

I learned that most of those we met and taught had barriers of various kinds that made it difficult for them to make a serious investigation of the restored gospel, much less make such a major life change as to convert to the Church of Jesus Christ of Latter-day Saints. Some of these barriers included satisfaction with the faith they currently had, religious tradition even without real belief or involvement, personal habits that were hard to give up, and apathy about religion caused by attachment to secular things.

And most of those who chose to investigate seriously faced significant opposition from friends, family members, faith leaders, and others. Many of those who did accept the gospel experienced minor or major miracles that helped them overcome these kinds of barriers. Indeed, the Lord poured out His tender mercies on me and many of those I met and taught and this made my mission a marvelous experience. And some of these experiences occurred in my very first area with two other brand-new missionaries in a very small branch that did not even have their own chapel to meet in. My mission began with miracles in the Gardner Branch.

CHAPTER 18

"We are going to double the size of your branch!"

The Gardner Branch consisted of about forty-five members who met in a large Methodist church in the city of Gardner, several miles from Fitchburg. Elder Buhler told me that the branch had not had a baptism in over a year and that we only had two active investigators to work with.

Missionaries set goals each month in a number of areas including the number of "contact hours" (time spent talking to people) and how many baptisms you will strive to obtain. Understandably, given the tiny branch and the small teaching pool, the baptismal goals for the Fitchburg area had been modest. On my second day in the area I wrote in my journal,

> *I feel as though the Lord wants a great many more people in his Kingdom than there now are and I believe that is why I am here at this time—I can't wait to baptize my first person and I am happy that the Lord loves me enough to let me serve him on a full-time mission. I know I am unworthy of all the blessings I have received but I am thankful for them all. (Mission Journal, page 2)*

In our first "companion inventory" Elder Buhler and I decided that we were going to set our goals much higher than what had previously been set in the area. A couple of weeks later we prayerfully set a goal that we would baptize eight people in the month of October. When Elder Buhler told the Zone Leaders about this they said there was no way we could set our goals that high—that it was unrealistic and would make the Zone goals unrealistically high. Elder Buhler told them this was our goal and they could turn in whatever they wanted to the mission but we were sticking with our goal. In our weekly "Letter to the President" Elder Buhler told him we were going to "tear this area apart and get baptisms."

The first Sunday in the Gardner Branch, I was asked to introduce myself to the members. I stood before the thirty or so members in attendance that day and told them about how the Lord had called me into the Church and how excited I was to be on my mission. I then said, in the fervor of faith and missionary zeal, "We are going work as hard as we can and with your help we are going to double the size of your branch."

The branch president, Chris Olson, was one of the most impressive young men I had ever met. He was only about twenty-six, had piercing blue eyes, and was the most "exact" person I had ever met in terms of his approach to living the gospel. He had just called several of his members—including himself—to serve "mini missions" for a couple months at a time. Thus, we had the chance to have him join us in our teaching often.

Our Elders Quorum president, Brother Horne, also was excited about helping with missionary work. Brother and Sister Horne had us over to eat often and always sent us home with some great healthy food. They were great member missionaries and we loved and respected them. Brother Horne invited us to speak at a luncheon at his Rotary Club. We wanted to do a good job and not embarrass him. So, over several days, Elder Buhler and I worked hard on the talks we would give.

We discussed various options, wrote and rewrote what we would say, but neither of us felt good about what we had prepared. We thought that, in order to not offend these associates of Brother Horne and thus put Brother Horne in an awkward position, we should be very diplomatic and perhaps just share a little about the Family Home Evening program. But ultimately, we decided we would "go by the Spirit" and say whatever came into our minds when we stood. Since Elder Buhler was the senior companion and more experienced in missionary work, we decided he should speak first and take more than half of the time.

We went to the large meeting hall, were introduced to a few people, and then seated at the head table. The room was filled with men who were drinking, smoking cigars and cigarettes, and flirting with the cocktail waitresses. After lunch, Brother Horne introduced us. Elder Buhler spoke first. He began by saying, "Since we are missionaries for our church, you might think that we are going to say that our church is the only true church on the earth, and that whatever church you belong to is not true, and that you need to repent and be baptized into The Church of Jesus Christ of Latter-day Saints . . . and that is exactly right!"

When he said this, I was stunned since I knew that he had intended to say that we were just there to be friends and share a little bit about Family Home Evening. But the Spirit had come over him and he then gave a powerful sermon calling these men to repentance. Then suddenly he stopped, almost mid-sentence, and turned the time over to me. He later told me he just felt prompted to stop and invite me to speak, leaving me well over half the allotted time.

I felt the Spirit strongly and while I did not know what I was going say, I felt that the Spirit would guide me. I looked out at the large room full of men and I told them about my youth and my conversion to the gospel. I talked about how many of the youth these days—including their own kids, were using drugs and ruining their lives. Many heads nodded at this. And then I said that it was not surprising that their kids would be doing this given the bad example of their fathers who were sitting there drinking and smoking and flirting with women they were not married to (the waitresses) and how could they blame their kids for following their example. I went on to call them to repentance and urged them to be more involved as fathers.

Elder Buhler later told me that, when Brother Horne heard what I had said, Brother Horne turned to him and whispered, "Well, I guess they won't be asking me to find speakers again." I did not notice this at the time, but Elder Buhler later told me that as I spoke most of the men put out their cigars and cigarettes and waved off the cocktail waitresses. After the meeting was over, most of the men left quickly. Brother Horne later told us he had never seen them leave so early since most usually stuck around smoking, drinking, talking, and flirting.

I suppose this may have been one of those times when my experiences in front of large groups during my months in the BYU theater department gave me confidence to speak with forcefulness to a group of grown men and not be intimidated by the fact that they were not predisposed to like what I was saying. But far more likely was that the Spirit simply used Elder Buhler and me to boldly call a group of men to become better husbands and fathers than perhaps they were currently.

We soon began to teach a number of wonderful people in great families. One of the families we taught was a part-member family named the Messiers. We were teaching Sister Messier's husband, Bud, and their daughter Patricia Lisle, and Patricia's son Chris. We were focusing our efforts on Bud since Patricia and Kris were progressing well and were committed to be baptized. But they wanted to wait for

Bud to gain a testimony. Bud was a truck driver and was gone a lot. He was a large man and very kind, very humble, but perhaps somewhat stubborn (in his words). He had been taught by several sets of missionaries and we were just the latest in a long line of Elders trying to help him commit to joining the Church.

He was concerned about tithing, but his big issue was that he had not yet felt the Spirit bear witness to him of the truthfulness of the gospel. Several sets of missionaries before us had made many efforts to get Bud to pray for a witness. But he was a very shy person and felt uncomfortable praying out loud. We had also attempted to get Bud to pray but each time he adamantly refused to pray out loud.

One evening, Elder Buhler and I determined that we were not going to leave Bud's home until he had prayed for a witness. When we came to the end of the discussion, we again invited Bud to pray. He again declined. We told him that we were not going to leave until he had prayed. He said that other Elders had tried to get him to pray and it did not work then and would not work now.

But we knelt and invited the family to kneel with us. Everyone except Bud knelt. We calmly and gently went over the four steps to prayer again and told him we had great confidence he would be able to pray. We talked Bud to the edge of his seat. Then we encouraged, nudged, cajoled, and otherwise plead with him to join us on his knees. After what seemed like half an hour he got on his knees. We then talked him through the steps of prayer again and asked him to pray.

Finally, he bowed his head and said a short, simple prayer, asking Heavenly Father if what we had been teaching him was true. Then he was silent. In only a few seconds, he literally jumped from his knees to his feet, thrust his hands in the air, and joyfully yelled out, "I did it! I did it! And it is true! It really is true!" All of us rushed over and hugged Bud and congratulated him. There were many tears of joy shed that night although Bud would not commit to be baptized—there was still the issue of tithing.

Sister Messier's father, Ed Thompson, lived in the home as well. He was an older widower—perhaps seventy-five years old—and a classic example of what we young folks would call "an old codger." Sometimes during discussions, Ed would sit in the chair seemingly asleep. Other times he would be in the other room reading or watching TV. And sometimes he would make an appearance at some point in our discussion, tell an off-color joke or story clearly designed to scandalize the young, innocent Mormon missionaries, give a great belly laugh, and then depart while chuckling. We thought of Ed as a fun old guy who made our discussions interesting.

TENDER MERCIES & LESSONS LEARNED

The Lord was very kind to allow me to work with the Messier family. They were extremely kind and humble people who not only were willing to accept the restored gospel but who also fed us like kings every time we came to their home. Sister Messier cooked the best Greek food I have ever had in my life. To see how the Lord was willing to pour out His Spirit on this humble family was a great blessing for me in my first area on my mission.

From this experience, I learned that the Lord prepares His children to accept the gospel in many ways and over many years. I also learned that persistent faith moves mountains, even if it is just moving a mountain of a man like Bud to humble himself and kneel in prayer to receive a witness from the Lord.

CHAPTER 19

Dreams, Blessings, Baptisms, & Confirmations

We worked extremely hard during the month of October 1979. We often worked until late in the evening contacting, teaching, and counseling with members and investigators (those we were teaching). We were invited to be on the radio and to speak with various groups. We also worked closely with members. Yet at the end of the month we had no baptisms. We again prayerfully decided to submit the goal of eight baptisms. Again, our Zone Leaders were understandably concerned at this seemingly ridiculously high goal. Again, Elder Buhler said that they were welcome to put whatever they wanted on the Zone report but we were sticking with a goal of eight. Then the real miracles began.

On November 11, one of the most important sequences of events in my mission and my life began. Our Elders Quorum president, Brother Corrigan, called us on Saturday evening to tell us he was bringing a friend to church the next day. On Sunday, he introduced us to Jackie McLean, a single mother of three children, Marie, Kelly, and Jimmy.

While we were in a Sunday School class, Brother Corrigan came and got us out of class and asked if we would assist him in administering to Jackie. She had been trying to quit smoking for some time. Brother Corrigan told her about priesthood blessings and she had asked for a blessing. We went downstairs into a classroom and gave Jackie a priesthood blessing by laying our hands on her head and speaking words inspired by the Holy Spirit.

Brother Corrigan stood behind her and was voice for the blessing, Elder Buhler stood behind her on her left and I stood behind her on her right. During the blessing, Elder Buhler and I felt the spirit very strongly. After the blessing, Jackie stood up and looked very white—as though she was going to pass out. She said she was not feeling well and wanted to go home. She accepted our invitation to take the discussions the next day and went home.

We began teaching the McLean family the next evening. The kids seemed to enjoy our visits and accepted what we taught. Jackie accepted everything we taught her although though she said she had been a Pentecostal Christian who had read and believed a great deal of anti-Mormon literature. In my journal that night I wrote, "I know that this area will blossom, very, very soon" (Mission Journal, page 8).

On November 14, Pat Lisle told us that she and her son, Chris, had decided to be baptized on November 24. On November 17, while the Zone Leaders were interviewing Pat and Chris for baptism, Elder Buhler challenged Bud Messier to be baptized and he accepted.

On the 21st of November, as Elder Buhler and I were teaching Jackie McLean about the Atonement of Jesus Christ, I began to have the strongest sense of déjà vu (the feeling you have experienced something before) that I had ever experienced. It became stronger and stronger. I stopped teaching, turned to Elder Buhler, and said, "I am feeling really strong déjà vu."

Elder Buhler said, "So am I!"

Then Jackie said, "Would you like me to tell you why?" We nodded and she told us that beginning a couple of years ago she began having a recurring dream that she was in some deep distress and there were two young men in dark suits with short hair who were praying over her. The dream was very vivid and it bothered her. She did not know the two young men and she did not know if, in the dream, she was dying or was dead. She was bothered enough that she asked a number of people, including her pastor and a palm reader, to "interpret" the dream. No one gave her a satisfactory answer. She continued to have the dream a number of times in the next two years.

She then said, "When you gave me the blessing on the day we met, the dream came to me again and I saw the faces in my dream. It was you, Elder Buhler, and you, Elder Dollahite." That was why she felt sick after the blessing—because she thought it may mean she was going to die. She told us that was why she agreed to be taught and accepted everything we had taught her even though she had been told by her Christian pastors that the Mormon Church was a cult and she should never listen to Mormon missionaries. Indeed, she was one of the most faithful members of her church and her current pastor could not believe she was listening to us. He was working very hard on her telling her she was going to go to hell if she became a Mormon. She said she knew that God had given her the dream to prepare her to accept what we were teaching her. Of course, Elder Buhler and I were amazed and thrilled by what Jackie told us, and she accepted the invitation to be baptized on the twenty-fourth, less than two weeks from when we met her at church.

On November 23, Fred Jakowski, a man whom we had been teaching for some time, called us and told us he wanted to be baptized. We turned him over to a new senior missionary couple, the Winklemans, who had just been assigned to our area. He intended to be baptized in December.

Also on November 23, the night before we were to baptize six of those we were teaching, we got a call from Carol Messier telling us that her father, Ed Thompson, also wanted to be baptized with the rest of his family. We were stunned. We had no idea he was at all interested in joining the Church. We had assumed his colorful jocularity with us was the extent of his interest in what we were in the home to do. It turns out he had been listening to us all along. When he was "asleep" he actually was listening. When he sat in the other room "reading" he actually was listening. And he believed what we were teaching his son-in-law, granddaughter, and great-grandson.

We went over and met with Ed to quickly review the discussions and the commandments and to ascertain whether he really understood the gospel and was willing to keep the commandments. Elder Buhler interviewed him thoroughly about the doctrines we had taught his family and he understood and believed them all. He committed to live the commandments.

Ed told us an interesting story. On his honeymoon several decades before, he and his wife were driving around and happened to stop in front of an LDS chapel. Ed said that he had known a Mormon guy when he was in the military and had respected his values and integrity. His wife also knew an LDS woman and respected her. Based on this alone, Ed and his wife decided that if they ever were to join a church it would be the Mormon Church. Ed's wife had passed away and they still had not joined any church. He also thought that since his entire family was joining the LDS Church, and since his deceased wife was probably a member now, he wanted to join with the family in baptism. We had the Zone Leader come over and give Ed a baptismal interview in the morning before the baptism. He passed!

Thus, on November 24, 1979, we baptized and confirmed Bud Messier, Patricia and Kris Lisle, Ed Thompson, and Jackie, Marie, and Kelly McLean (Jimmy was younger than eight years old—the minimum age at which people are baptized in the LDS Church). The baptism was amazing. Seeing so many people in white was wonderful. To see three wonderful families now joined in the gospel was marvelous. I was able to baptize and confirm three of those who entered the Church that day (Nancy, Bud, and Chris). The next day, in my journal, I wrote,

> *It was so neat to go into the waters of baptism and have the authority to admit someone to the Kingdom of God. I loved being able to lay my hands on someone's head and confirm them a member of the LDS Church and let them receive the Gift of the Holy Ghost. I am so happy to be on a mission and being able to learn so much in such a short period of time. . . . I love serving the Lord and I know the Gospel is TRUE. (Mission Journal, page 8)*

Nancy Alexander, who we thought would also be baptized in November, decided to wait until December. So, for November we did not quite reach our goal of eight baptisms but we were able to see seven wonderful people come into the Lord's church. President Tempest told us there had never been so many baptisms on one day in one area in the mission.

It was interesting when Ed began coming to church in the little branch. He could not hear very well and the acoustics of the large Methodist Church we met in were not very good. So, during Sacrament Meeting talks (i.e., sermons), Ed would sometimes ask those sitting next to him, in a loud voice, "What the hell is he saying?" or if someone would make an especially good point he might say, "Damn right!" or something like that. All members of the branch welcomed Ed along with the rest of his family and, although members were not used to hearing outbursts in Sacrament Meeting, much less swear words, most members took this in stride.

TENDER MERCIES & LESSONS LEARNED

While having the first set of baptisms on my mission was a marvelous
experience, the experience with Sister McLean's recurring dream about
Elder Buhler and me was an even more profound and tender mercy.
For me this was an extremely important revelation since when she had
begun having the dream I was not even a member of the Church—in
fact I had not even heard of the Church. Thus, the Lord knew before I
did that I would accept the gospel, that I would serve a mission, that I
would be called to New England, that I would be assigned to that area,
that Elder Buhler would be my companion, and that we would give
Jackie McLean a blessing during which she would recognize us from
her dream.

   Elder Buhler told me that he was not active in the Church when
Jackie began having the dream. This was very moving to Elder Buhler
because it meant the Lord knew he would become active in the Church
and serve a mission. Elder Buhler's patriarchal blessing, received a
little over a year earlier, said that on his mission he would go to people
"who are being prepared to receive the message you will have." Indeed,
they were being prepared at that very time. This was direct evidence
to Elder Buhler of the prophetic truthfulness of his blessing and the
Lord's hand in his life.

   A couple of months later in my personal interview with President
Tempest I told him about this experience. He said, "Now I know
why I felt so strongly to put you with Elder Buhler!" He said it was
his strongly held belief as Mission President that you should put "the
strong with the weak" in missionary work. Thus, when he looked at
the large board of all companionships in the mission that was mounted
in the mission home, and thought about where he should assign me,

he kept putting my picture next to Elders who were struggling in some way.

But he kept feeling that he should put me with Elder Buhler. This made no sense to him since Elder Buhler was doing great and had only been in New England for two months and President Tempest's policy was that no one should train a new missionary until they had been out at least five months. He said he had such repeated and strong impressions to assign me to work with Elder Buhler that, even though it went against two of his cardinal principles, he sent me to Fitchburg.

To me this meant many things: it meant that God knew me and knew my heart even before I knew and believed in Him. It meant that the Lord had guided every aspect of my preparation to hear the gospel. And it meant that my call to this particular mission was not of man. It was not coincidence. Every part of it was of God. My neighbor, Bob, would have sent me to some exotic jungle; my mom would have sent me to Cambridge rather than this small factory town many miles away from any major university; and I would have sent me to Ireland, England, or Australia. But the Lord knew exactly where He needed me to be to accomplish the purposes He had for me and others of His children.

This has been one of the greatest tender mercies the Lord has granted to me in my entire life. Because of this experience, I have never doubted that the Lord is guiding my life—and other people's lives. I have always known that the Lord knows the beginning from the end and I have always tried to have faith in the Lord's divine plans and purposes for me and for others, despite challenges and seeming setbacks. And in another tender mercy, November 24, the day of my first baptisms in the mission field, was two years to the day from when I first read the Book of Mormon.

CHAPTER 20

"Let us take strides together."

At the end of November, we set a goal to baptize nine people in December. We were working extremely hard in difficult circumstances. The weather was bad, most people rejected our message, we were fatigued from so many long days and our apartment had little heat.

Each evening when we went to bed we tacked a blanket over the door to our bedroom and put on the space heater to keep warm. When we left that room in the morning the rest of our large apartment was freezing. One morning, when I went to use the bathroom, there was a thin sheet of ice on the water in the bowl. I woke Elder Buhler to show him. Even a missionary as enthusiastic as I was sometimes became discouraged.

We did a lot of door-to-door tracting in my mission. I do not know how many thousands of doors I knocked on during my two years in New England but it is one of the abiding memories I have. Tracting in the bitter cold winter months was always a challenge. Few people wanted to let us in and many would only crack open their storm doors just enough to tell us they were not interested.

Yet there were many times when the Lord clearly led us to those He desired us to speak with. Sometimes the Spirit led us so clearly that we and those we were led to could have no doubt about the hand of the Lord. Often, before we were blessed with miracles, we were tested with challenges. And some of the challenges led to marvelous spiritual experiences as well.

One time Elder Buhler and I had been out tracting all day in near-blizzard conditions. We had very little success and were rejected by most whose doors we knocked on. We got home and there was a postcard for me from my old tennis buddy Jim Lowell. The picture was of a beach on the French Riviera. On the other side of the postcard, Jim wrote that he was traveling around Europe playing tennis tournaments like we had planned to do together and was having a great time, making some money and meeting some cute girls. He said he wished I was with him.

I was glad Jim was having a good time in Europe. And although we had just had one of the toughest days of my mission, I did not in the least degree wish I was in Europe playing tennis in the sun instead of being in New England knocking on doors in a blizzard. Jim went on to become the head tennis pro at the Pebble Beach Racquet Club in Monterey, California. I keep in touch with him on occasion and got to play tennis with him at the Pebble Beach Racquet Club one time (he avenged his loss in the finals of a tournament we played as kids by beating me badly).

Another day with similar weather conditions led to one of the most sacred and important experiences on my mission and in my life. It was a particularly difficult and discouraging day, brutally cold and windy. Many slammed their storm doors in our faces, no one expressed interest in hearing our message, many were quite rude, and some were downright abusive to us and our religion. In addition, we had a couple of investigators who had been making progress but who had told us they were no longer interested in having us teach them the gospel. As I look back now I can certainly understand why having two Mormon missionaries knock on your door in the middle of a blizzard would be quite irritating.

That evening we sat in our old, ugly, freezing apartment reading the scriptures and talking about how discouraging that day had been. As we read the scriptures, we came to D&C 84:88 which states, "And whoso receiveth you, there I will be also, for I will go before your face. I will be on your right hand and on your left, and my Spirit shall be in your hearts, and mine angels round about you, to bear you up."

As we discussed this verse, a sweet, powerful spirit came over both of us and Elder Buhler said, "I bet there are angels right here right now." When he said this I felt a powerful rush of the Spirit and felt the veil was very thin. Then I said, "Yes, I believe there are," and experienced another powerful rush of the Spirit confirming that this was true. Elder Buhler told me he felt the same rush of the Spirit and the same confirmation that we were, in actuality, being attended by angels.

One day, we realized that we had tracted out many of the neighborhoods in the areas around our apartment, yet we had not spent any time in a town on the outskirts of our area. So, we decided to spend the entire next day in that town. We packed a lunch and arranged for a dinner appointment with a member in the town. We were excited to spend the day in this town.

As we drove out of Fitchburg and got on the major road toward the town we crossed some railroad tracks. Immediately after crossing the tracks I felt a clear spiritual prompting that we needed to go work the street just before the tracks. I turned to Elder Buhler, who was driving, and told him of my impression. He looked at me and said he just had the same impression.

We drove for another mile or so and I felt an even stronger prompting that we needed to go to that street. I relayed this to Elder Buhler and he said he had the same stronger impression. I said, "Well, we better write that street down so we don't forget," and pulled out my pen and Franklin Day-Planner to write it down. Then, very quickly, I had a strong impression that we needed to go right then. I looked at

Elder Buhler and he looked at me and at the same time we both said, "We need to go back now." We turned around and went back.

We turned left at the street, drove a block or two, and pulled off to the right to park. We saw a man with his back to us raking his leaves on the other side of the tree-lined street. We got out and walked toward him. When we stepped up on the sidewalk in front of his house he turned around and saw us. His mouth dropped open and he looked surprised.

We introduced ourselves and he said, "Boy, you guys sure got here fast." When we asked what he meant he said, "My brother sent you, right?" We said that no one sent us but that we had a message from the Lord for him. He said, "Come on guys, I know my brother sent you. You can admit it." We said that we did not know his brother but that the Lord had sent us to him. He said, "Come on in. I want to show you something."

He invited us into his home and went and picked up something off the table and brought it over to us. It was a postcard with a picture of two LDS missionaries walking down a street that looked sort of like the one we were on. At the bottom of the postcard was a caption that said, "Let Us Take Strides Together." He showed us the other side of the postcard and said that his brother and sister-in-law had just moved to Idaho Falls and were investigating the LDS Church and said they were excited about what they were hearing and strongly urged him to seek out the LDS missionaries so they could teach him.

Then he said, "Okay, so come on guys, you can admit it; my brother sent you, didn't he?" We then assured him we had not been contacted by his brother and told him exactly what had happened as we had passed his street. He then said, "Really? I guess that means the Lord really wants me to listen to you, doesn't it?" We said it sure seemed like that.

He invited us to sit down and we taught him the first discussion. He said he had time to read and would read the Book of Mormon and call us when he was finished with it. Later when we returned to his house, he did not respond well and did not invite us to come back. I certainly hope that this tender mercy from the Lord made an impression on him and that his brother continued to extend invitations to him to learn more about the restored gospel.

Since I did not receive many letters from family and friends, sometimes I became discouraged. Elder Buhler's letters made it clear that his family was praying for him. I sometimes yearned for the knowledge that my family was praying for me on my mission. I cherished the letters I received from the Leiningers and from a few of my LDS friends and a few others in the ward who would sometimes write.

But there were also fun times—even in the midst of a rough New England winter. One time we came home from an especially tough day in lousy weather. While I made "call-backs" (phoned people we had met to see if we could come and teach them), Elder Buhler made an incredible dinner with chicken, gravy, stuffing, potatoes, and green beans. As we sat down to eat I commented on how great the dinner looked—almost like a Thanksgiving feast. One of us—we still disagree on who it was—offered the prayer and simply said, "Heavenly Father, thank you for this food. Please bless it that it will taste just as good as it looks. In the name of Jesus Christ, Amen." We both laughed at that simple prayer—which was definitely answered.

TENDER MERCIES & LESSONS LEARNED

While investigating the Church I was taught about all the commandments: The Word of Wisdom, the Law of Tithing, the Law of Chastity, the Ten Commandments, the Sabbath Day, the Law of the Fast, and so forth. Because of the powerful, indeed undeniable, spiritual witness that the Lord had granted me, I was willing to commit to obey all these demanding laws of God.

What the missionaries could not have known about was that in joining the Church I was also committing to leave behind the warm California "winters" I grew up with and endure twelve consecutive years of brutal winters. For the first dozen years after I joined the Church I spent winters in Utah, New England, and Minnesota (while getting a doctorate in family studies). Had the missionaries told me this was part of the package I was committing myself to in accepting the gospel, I think I would still have happily joined the Church—but it would have been harder!

I do not like snow, sleet, and cold. So, the many months I spent tracting in New England winters were not easy for me. But I am deeply grateful to the Lord for His tender mercies in blessing me with wonderful experiences in the midst of those climatic trials. Although I had spent years hoping, dreaming, and planning to play professional tennis on warm, sunny tennis courts around the world, when I received Jim's postcard I had no desire to be there instead of where I was. This is clear testament to the power of the Lord to completely change hearts, minds, and spirits.

When I think of how the Lord repeatedly prompted Elder Buhler and me about going back and tracting that particular street right then, it reminds me that the Lord knows exactly who is ready to (or needs to) hear the message of the gospel. It reminds me that I need to continually seek the promptings of the Spirit so that I might go and do what the Lord needs done when He needs it done.

I cannot think of the experience Elder Buhler and I had, while reading from the scriptures about missionaries being attended by angels, without feeling tremendous gratitude to the Lord. His willingness to manifest to two discouraged missionaries that we were, at that moment, attended by angels, is one of the greatest tender mercies I have ever experienced in this life. I have no doubt that all missionaries, and all Saints, and perhaps all people, have guardian angels watching over them. I have had a number of experiences over the years that have made it clear that the veil between this earthly sphere and the spiritual realm is often quite thin. But none of them have been more welcome and more needed than on that bitter cold evening in a freezing apartment in Fitchburg, Massachusetts.

CHAPTER 21

The Disappearing & Reappearing Pamphlet

In December, the Lord led us to one of the most wonderful families I had the joy and privilege of teaching during my entire mission and with whom we had one of the most interesting minor miracles of my mission. We had baptized so many of our investigators that we needed to build our teaching pool back up. Elder Buhler was feeling like the area was in a lag and was determined to do something to jump start it. For some reason I was "down" and was not my usual enthusiastic self. With the weather, the cold apartment, not receiving many letters, and continual rejection, I suppose down days were inevitable, but Elder Buhler was concerned and wanted to deal with it. Elder Buhler consulted with the Zone Leaders about the situation and they suggested taking me out to work (meaning tract for hours in the New England winter).

We went out and tracted all day on December 4. After doing a couple of member presentations, Elder Buhler felt strongly that we should tract a certain street in a neighborhood where we had been working. He felt like there was someone there for us to teach. It was already late in a very cold day at about the time we would normally be heading back to our apartment for dinner.

In addition, I really needed to use the bathroom. But when I told Elder Buhler he said, "Let's just tract one last street before we head home." After knocking on the doors of several houses I said I really had to go to the bathroom and asked if we could come back and do the street tomorrow. He said, "You'll be alright. Let's just finish this street." After knocking on several more doors I now really needed to go badly and told Elder Buhler we really needed to get me to a bathroom. He said, "Come on, just hold on, I feel like we need to finish tracting this street." Fortunately for me there were few people home.

Finally, at one door near the end of the street, a very nice woman with a couple of young children answered and we told her we had a Christmas message we would like to share with her family. She told us she and her husband had been looking for a church and had been attending various churches to try to find one to join. She said they had known an LDS family and were impressed by them. She agreed to let us come by and we scheduled an appointment for a couple of days later.

We learned that her name was Patricia West and her husband's name was Gary. She said she would need to talk with Gary to make sure it was okay for us to come but she said she was sure he would be happy to meet with us. We gave her a pamphlet about the Prophet Joseph Smith on which we wrote our names and phone number. We told her that if something came up she could call us and we could reschedule the appointment. After we left Pat's home Elder Buhler said he felt that she was the one we were supposed to find so we headed straight for the car and got me to a gas station to use the restroom.

A couple of days later, we came back to share our message with Gary and Pat West and their two little boys, Chris and Andy. The Spirit was very strong. We felt it and we knew they felt it. They invited us back to teach them and each lesson was wonderful. They were humble and faithful. They read the Book of Mormon and gained a witness it was true.

When we taught them that there were living prophets and apostles on the earth at the head of the Church, Gary looked at us in amazement and said, "Why haven't we heard this on the evening news?" A little over a week after we began teaching the West family, Elder Buhler was transferred and I received an assignment to train a new missionary—Elder Sorensen. He came on Thursday and on Saturday I baptized and confirmed Nancy Alexander. Saturday, we also taught Gary and Pat West and the Spirit was strong. It was a nice way for Elder Sorensen to be introduced to missionary work. On December 16, I wrote the following in my journal:

> *Tomorrow I will be 21 and I don't care if I have a birthday party or not. I love where I am and what I am doing. I love the West family. They are truly loving, faithful people and they bore their testimony of the Savior tonight and I could have cried. The Spirit of the Lord has moved in them and prepared them so well to hear the gospel and accept it. They said we could come by every night and teach them, and I am so excited they are going to be baptized on the 29th. I love the Lord. I love missionary work. I love my companion. (Mission Journal, page 10)*

The next few weeks brought two of the most memorable prayers I heard uttered on my mission. One time Elder Sorensen and I tracted all day in bitter cold, windy weather with little success. In his blessing on our dinner that evening, Elder Sorensen said, in a playfully sarcastic tone of voice, "Heavenly Father, we would like to thank you for sending us such lovely weather to do your work in."

I was both stunned and amused and actually burst out laughing at the audacity of someone speaking to the Lord like that and said, "You can't talk to the Lord like that!" and Elder Sorensen just laughed. At the same time, I really enjoyed his honesty and his spunk since I had had similar types of thoughts but would never have expressed them to the Lord in prayer.

Elder Sorensen later told me that part of the reason he prayed that prayer was that he was feeling like I was taking my responsibilities as his trainer too seriously and that I needed to lighten up a bit. I am sure he was right as I did take my new responsibilities very seriously. I had only been out for three months when I was asked to train him and I was trying to follow the great example of hard work that Elder Buhler set for me.

The Wests had us over for dinner a few times during the weeks we taught them. One time Gary called on his little boy, Chris, to say the blessing on the food. Chris was two or three years old. We all bowed our heads and Chris said, "Hebenwy Fawder, we ask dee to bwess da food. Pwease bwess da meat and bwess da peas and bwess da potadoes and bwess da catsup and pwease da wadder, and bwees da salt and pwease bwess da peppa and bwess da forks and bwess da napkins . . ." He blessed everything on the table as each of us at the table desperately tried to hold our mounting need to burst out laughing.

Just a little over three weeks from when we first met Pat at the door, the Wests were baptized. On the night before their baptism, we had a wonderful discussion with them and as we were getting ready to leave Gary said to Pat, "Should we tell them?" and Pat nodded. They said that on the day we had first come by their home and met Pat, when Gary got home from work, Pat told him that the Mormon missionaries had come by and wanted to return to share a message. Gary said that he was tired of "church shopping" and did not want to meet with us. He asked her to call us back and tell us not to come.

Pat was disappointed by this since she had had a dream about me before this and strongly felt they should listen to us. She went to the mantle where she had put the pamphlet we had given her so she could call us and tell us not to come. But the pamphlet was not where she had placed it. She then spent the next couple days searching high and low in their house for the pamphlet. Although she scoured every inch of their small home she could not find the pamphlet.

On the day of our appointment, Gary had intended to tell us they were not interested in hearing our message after all but when we showed up at the door, inexplicably he decided to let us in. That evening, just after we left their home after our very spiritual first visit, they turned to each other and each said that they had felt something very strong and felt they should continue to have us come.

After this discussion, and this decision, they looked over at the mantle and there was the pamphlet we had left with Pat that first day—in exactly the same place Pat had placed it. She was absolutely positive that it was not there during the two days she searched for it. Pat asked us what we thought happened. Of course, we were amazed at this minor miracle and jokingly said that we had some angels that took pamphlets from those who planned to cancel appointments.

On December 29, we baptized Gary and Patricia West. Their families came to the baptism and the Spirit of the Lord was there. The Wests began being missionaries right away and invited Pat's younger sister Kathy to listen to the missionary discussions. We loved teaching Kathy because she was very humble and open to the truths we were teaching her. She also decided to be baptized at the end of January. Gary received the Aaronic priesthood right after his baptism and thus he was able to baptize his sister-in-law. She asked me to speak at her baptism and confirm her as a member of the Church. It was a wonderful experience to see a new convert be able to baptize a family member less than a month after he himself had been baptized.

Gary, who worked in the budding computer industry, said he was in a corporate training meeting and the trainer had asked each person to imagine they were on a desert island and asked what one thing they would want to have with them. Others suggested a knife, or matches, or a gun, or a fishing pole. When it was Gary's turn, he said he would want to have the Book of Mormon with him since then he would have truth and salvation. We were amazed with his faith. After his baptism, Gary later left his employment there and went to work for the Church on a welfare farm. He had always wanted to be a farmer.

During this same period of time I spoke with Jackie McLean who had been having some very difficult times after her baptism. Continued resistance from those closest to her and other challenges were making it hard for her to remain active. She told me that the fact she had seen my face in her recurring dream was what inspired her to remain active despite the fierce trials she was having.

TENDER MERCIES & LESSONS LEARNED

It was a great blessing to be able to teach and baptize such wonderful people while training a new missionary. I was in my first area for five months and I was able to be involved in the baptism of nearly half of the total number of the wonderful people my companions and I were able to baptize my entire mission. It turned out that in the five months I was in the Gardner Branch, we were able to baptize eleven wonderful people. We did not double the size of the branch but did increase its size by a third. Ten of these converts were in three families and another woman was married to a branch member in the military. We were happy to help unite families in the gospel that allows families to be joined eternally.

We met the West family because Elder Buhler followed the counsel of the Zone Leaders to head out to work despite the fact that I was feeling discouraged. Because of Elder Buhler's faith we persevered until we found the family the Lord wanted to bless with the gospel. At the same time, the Lord answered the prayers of the West family who were diligently and patiently seeking the truth.

The disappearing and reappearing pamphlet was a tender mercy for both the West family and us. Had it not "disappeared" they would have called us to tell us not to come over. Had it not "reappeared" after our first lesson, they would not have received a powerful message that there was a higher power that was very interested in their knowing this was the right thing for them to be doing.

Of course, I do not really know what happened with the pamphlet. Did an angel actually remove and then replace the pamphlet or did some power prevent them from seeing it until after we left? (Like the power that prevented those who wanted to stone Jesus from seeing him as "he passed through the midst of them" in Luke 4:30.) This is one of many things I hope I will be shown in the hereafter!

However it was done, it was evidence to them that they should listen to us. I have kept in contact with the Wests over the forty years since their baptisms and watched their family grow and progress. Their sons have all served missions and all of their children have married in the temple. They have been a great strength to every ward and branch they have served in.

CHAPTER 22

Discouragement, Despair, & Comfort

In February of 1980 I was called to be a District Leader in Marlborough, Massachusetts. My companion, Elder Tom Boyer, was also new to the area. Elder Boyer and I came into an area that had been having some problems with the missionaries and so the mission president decided to transfer out both of the missionaries who had been in the area and bring Elder Boyer and me in to try to "clean things up."

We worked hard to get the area on the right path. We quickly built up a teaching pool of good people who were willing to listen to the gospel. Despite how hard we worked we faced a number of serious challenges. Not all the missionaries in our district were working hard and keeping the rules and we tried to help motivate them to greater effort and obedience.

When I reported to President Tempest what we were experiencing he said he had "handpicked" us for this area. We seemed to meet a number of people in the area who were dealing with a number of strange spiritual phenomena and some of them were quite troubling. I wrote in my journal that,

> *I am really being tested on my mission and I am really being strengthened. I love God and I know that he loves us and what a struggle a mission really is. I will come home a strong person and a real knowledgeable person if I continue to learn and grow. (Mission Journal, page 21)*

I experienced some of the worst illness of my mission in this area. We also had to move to a new apartment since the older woman we were living with was used to the missionaries spending a great deal of time with her rather than being out doing missionary work. She was very upset that we decided to move to another apartment.

We met and began teaching some people that were having unusual spiritual manifestations. One was a woman who shared with us some experiences she had been having. She was sitting in the dark when "spirits" began to speak to her through her pencil by causing her hand to make words and sentences. She would ask questions and receive communications from the "spirits" every day around 3:00 p.m.

The "spirits" told her that the two men were sincere and teaching her things to help her spiritual growth. She asked us what we thought they were. We really did not know what to make of it. In my journal I wrote,

> *I am really learning how important the church really is in my life. I am learning how much people lack in their life and how happy they could be if they were active in the Lord's church. It is really a sin that Satan has so many of his brothers and sister[s] in bondage. He really is tricky. Norma* is still having her "communications" with "them." [T]hey said that she should listen to us. They said, "Dolomite, a mineral; Dollahite, a man of ideals." I don't know who "they" are but they really have a hold on Norma. (Mission Journal, page 22)*

The "spirits" or "voices" Norma received communications from were very confusing. We were not sure if they were good people from the other side of the veil who were trying to lead her to the truth, or if they were what the Bible calls "familiar spirits" with unholy influence.

On the one hand, they were telling her we were sincere and that she should listen to us. On the other hand, she could not seem to stop the influence they had on her. After working with her for a couple of weeks, we found that they were not a wholesome influence and we decided to stop going to see her.

I was also thinking a lot about a couple of girls I had dated before my mission. Thinking about whether I might marry one of them, thinking about what to write in letters to them, and thinking about what they had written in letters to me distracted me from fully focusing on the work of the Lord. In short, I spent too much time worrying about things other than what I was in the mission field to do.

In addition, there were things happening in the broader world that were distracting me. This included the hostage crisis in Iran. It seemed like war might break out and I worried I might be called into the military and be sent overseas. A more immediate distraction was the political battle over the passing of the Equal Rights Amendment which the Church had taken a position against. Many people we met were upset with the Church over this and many would not speak with us while others only wanted to discuss the political issues and were not willing to listen to our message about the gospel of Jesus Christ.

Despite the fact that we were working hard and having some success and despite my basic optimistic and happy nature, I was struggling with feelings of extreme unworthiness and discouragement. And, because of an earlier bad experience with an Evangelical Christian pastor who was a "professional anti-Mormon" and who targeted us with his anti-Mormon tirade, for the only time in my life I was actually struggling with my testimony. During this time, I wrote the following in my journal:

I feel very sinful and weak and unprofitable in the Lord's eyes. I do so many things wrong, I don't love God as I should, I don't love my fellow man as I should, and I don't work as hard as I should. I feel [as] though I am being prepared for a leadership calling in the mission and I feel so unworthy and unqualified to fulfill the call the way it should be fulfilled. Who knows where I will be three or four years after my mission. I might be needed to serve as a branch president or something oversees [sic]. The hostages in Iran have been there for 175 days. Yesterday the U.S. tried to run a mission to rescue them — it failed! The Soviet Union is saying they will protect Iran if we try anything. I am fearful that a small war might break out if we are not very careful. (Mission Journal, page 23)

All of this culminated in my feeling the worst darkness and discouragement in my life. The deepest and most difficult cause of my discouragement was that I felt like I would never be as good as all the wonderful missionaries and members I was serving with. I had a recurring sense of spiritual self-doubt about my ability to ever measure up to the wonderful LDS people that I saw around me. I thought of myself as spiritually second- or third-class. I saw these wonderful missionaries and members as "celestial people" and saw myself as a telestial person or terrestrial at best.[3] I thought that since I was just

---

3. In LDS theology, heaven includes three "kingdoms of glory" with the Celestial Kingdom being the most glorious followed by the Terrestrial Kingdom and the Telestial Kingdom. It is believed that the vast majority of human beings will inherit one of these glorious kingdoms with only an extremely small number being cast out of God's presence.

not a celestial person, I was just fooling myself to think that I could ever measure up. I figured that if I were a celestial person I would have been born into a great LDS family and not have "wasted" almost nineteen years of my life without the gospel.

These feelings increased until I thought that I should just go home from my mission and forget about ever trying to find a great LDS girl to marry. I thought that it would be unfair to whomever I married since I would never measure up to her and to what God expected of me. I thought that if I continued on my mission and returned and married an active LDS girl and had children it would mean they would make it to the Celestial Kingdom and I would not. And that would be unfair for them.

All these kinds of thoughts and feelings came to a head one day. I felt a pervasive spirit of darkness and discouragement about me and so I went into our backyard and spent about thirty minutes in prayer. I repented of my sins and told the Lord exactly what I was thinking and feeling. I poured out my soul in prayer in the greatest despair I had ever experienced.

In response, the Lord sent the strongest outpouring of His Spirit since I first received my witness of Christ and the Book of Mormon. I was overwhelmed with the power of the love and mercy and acceptance I felt from the Lord. I felt a clear message that I was in no way spiritually inferior to any others of Heavenly Father's children, and that if I continued to be faithful to what I had been taught, and continued to repent and progress along the path the Lord had placed me on, that I would inherit the Celestial Kingdom, and would be with my wife and children forever.

There is no way I can describe the power of this spiritual outpouring in searing into my soul a sense of spiritual peace and confidence. I wrote in my journal:

I don't know what life is going to be like in twenty years but I
don't think it will be much like it is now. I can see as clear as
noon-day the fulfillment of the Lord's prophecy about the last
days. I had the spirit bear witness to my soul that Joseph Smith is
a prophet and that what I am doing is right in the Lord's sight.

I have had many fears and worries about being wrong about
my testimony but every time I am challenged the spirit whispers
to me, "It is so. It is true." The gospel seems just too good to be
true, to think that we are here on earth to prepare for godhood
is such a noble goal and so very far off from view. To think that
we really have an important place in the whole situation of the
universe is glorious. To think that I can literally perfect my soul
and live with my Father, Jesus, and my wife and children in
eternal burnings is beyond comprehension to the mortal, sinful
soul. To know that you are a noble son of an eternal Father
and Mother is so comforting. To see so many people day after
day that know not who they really are and why they are on the
earth is sad at least, painfully awesome at most. To know that
the Savior of all men knows you by name and that you are his
legal representative on the earth and that you hold the same
priesthood which he held is humbling and sobering and almost
soul bursting. (Mission Journal, page 24)

As a result of this experience, I was able to move forward and
continue to work in that area. I then was called to serve in another
area. My new companion was only two months from completing his
mission and, to use the LDS missionary jargon for those whose focus
was on home, he was extremely "trunky" (sitting on his packed trunks).
My companion was so trunky that he had obtained a subscription to
his home town newspaper and read it every day. He did not want to

wake up on time, did not want to go out and contact people, and when he was willing to go out he preferred to argue with people rather than to teach them.

I had a very difficult month in this area. In addition to the work not going as well as I would have liked, I found out that one of the girls I was thinking about a lot was engaged to be married. This turned out to be a very good thing for me since, as I wrote in my journal, "At last I can forget about her and just think about nothing but the Lord's work."

Despite my ability to forget about a girl, my problems with my companion continued to the point where I experienced the greatest conflict with any companion during my entire mission. I am sure I did not handle it as well as I should. I should have been more patient and humble and helped this Elder to have some success. But our personalities clashed and my desire to work and his lack of desire to do missionary work was difficult to reconcile. It got to the point where I lost my composure and actually told him that if he did not change his behavior I was "going to have to hit him!" Of course, I then felt bad for this very un-missionary-like behavior on my part.

In my third week in this area I sent President Tempest the only negative Letter to the President that I wrote (out of the nearly 100 that I wrote on my mission). I complained about my companion, even saying I had been very close to hitting him. I received a note back from the mission president in which he said, "Elder Dollahite, it is always darkest before the dawn. Work hard!" So, I just worked as hard as I could for the next week.

In June, President Tempest called me to be a Zone Leader with Elder Mark Manley as my companion. I was very excited to see the light at the end of the tunnel and wrote in my journal:

There will be a lot of neat experiences for me in the next year and two months. I am so thankful to my Father in Heaven for allowing me to participate in this great latter day work in New England. This is the greatest mission in the world and I can hardly believe I am able to play a part in the greatest age in history. I don't know what I did in the premortal life to allow me to have such a great life here but I do know this: I love God and I want to serve Him, be like Him, and be with Him some day. I pray God to help me fulfill my responsibilities in a way pleasing to Him. I know the Gospel is TRUE! I love the Church. I love President Tempest. (Mission Journal, pages 28– 29)

It turned out that this next area—Weston, Massachusetts, in which I was to spend seven months—was a marvelous experience for me in which my companions and I were able to teach and baptize some great families and learned many important things. It started out with our teaching a wonderful family: the Lewis family.

TENDER MERCIES & LESSONS LEARNED

I realize now that I was exhausted from several months of very hard work over very long hours in very challenging weather and physical surroundings. It was not until I was writing this account in 2008 that my first companion (Wayne Buhler) showed me his journal in which he had recorded what time we arose (by 6:30 a.m. nearly every day) and what time we went so sleep (rarely before 11:30 p.m.). I have learned that it is very important for the Lord's servants to get enough rest and exercise and to eat well. In addition to the normal emotional stress of missionary work, I was hit with a barrage of spiritual opposition and relational challenges in this area.

The experience in prayer I had during this part of my mission remains one of the most important communions I have had with my Heavenly Father. I continue to struggle with a sense of spiritual and intellectual inferiority but that is not surprising given my amazing colleagues and students at BYU. Nonetheless, I try to remember that day and that prayer and I know that we are "all alike unto God" (2 Nephi 26:33).

In my journal, I wrote that "I really am happy that I had the experience of being in Downsville* for a month because I learned a lot of things there I would not have learned anywhere else." That was certainly true. President Tempest was certainly correct when he said it was always darkest before the dawn. The next area I served in was filled with more of the kind of miracles and blessings that I experienced in my first area.

CHAPTER 23

The Lewis Family & Friends

I was transferred to Natick, Massachusetts (Weston Ward) where my next companion, Elder Manley, was wonderful to work with. We had a couple of rooms in a nice home owned by an old widow who had a dog and cat. We had twelve missionaries in our Zone and it was fun to go on "tours" where we went and worked with the missionaries in different areas. We conducted monthly training meetings with the missionaries in which Elder Manley and I gave training workshops on improving missionary work. We also went to Zone Leaders meetings with the president and his assistants that were always exciting and edifying. I loved my service as a Zone Leader.

Early in my time with Elder Manley we began teaching the Lewis family. Before I arrived, Elders Manley and King had received a "member referral" from an LDS family in Arizona who had joined the Church about four years before and sent the missionaries a note indicating they wanted missionaries to visit the Lewis family, who were friends of theirs. Elder Manley and Elder King had been by a couple of times. The first time they went Peg (the wife) was away and the Elders spoke with Peg's mother who told them Peg and John (the husband) were happy in their faith (they actually were not but had not yet informed Peg's mom). The Elders went by again and spoke with John who was friendly and invited them back.

We drove down a long, winding, tree-lined road until we got to the Lewis's large home which was on a couple of acres of land. For the first couple of visits, Peg did not seem interested but she was a friendly person who warmed to us and to the gospel in time. Peg and John had been active members of a mainline Protestant church in which they were very involved in music. But they did not find much truth in that church and had decided not to be associated with organized religion.

They were extremely interesting people and we loved teaching them. John was a professor of planetary science at the Massachusetts Institute of Technology (MIT) and one of the most brilliant people I had ever met. At first John and Peg only wanted us to teach them but not their children. After a couple of discussions with the parents, we asked if we could show the kids a film strip and they allowed us to show them Man's Search for Happiness—a film strip about the Plan of Salvation. [4] The kids seemed interested and we learned later that Van, the oldest child at age fourteen, told Peg he thought it was "the truest thing he had ever seen." From then on John and Peg had the kids join in our lessons. The kids were very bright and fun and responded very well to what we were teaching their family.

Peg and John were also heavily into Transcendental Meditation (TM), a form of meditation that had been brought to America from India by a guru named Maharishi Mahesh Yogi. Their practice of this form of mediation helped them discern the truth. In fact, as we taught them the gospel they already believed much of it and had little trouble accepting most of the rest. They were really into health foods, were mostly vegetarians, kept goats (and drank goat milk), and kept ducks and geese.

After her initial hesitation to reconsider the worth of organized religion, Peg progressed more quickly and gained a testimony and a desire to be baptized sooner than John. The kids were also progressing along well and ready to be baptized. John progressed more slowly.

---

4. lds.org/media-library/video/2016-10-0001-mans-search-for-happiness-1964

He took a more scientific, cerebral approach. He was open-minded and willing to study the things we were teaching, but did not gain a spiritual witness as quickly.

John read several languages, including Sanskrit, the language in which the Hindu scriptures (the Vedas and the Bhagavad Gita) were written in. As we were teaching the Lewis family some doctrine of the restored gospel, Elder Manley and I found it very interesting that, several times, John would get his copy of the Bhagavad Gita and search until he found a certain verse and then translate from the Sanskrit a passage that said something very similar to what we had just taught them. This happened with gospel doctrines such as the pre-mortal life, becoming like God, the glory of God is intelligence, all spirit is matter, and others. [5]

They also told us that the most dedicated practitioners of meditation can do amazing things like levitate. Yes, briefly float in the air while meditating. We had a hard time believing this, but the Lewises were so bright, educated, normal, and sane that we had to try to give credence to what they were saying. John was then a professor of planetary science at MIT and Peg was a brilliant person and we wanted to give them the benefit of the doubt. And we knew that Jesus had made food multiply, walked on water, appeared through walls, healed all manner of diseases, and other "amazing" things that seemed contrary to the laws of nature.

---

5. A number of LDS doctrines—including the nature of the soul (that every person is literally the spiritual offspring of heavenly parents), the Plan of Happiness (that answers the questions of where we come from, why we are on earth, and where we are going after death), and eternal progression (that human beings can become like God)—are distinct from the beliefs of most other Christian faiths.

But what they were saying was strange enough to us that Elder Manley called President Tempest to ask him what he thought. In his previous area, Elder Manley had found and taught some unusual people that the President knew about. When we told President Tempest about the levitating part of meditation, he laughed loudly and said to Elder Manley, "Elder, here's what I want you to do. Tomorrow I want you and Elder Dollahite to go out and knock on some doors and find some nice, normal families to teach the gospel to."

But we felt such a good feeling about the Lewis family and they were making such good progress and President Tempest did not say that we could not continue teaching them, so we did. Another issue was that they believed in reincarnation. We explained the LDS doctrine of how human beings all progressed from being self-existent intelligences to becoming spirit children of God, to gaining a body through birth, through the spirit world after death, and finally to receiving a resurrected body. John opened his Bhagavad Gita and found the verses that are typically interpreted as reincarnation and he realized that this "eternal progression" from one sphere to another was taught in the Hindu scriptures and was simply misinterpreted by the Hindu scholars who came up with the idea of reincarnation.

After a few weeks Peg and the kids were ready and anxious to be baptized, but John was still studying the doctrines from a more intellectual standpoint. During one lesson, Elder Manley and I were "working" on John, trying to answer his questions and resolve his concerns. It was hard for us because he was so much smarter and better educated than we were and was asking so many really good questions.

We were doing our best to address his concerns but we were not really able to provide all the answers he needed. After an hour or so of this type of discussion, Peg was sitting on the edge of her chair and at a certain point she burst out, with encouragement to us, "Come on, boys!" She really wanted to join the Church and was just patiently waiting for John to gain his testimony.

We were very blessed to have some wonderful ward members like the Garlands and the Lavins that had befriended the Lewis family as well as a very bright professor named Fred Bowman who helped us teach them. We began emphasizing the importance of gaining a testimony of Joseph Smith and the Book of Mormon. I quote here from an account of their conversion that Peg wrote for me:

> *Along about this time the missionaries were insisting that we read the Book of Mormon and gain a testimony of it and of Joseph Smith. That Joseph Smith story was rather upsetting, and I really didn't have any confidence in it. But eventually I decided to read a little of the Book of Mormon and then pray if the church was true. This undertaking was a challenge for me.*
>
> *I was greatly embarrassed at the thought of praying, so I took the kids to the beach; then drove the long way home to pray in private. I was so embarrassed that my prayer came out hostile and challenging, and—I didn't get an answer! I picked up the kids, and tried again the next day, same pattern. Except in between I realized how disappointed I had been when I didn't get an answer in the affirmative. When I tried the second time, I pleaded to know if the church was true, with true intent, nothing wavering. And I received such a spectacular answer that I had to go look it up in the scriptures—I knew I had read it somewhere. It was a swelling in my bosom . . . So, I had my answer, and I rejoiced in it.*
>
> *I knew John liked all the stuff that was happening, but he didn't have an answer, even though he apparently had prayed about it in some fashion. I remember a hot, sticky summer*

*afternoon when we were all craving a thunderstorm. John was
lying on the floor of the family room and I was sitting next to
him, pleading with him to acknowledge the good things that had
happened since we had started investigating. He pondered it all
silently. He wasn't ready. In fact, good things and bad things
were happening. We were all nicer to each other and so on, but
in the bad department, all our appliances were breaking and we
didn't have any money to repair them. It was at about this time
that I realized that I'd have to give up my business if we joined
the church, because I worked mostly on Sundays, the rest of the
days being taken up with caring for a farm and four children.
And now we were supposed to honor the Sabbath day and keep
it holy.*

*But we also understood the bad things. One day when we
were sitting after meditation and having a chat, we combined
our thoughts about the obvious ploy the adversary was using to
try to discourage us and had a good laugh about it. It just added
to our testimony. Somewhere in all this period of intense study
and odd happenings, John gained his testimony. Good thing,
too: I decided to write to our old minister to tell him what was
happening, and he called from his vacation spot in Maine to
argue about it. I asked if he could say our old church was 100%
true. He said no, of course not, maybe 30% true (or whatever
inadequate number he used). I said that wasn't good enough. He
asked to talk to John and got the same response. We never heard
from him again. But after he hung up we noticed that the bright
sunshine that had been streaming in the window was now
obliterated. The room was filling with darkness, beginning from
one end and moving toward us in a sickly cloud. We looked at
each other and somehow knew what it was. John turned toward*

*it and said in a loud and firm voice, "Be gone. This will make no
difference to us. Get OUT." And the darkness disappeared. That
put the finishing touches on our testimony. If our joining the
church were worth that much attention, the church must be true.
(2008 email in possession of author)*

Soon after this John told us he had decided he wanted to be
baptized along with his family. We asked him how he had gained his
testimony. He said he had been praying for a spiritual witness of the
truthfulness of the gospel and the spirit prompted him to think about
the changes in his family since the missionaries had begun teaching
them. He realized that his kids were happier, they all got along better,
they all had a new sense of purpose in life, and when they held Family
Home Evening like we had taught them to, there was a great feeling
in their home. He said this was witness enough for him that the things
we were teaching him were true and he would just have faith that his
intellectual questions would be answered in due time. Of course, we
were thrilled and so were Peg and the kids. The Lewis family was
baptized a couple of weeks later. As I was writing this account, I asked
Peg if she would send me a written account of their conversion. About
their baptism, Peg wrote to me:

*We set a baptism date. The bishop came and interviewed us in
our home. As he left, the missionaries, who had left before him,
came driving back in the driveway with a great impression of
needing to convey something urgent. We were mildly alarmed.
They sat us down and taught us the principle of tithing, which
somehow had gotten left out of our many discussions. John and
I looked at each other. We had no money, we were going into
debt every month—and yet we knew it was a true principle.*

We acknowledged that we already had a testimony of tithing,
and the baptism went ahead as scheduled, on our 16th wedding
anniversary. The ward turned out in force for the baptism of our
family, which was very heartening. We felt loved. (2008 email
in possession of author)

The Lewis family was baptized on August 1, 1980. John and Peg
and three of their kids, Van, Meg, and Chris, were baptized. A couple
nights after their baptism, we were teaching them when Van came
running into the house, having just come from attending the LDS
youth group (Young Men) and said, "Mom, guess what, they have a
basketball team at the church!" Peg then said, "Yes, Van, they have
EVERYTHING at the church; they just haven't told us all of it yet!"

The Lewises were so excited about the gospel that they gave us a
referral to teach some very close friends of theirs, Peter and Valerie
Daniel, who were also really into Transcendental Meditation. Peter
was a chemist with a PhD. We began teaching them and the Daniels
progressed quickly with John and Peg fellowshipping them and
helping us to teach them and resolve their concerns. A little over a
month later the Daniels were baptized. John Lewis, who had been
ordained a priest in the Aaronic Priesthood, was able to baptize them.
We then began teaching some other close friends of the Lewis and
Daniel families named Heather Kindness and her daughter, Alana
(Lani). The Kindness family also was very open to the gospel and was
already living the same kind of spiritually- and family-oriented life
that the Lewis and Daniel families were.

After we had been teaching Heather and Lani for a few weeks,
and things were progressing nicely toward their baptism, we went with
them to a nice wilderness park for a walk. On our walk Heather said,
"Elders, I am sorry but I just don't think I can be baptized after all."

We were crushed and asked why. She said, "Well, if I join the Church everyone will call me 'Sister Kindness' and that would be like being called 'Brother Love' and it would just be too strange." We said we would ask the members not to call her "Sister Kindness" and looked expectantly at her for a few seconds. Then she smiled and said, "I'm just kidding. I'm going to be baptized and it's okay if Church members call me 'Sister Kindness.'"

In December, we baptized Heather and Alana Kindness. Peter Daniel baptized Heather and I baptized Lani. In addition to the marvelous experience of teaching the Lewis, Daniel, and Kindness families, we were also able to baptize a couple, Susan and Greg Woodworth, friends of a family in the ward, along with John Wahnon.

TENDER MERCIES & LESSONS LEARNED

This was one of the greatest times in my mission. Elder Manley and I got along great and we were able to have a lot of success in teaching and baptizing and were able to work with a lot of great missionaries in our zone. Teaching the Lewis, Daniel, and Kindness families was one of the greatest experiences of my life. Each family member was filled with light and love. I learned as much or more from them as they learned from Elder Manley and me. John, Peg, Peter, Valerie, and Heather were and are among the most intelligent and Christian people I have ever met.

One evening, President and Sister Tempest hosted a gathering in the mission home, where Truman Madsen—a brilliant BYU professor of philosophy (with a PhD from Harvard) and well-known writer, speaker, and former New England mission president—gave a talk. John and Peg Lewis, who had been members of the Church for some time by then, came to the talk. After the talk, I introduced them to

President Tempest and Brother Madsen as one of the families I had had the blessing to teach. They visited for a while and John was able to talk with Truman Madsen about some deep ideas and both President Tempest and Brother Madsen were very impressed with John and Peg.

Later, President Tempest said, "Now those are the kind of wonderful people we need more of in the Church." When I explained that this was the couple who practiced TM and levitated, the president was incredulous. I was impressed when he said he was obviously wrong about them and he was very happy we kept teaching them.

It has been a great blessing for me to have remained friends with the Wests and the Lewises and to have been able to have their kids in our home as they have come out to BYU and come to the MTC before their missions. Our family has been greatly blessed to hear from these wonderful converts how the gospel changed and blessed their lives. Both the West and the Lewis families ended up having more children than they likely would have had if they had not joined the Church. Their faithful lives have been a blessing to many Saints, not the least of which are my family and me.

During my mission, there gradually evolved within me a deep desire to drink deeply from the fountain of knowledge that God had revealed and that man has discovered. The months that I spent in the Weston Ward increased these desires because there were a number of professors and graduate students in the ward. In addition to those we taught, many Weston Ward members, such as Fred Bowman and the Goldberg family (who had converted from Judaism years before), also inspired me to seek to learn as much as possible about everything I can. This deep commitment to learning was increased even more when I was transferred to be a Zone Leader in Boston.

CHAPTER 24

Serving in Boston & Cambridge

On Christmas Eve in 1980 I wrote the following in my journal:

*Today I was transferred to Somerville, Massachusetts, to be with
Elder Finch. . . . I am looking forward to working in Boston
and really meeting a lot of interesting people. I don't know
what's in store for me but I am looking forward to whatever it
is. . . . I have been out 16½ months now and I cannot believe
it. They said your second year goes by quickly but that is an
understatement and a half. I am really going to work hard my
last 7½ months and do all I can to make up for any lack of work
I might have had so far. I feel pretty good about my mission so
far and I have worked hard almost all the time. I am going to
really stretch my soul for the rest of my mission and exercise faith
in God and really have success. . . . My testimony of the gospel
continues to grow every day and as I serve the Lord diligently I
feel the joy that passes all understanding. . . . I love the Savior,
I know He lives and I know He guides this church and I know
he will come again soon. I look forward to that day with all my
heart. The gospel is TRUE! (Mission Journal, pages 36–37)*

One of the greatest parts of serving a full-time mission is the
chance to meet so many interesting people from so many backgrounds.
Missionary work is rarely dull and a great variety of people and
experiences are packed into the two years. I had interesting experiences
and met fascinating people throughout my mission.

But my last eight months were spent mostly in the exciting
and diverse cities of Boston and Cambridge which included many
university campuses (e.g., Harvard, Wellesley, MIT, Boston College,
Tufts, and the University of Massachusetts). Thus, many of the
most interesting people I met and experiences I had were in the last
eight months of my mission in which I served as a Zone Leader in
Boston and as an Assistant to the President in Cambridge (and then
Belmont). I also traveled throughout the mission during the last four
months, training and touring with missionaries and attending stake
conferences. I share some of those experiences in this and the next
chapters.

One time my companion and I were tracting in an exclusive
neighborhood in Belmont, which is in the greater Boston area. We
usually found that folks in the wealthier parts of the towns and cities
were less likely to be willing to allow us in to share our message. In
the most exclusive neighborhoods, the homes had fences and gates and
we might not be able to speak to anyone except through an intercom
system. We usually had more success in the neighborhoods of middle-
and lower-income families.

At one mansion, we rang the doorbell and a few bars from the
national anthem played over speakers we could hear. A woman in a
full-blown maid uniform came to the door and asked who we were and
what we wanted. We told her who we were and said we had a message
about Jesus Christ that we would like to share. She said she would get
"the lady of the house" and left us standing at the door.

A couple of minutes later a middle-aged woman dressed and
coiffed to the hilt came to the door and looked at us suspiciously. We
told her who we were and asked if we could share a message about
Jesus Christ with her. She looked at us disdainfully and said in a
haughty voice, "Look around you. Does it look to you like I need

religion?" Then she slammed the large heavy door. My companion and I looked at each other and laughed. She had baldly stated what many people of her class probably felt and it was quite refreshing to hear it clearly said out loud.

One time we were "street contacting" in Harvard Yard (a courtyard between the dorms at Harvard) and we were talking with a couple of students. A woman in her twenties who was wearing a ski hat propped on her head in conical shape came up to us. On the hat was attached a large star made from aluminum foil. She came up to me and looked at my name tag and said, "Who are you?"

I said, "We are missionaries with the Church of Jesus Christ of Latter-day Saints."

She said, "Oh, I'm a missionary too!"

"Which church are you a missionary from?" I asked.

She said, "I'm a Space Catholic."

Sensing she was not altogether in her right mind, I am very ashamed to admit that I said, "Do you mean Space Cadet?"

And she, without realizing I had just been rude, said, "No. Space Catholic."

I said, "Space Catholic? What do Space Catholics believe?"

"Well, we believe that Jesus came in a spaceship from another planet. And he taught the people and then he ascended to heaven in a spaceship. And he will return soon in a spaceship."

I said, "Interesting. So how many Space Catholics are there?"

She said, "750 million."

I said, "750 million? Isn't that the number of Catholics in the world?" (I had just read this statistic a few weeks before.)

She said, "Yes, all Catholics are Space Catholics. They just don't know it yet. That is why I'm a missionary."

Then she walked off in search of converts.

One of the great recurring aspects of my mission was the chance to "tour" with other missionaries for a day or two. Most of the time when we went on tours with other missionaries (worked with them for a day or two in their area), the Lord blessed us with great success in finding new folks for the Elders or Sisters to work with. It was amazing how often we went to an area that had very few people in their teaching pool (those they were actively teaching) and, by the end of our time with the missionaries, they had a number of good prospects to teach. The Lord wanted to give them encouragement and success and often used a tour with mission leaders to jump-start their area. In addition to great success, we also often had unusual experiences while touring.

One day we went with the Sisters to teach an African-American girl in Dorchester which was one of the most impoverished and dangerous parts of Boston. Sister Horlacher was teaching this girl about Joseph Smith when the girl's obviously drunk father walked in. He had just lost his job so he was quite upset. He started to yell at us for teaching his daughter. He then sat down in the chair and listened to us teach for a few minutes. Then out of the blue he asked us if we knew about "roots."

There was a popular television mini-series called Roots about an African man taken into slavery which had spurred a lot of African-Americans to become interested in their genealogy. We said we knew about Roots and that we believed it was important to search out our ancestors. But then he started talking about Voodoo doctors who use plant roots in their potions and went on for a while about that. Then, suddenly, he dropped his head and fell asleep in the chair. We were then able to have a very spiritual gospel discussion with his daughter and told this young lady and her mother about baptism.

When I had about six months left on my mission I wrote the following in my journal:

Well, I have been feeling good lately. We had the Mitt Romney fireside and a lot of people came to it and enjoyed it. Jill, Paul, and Bob will be baptized this month and hopefully Gary Garth and others next month. I have been with Elder Kelly Pond for a little over a week now and he is great. We get along well and work well together. I am feeling strange feelings knowing I am nearing the end of my mission.

I feel excited to return to school and work at the MTC and use the things I have learned to help people. And, of course, I am sad at the thought of leaving the mission field. I am striving to really work hard this last six months so that I can help the Lord's work go forth as much as possible. . . . I am so very grateful to Father in Heaven for allowing me to be a member of His Church and serve him on a mission. I really love the Lord's work and I love to see the change in peoples' lives as they find the truth. . . . [E]veryone keeps telling me that I am going to be the next Assistant. I don't feel worthy to even be a member of the Church, much less to be an Elder, much less an Assistant to the President. I personally think Elder Pond will be the next Assistant. (Mission Journal, page 41)

In fact, Elder Pond was called to be an Assistant to the President. About a month later, I wrote in my journal:

This morning is transfers. President Tempest called me at 6:30 to call me to be one of his Assistants. I am grateful for the chance to serve the missionaries in the mission and to teach the gospel to the people in my new area. I am excited to work with the office staff and learn from each of them. The President said he had been watching me for a long time and felt I was ready for this responsibility. I hope I can magnify this calling and be the best Assistant in my power. I am so humbled to think that 150 missionaries will be looking to me for guidance and strength. I have got to be at my best at all times. I am so excited about the next four months! (Mission Journal, page 44)

One of the responsibilities of the Assistants was to tour the entire mission. Thus, we drove throughout New England spending a day or two with a large number of missionaries, working in their area trying to help encourage and assist them to find new people they would be able to teach the gospel of Jesus Christ to. Some of the missionaries we toured with were a bit intimidated to have the Assistants coming to work with them and so they were a bit tense. We tried to help them relax by having some fun. One time Elder Pond and I were touring with a couple of Sisters who were very nervous about having the Assistants work with them. Elder Pond and I were with Sister Parsons, who happened to be a fine singer.

We came to one door and a sweet little old lady with laughing eyes answered the door and I said, "Hi, my name is Elder Dollahite, I'm a missionary from the Church of Jesus Christ of Latter-day Saints," and then I said, in a kidding voice with a big smile, "and I have two special guests with me, Donny and Marie Osmond. Donny and Marie, why don't you sing something for this nice lady?" They then sang "I Am a Child of God."

They sang beautifully and when they finished the woman said, "Well, I don't think that is really Donny and Marie since I watch their show. But they were pretty good and that was a pretty unique pitch, so why don't you come on in and we can chat for a while." We went in and she gave us something to drink and we taught this lovely lady about the restoration of the gospel.

One time we were working with the Sisters teaching a woman named Jo Erin. We had planned to teach her about the priesthood and baptism, but as we started Sister Reeves did not feel right about it so she started teaching the Plan of Salvation. As I was talking about the purpose of life, I mentioned that I had joined the Church three years before. Jo Erin immediately asked me to tell her how I came to join the Church. I related to her my conversion story and the Spirit was very strong. Afterward, Jo Erin said that was exactly what she needed to hear and that it helped her a lot. I was grateful to Sister Reeves for being in tune with the Spirit so that Jo Erin could be taught what she needed.

In May, Elder Pond and I toured and worked with the missionaries in Cape Cod and, on our P-Day,[6] went to some historic sites in Plymouth including the Mayflower II,[7] Plimoth Plantation (a place where people dress, speak, and act as if they were actual people from that time), and Plymouth Rock. There was a protective barrier around Plymouth Rock with clearly posted signs about NOT climbing the fence to stand on Plymouth Rock. I am ashamed to say that, in a moment of youthful impetuousness, I hopped the fence and stood on Plymouth Rock briefly, and then hopped back over the fence. I realized later that this was a stupid, selfish, and wrong thing to do.

We began teaching Bob Scannell, a young man about our age who was very bright and extremely interested in the Church. He read the entire Book of Mormon in the first few days of our teaching him. He

---

6. P-Day stands for Preparation Day when missionaries get a little break from missionary work, see some tourist sites, write home to their family and friends, and do their laundry.

7. The Mayflower II is a replica of the original Mayflower.

was excited about everything we taught him and believed most of it. He was a highly religious person with an inquisitive mind and had a lot of questions.

We taught him that he needed to obtain a testimony of the truth and described for him what a "burning in the bosom" was like. He seemed to want to be baptized but he also had a number of doctrinal questions and issues. Each time we met with him, we asked if he had obtained a testimony or a witness of the truth. He said he had prayed but had not felt the "burning in the bosom" that we had described which is mentioned in LDS scripture.

After a few weeks, one day we came to the appointment and Bob was very excited. He told us about an experience he had the night before. He said he had prayed before bed for a witness of the truth of what he was being taught. In the middle of the night he awoke and sat up in bed and rather than being confused about what he had been learning with questions swirling around in his mind, he said somehow all the questions were gone and his mind felt at complete peace, he felt like his mind was like cement that had become rock solid in knowing the truth.

Then Bob said, "I know this is not the 'burning in the bosom' feeling that you described, but I think I know the gospel is true and I really want to be baptized. Does that count as a testimony?" We assured him that it did and set a baptismal date. Bob was the last person on my mission that I was privileged to go with into the water and baptize but we were later to teach and baptize one of Bob's close friends as well.

One time we were in the Cambridge chapel when a man named John Hussain walked in. He said he was from Lebanon and had become a Christian there but had been persecuted by Muslims in his home village, and had fled from Lebanon and come to America so he could practice Christianity.

We did not think there were any LDS missionaries or branches in Lebanon and we asked him which Christian church he had joined. He said he had obtained a copy of the New Testament and been converted to Christ through reading it but had not yet joined any church. We asked him how he decided to come to our church. He said that when he arrived in Boston he found a telephone book and looked for the "Christian Church" in the phone book. He said he was surprised to find so many churches under the "Christian" section in the phone book but when he found "The Church of Jesus Christ of Latter-day Saints" he knew he had found the right church.

He was humble and accepted everything we taught him. When he prayed, it seemed like the Lord was his friend and was in the room. Since his English was quite limited, it often took some time for us to teach him even basic Christian concepts. One time we were teaching him about the Fall of Adam and we asked if he had heard about the "forbidden fruit" that Adam was not supposed to eat. He smiled and said, "Ah, yes, the apple."

We said, "Yes! And do you know the name of the tree that the forbidden fruit was on?" We were trying to get him to say the Tree of Knowledge of Good and Evil.

John looked at us kind of funny like we had asked him sort of a silly question and said, "Yes. Tree Apple." We laughed and said yes and that another name for the tree was the Tree of Knowledge of Good and Evil. John was making great progress and had committed to be baptized when one day he called us and said that his visa application had not been approved and he was being deported back to Lebanon. We never heard from John again. I hope and pray that perhaps he was able to find the restored gospel.

While I was in Cambridge, my companion and I taught a seventeen-year-old Jewish girl named Andrea. She had learned about and become interested in the Church because of the Osmond family, a well-known LDS performing group. She was receptive to our message but her parents were very upset about her investigation of the Church. She progressed well and set a baptismal date for the 24th of July, 1981, and asked that I baptize her. The Osmonds were going to perform a concert in Boston on the twenty-fifth and so she wrote and invited them to attend her baptism.

Given how much fan mail the Osmonds likely received, I did not expect that they would read and respond to her letter. I was wrong. Alan Osmond called to apologize to her that they could not make her baptism. However, a few days before Andrea was to be baptized, her mother insisted that she call it off. I do not know whether she was later baptized but I certainly hope so.

TENDER MERCIES & LESSONS LEARNED

While most of the experiences I mention in this Chapter were simply interesting interactions with diverse people, I learned some important lessons during my time in Boston and Cambridge. In the first 16 months of my mission I was primarily in suburban areas and while I met a range of people, it did not compare to the tremendous diversity I witnessed in the big city.

One of the greatest lessons I learned was that there are an almost infinite number of ways you can live and believe that leads to unhappiness or merely worldly pleasure. Indeed, "broad is the way that leadeth unto destruction" (Matthew 7:13) and "I cannot tell you all the things whereby ye may commit sin" (Mosiah 4:29). During my time in Boston I wrote the following in my journal:

I am learning much from this experience in Boston that I wouldn't learn anywhere else. I am seeing first-hand what life without the gospel produces—not very much. I will be a missionary for the rest of eternity because that is where the greatest happiness comes from and that is how I can be a useful person. I love the Lord very much and I know Joseph was and is and always will be a Prophet of the Living God. (Mission Journal, page 40)

Seeing so many diverse people in so short a period of time allowed me to see many ways that people can seek for happiness in ways that will never bring it. I saw clearly every day the truth of the scriptures from the Book of Mormon that "wickedness never was happiness" (Alma 41:10) and "ye have sought for happiness in doing iniquity, which thing is contrary to the nature of that righteousness which is in our great and Eternal Head" (Helaman 13:38). The Lord, in His tender mercy, allowed me to see for myself that "the wages of sin are death" (Romans 6:23).

From working with Bob Scannell, I learned that the Lord communicates with each person in whatever way the Lord deems best. Just because one person receives a testimony in one way does not mean someone else will have the same type of experience. The Lord said he would speak to us "in your mind and in your heart" (D&C 8:2) and for Bob in was mainly in his mind. Bob has remained very active in the Church and we occasionally correspond.

CHAPTER 25

Experiences with Leaders from Other Faiths

On various occasions during my mission I had experiences with leaders of other faiths. Most of these were positive. For example, in my missionary journal, on January 11, 1980, I wrote: "I had the chance to speak with Pastor Burke yesterday. He is a very powerful man who loves the Lord and has very strong ideas. I learned a lot from him and was able to bear my testimony to him."

A few of these experiences were not positive. Often my interactions with leaders of other faiths was tinged with competition in that they felt that because I was a missionary out to make converts, they thought I was trying to "steal their sheep" from them.

Early in my mission I had an unpleasant experience with an anti-Mormon preacher. There was a minister in our mission who spent his entire ministry traveling around preaching and writing anti-Mormon material. He and/or his wife would drive around looking for LDS missionaries and, when they found them, would invite them over to the car and tell them they had been looking for the missionaries to teach the gospel to them and invite the Elders over.

We had not heard of this, so when the wife drove up to us and invited us over we thought we were going to get to teach some "golden" investigators. When we got to their home, the minister had us come into his study. He showed us the many LDS books he had (*Jesus the Christ* and *Articles of Faith* by James E. Talmage and *A Marvelous Work and a Wonder* by LeGrand Richards as well as others). He then proceeded to preach to us the standard Evangelical Christian anti-Mormon stuff that I had heard before, although he was particularly articulate and passionate. As soon as we realized this was an anti-Mormon ambush, we bore our testimonies and excused ourselves.

We had another negative experience with an Evangelical Christian pastor. One of our investigators was progressing in the teaching process and was accepting what we taught. She told us that her minister, Pastor Jones*, often preached against "cults like the Mormons" and said we were going to go to hell. Of course, Pastor Jones was extremely upset that one of his most faithful youth was listening to the Mormon missionaries and seemed to be accepting what they were teaching. He tried various ways to persuade and even pressure her to stop taking the discussions from us.

One day we received a phone call from his secretary asking us to come to the church and meet with Pastor Jones. With some trepidation, we went to the church. It was a large building that included a spacious auditorium, the school, a day care facility, and other amenities. After the tour of the church we were ushered into Pastor Jones's spacious and well-appointed office.

He lost little time in beginning his assault. He brought out a big Bible and began railing on us, attacking the Church, and calling us various names. When we did not back down, he became angrier and the "Bible-bashing" session heated up. He finally ended by standing up and cursing us to hell in the name of Jesus Christ and kicking us out of his church. His assistant ushered us out the door to our car.

I was very upset that he was preaching anti-Mormon sermons, telling our investigator not to listen to us, and had cursed two of the Lord's servants. I felt a great deal of what I considered "righteous indignation." I had read a number of scriptures saying that the Lord's servants should "cast off the dust of their feet" against those who had rejected and cursed them (Matthew 10:14–15; Luke 10:10–12; D&C 24:15–16; 60:15; 75:19–22).

I called President Tempest and told him about what this pastor was doing and asked him how I would go about "dusting my feet" against this pastor, saying that I wanted to see his church "burn to the ground." President Tempest laughed heartily and said, "Elder Dollahite, we don't do that anymore." I said I thought this was exactly the kind of situation that the Lord was talking about in the scriptures, but President Tempest just laughed again and said to forget about him. I am sorry to say that our investigator succumbed to the pressure brought by her pastor and family, and told us she could not listen to us anymore.

On the positive side, we got to know a number of Catholic priests on our mission in heavily-Catholic New England. I remember fondly the kindly priests we met, one of whom invited us to eat with him on occasion and another who gave us tickets to attend a Boston Red Sox ball game at Fenway Park. I remember one particular lengthy conversation with a Catholic priest we met. It was my first real conversation with a priest. I told him that Latter-day Saints were expected to pay a tithe of one-tenth of their annual income, and asked him what percentage of income he thought most Catholics gave. He laughed and said it was far less than one-tenth, probably less than one percent, but that he would love to see them give more. I mentioned to him about the LDS home and visiting teaching programs in which members were in each other's homes about once a month, and asked him how often he thought he was in the homes of his parishioners. He said that his was a large parish (a couple thousand members) and he really only got into the homes of those who had experienced a family crisis of some kind, but that he wished his parishioners would take care of each other like the Mormons did.

I told him about other LDS beliefs and practices and asked other questions about Catholic belief and practice and was happy to hear him say how much he respected the kind of religious life his Mormon neighbors lived. I felt good feelings for this good man and appreciated his honest admiration for a faith that was quite different from his, and for his kind treatment of missionaries that he knew were going around trying to convert people from other faiths—including his own.

One time my companion and I were tracting in a neighborhood and a gregarious and fun Episcopal Priest invited us in, gave us something to drink, and listened to our message. I told him that my mother wished that I had become a military officer or an Episcopal Priest like my uncle. He enthusiastically said, "Hey, why don't you put on my priest's collar and I'll take a picture of you and you can send it to your mom and tell her you converted back!" Something about his enthusiasm and my lack of thinking about this caused me to say, "Sure, why not!"

He went and got his priest's collar (black shirt and round, white, stiff clerical collar) and I put it on. He gave me a big Bible and I stood with it open while he took a Polaroid photo of me. I wrote on the back, "Mom, I converted back!" and sent it to my mom with a letter explaining what had happened (including telling her I was just kidding about converting back). I later realized I should have politely declined this good man's offer to wear his clerical garb even though Mom got a kick out of this, and I treasure the photo of me in Episcopal priestly clothing.

One of the most interesting encounters I had with a leader of another faith was while I was serving as an assistant to President Tempest and touring around the mission working with the missionaries. I was in Brattleboro, Vermont, working with the Elders there and we saw a huge semi-truck being unloaded in an open field.

Painted on the side of the truck in big red letters was, "Brother Love's Born in the Blood Ministry" (yes, the same "Brother Love" that Heather Kindness mentioned). Beneath this was written in huge, red letters: "Healings, Tongues, Prophecies" and other things designed to let the reader know what would happen at the meeting. On the grounds, there was a huge sign that said, "Old Fashioned Tent Revival Meeting Tonight! All Invited."

We decided that this was too good to miss, so the four of us attended the tent meeting and sat in the back row. When the time came for the revival to begin the tent was absolutely packed. Brother Love, dressed all in white, was a spell-binding preacher. His southern drawl lingered over certain words and he had his audience in the palm of his hand. His wife, Sister Love, was also dressed in white and played the organ. It was highly entertaining as Brother Love worked the crowd, laid on hands for healing, spoke in tongues, led enthusiastic singing of gospel songs, and called everyone there to repentance.

Then he surprised us by looking directly at us and saying, "My friends, I see some Mormon missionaries here," and pointed to us (we were in the back row). He then said, "Now, I understand that you Mormons believe in prophets? Ain't that right?"

I stood up and said in a loud, clear voice, "Yes, sir, we do!"

He then said, "Well, I believe in prophecy too. In fact, I'm a prophet and I'm going to prophesy right now! I prophesy that Jesus Christ will return sometime between 1988 and 1990 and I prophesy that the United States will cease to exist by 1990 [this was July 12, 1981]. And I want you Mormon missionaries and everyone else to write that down in your little black books!" I went home and wrote it in my black missionary journal (page 120 of written journal).

After the meeting, we waited around and spoke briefly with him. When I tried to teach and testify of the restoration to him, he yelled at me and told me he would meet me at the judgment bar to condemn me to hell. As much as I did not appreciate being told by various Evangelical pastors and people that I would be going to hell, I would much rather speak with someone who had strong religious commitments and feelings than speak to those who were apathetic about their faith. Sadly, those turned out to be in far greater numbers than the truly committed.

One of the families we met invited us to attend their meeting of "Charismatic Catholics." We came to the parish on a Sunday evening and found 40–50 people meeting in a room on the floor below the main sanctuary. After some singing and praying they began "speaking in tongues" which sounded like gibberish to us. Some people would stand and "interpret" what was said and while some of it made sense, much seemed not to be edifying.

When I was in Boston I came to know Mike Davis, a marvelous Christian Science gentleman, who gave tours at the Mother Church of the Christian Science faith. Mike knew a lot about the Latter-day Saints and he was very friendly to the missionaries, who he saw when they came to tour the Mother Church. Mike took us out to lunch a couple of times and we chatted with him once or twice in addition to that. I attended a "testimony" meeting at the Mother Church—a large round building that holds thousands of people. In the testimony meeting Christian Scientists stand and tell about a healing they have experienced and bear testimony of God's power and love. They are quite similar to LDS testimony meetings.

TENDER MERCIES & LESSONS LEARNED

Since my mission, I have been able to spend nearly four decades carefully studying other religions. I have been blessed with understanding and empathy gained from decades of studying the beliefs and practices of various faiths along with my research for the American Families of Faith project (see americanfamiliesoffaith. byu.edu). In this research, we have carefully studied the faith beliefs and practices of more than twenty denominations of the three major Abrahamic faiths (Judaism, Christianity, Islam). I now have great respect for those of any faith who devote their lives to serving the Lord. As a young, new-convert missionary, however, my feelings toward religious leaders of other faiths were that they were leading their people astray and I wanted to teach them and their congregants the restored gospel.

The Lord was very kind to me in allowing me to meet a number of great leaders from other faiths. Although there were some exceptions, most of my interactions with leaders of other faiths were fairly positive. Because my uncle Gene was a priest and a very good man, I was predisposed to have good feelings about other religious leaders.

Of course, these leaders thought we were wrong theologically and did not appreciate that we were representatives of what we believed was the only true church on the earth. Since we were attempting to convert their congregants to Mormonism, there was a natural tension between us and our friends who led congregations from other faiths. But usually we were able to maintain good relationships.

I learned that it is possible to be kind and loving toward those who have very different religious beliefs and practices. I also learned that there are some faith leaders who consider themselves to be our enemies. I saw that my patriarchal blessing had been fulfilled when, referring to my mission, it stated that, "You shall travel among strangers and even enemies to your faith, but inasmuch as you hearken unto the whisperings of the Holy Spirit, you shall be guided aright and be protected from harm."

As part of my research as a professor of family life at Brigham Young University, I have personally interviewed almost three dozen pastors, priests, rabbis, and imams as well as almost sixty Christian, Jewish, and Muslim families about how their faith influences their family life. I have greatly enjoyed my conversations with all these devoted and faithful men and women. Having served as an LDS bishop, I have some appreciation for what it means to devote your life to the well-being of a congregation and how challenging that can be.

As part of my research, I have also attended dozens of religious services of many faiths in several states. I have brought my kids to attend a number of these services and we have always been treated with love and respect. (Well, there was one Evangelical congregation that had one person who was not particularly polite to my daughter and me when he learned we were LDS.)

I developed and teach a class at BYU called "Families in World Religions" (SFL 345) where we respectfully study the beliefs and practice of our friends of other faiths and how they live their faith in their homes and families. I try to teach about these faiths in the way I would hope others would teach about my faith—with respect, accuracy, and focusing on the positive virtues of the faith. I have folks from other faiths come in and speak with my students as guest lecturers. My students love learning about what our friends believe and do to live their faith.

All in all, my mission turned out to be all that I had hoped for—and more. I am eternally grateful that I was able to serve a two-year full-time mission in New England representing the Lord Jesus Christ. I worked closely with many wonderful people who made courageous changes in their lives. I experienced some minor miracles, grew spiritually and intellectually, and increased in love of the Lord and in my testimony of the restored gospel of Jesus Christ. ✶

PART IV

Courtship, Marriage, & Testimony

CHAPTER 26

Back at University &
Meeting Mary

When I returned to BYU, I lived with four guys who were fellow returned missionaries from New England in a house we called the "Boston House." We had a great time and made the transition back to "normal life" fairly easily. As soon as I got to Provo I went to the MTC and told them I was in town and updated my application with local contact information. I was told that there were hundreds of applicants and that I would likely have to wait several months or longer before I might expect to receive an opportunity to have an interview.

I went home and again prayed that I would be able to work at the MTC and train missionaries to become the best missionaries they could be. I prayed that, if it was His will, I would love to begin teaching there as soon as possible, since I would much prefer to teach at the MTC as opposed to flipping burgers or something. A couple of days later I received a call from Jim Kasen, who said he was a Zone Administrator at the MTC. He asked if I could come in for an interview. We arranged a time for me to come to visit with him.

When I met with Jim, he told me that he had felt spiritually prompted to go and look in the file drawer with applications. As he looked at the drawer with hundreds of applications, he noticed my name near the back and felt inspired to pull my file. He said he had a strong spiritual impression that I was supposed to be teaching at the MTC, and so he gave me a call. I told him about my conversion and my impression, when I was a new missionary at the MTC, that I would teach there after my mission. He offered me a position and I gladly accepted. Although I had faith the Lord would answer my prayer, I also knew there were almost certainly many other BYU students offering the same prayer so I had been resigned to wait much longer. Thus, I was thrilled to be able to begin teaching at the MTC sooner than I thought.

I had a great experience working at the MTC. I spent a year as a classroom teacher working with more than a dozen districts of missionaries going to English speaking missions. I loved every minute of it. After a year in the classroom, Lane Ward, my boss and the Director of Training, asked me to come and work with him in the Research and Development Office. He had just received an assignment to develop new materials for all Visitors' Centers throughout the Church. Until then each Visitors' Center had its own script that missionaries memorized. The script had typically been written by one of the directors or the missionaries at the center and varied widely in the quality of writing, the soundness of history and doctrine presented, and in the length of the presentation.

My assignment was to help write lessons for a new "modular" approach where we wrote brief lessons focused on basic doctrines such as the Atonement, the Book of Mormon, the Joseph Smith story, and the Plan of Salvation. I also helped senior couple missionaries who were assigned to go to Church Visitors' Centers throughout the nation to learn the modular presentations we were writing. It was partly as a result of my work at the MTC that I met the person who became my wife. But before I met her I had a challenging year of college and some challenges with relationships.

Having decided that I wanted to help families as a family counselor, I was now serious about my university studies. I decided to go to school full-time year-round for two years and finish my bachelor's degree two years after my mission. This way I could begin graduate school as soon as possible. I changed my major from theater to family life and worked hard to do well academically. I loved my major and I felt that the Lord was guiding me in the choice to learn how to strengthen families.

As far as my own progress toward courtship and marriage, I had dated a few women and had become very involved with one wonderful person that I thought I wanted to marry. We went out for eight months and although we became engaged, we both had conflicted feelings about getting married. We cared deeply about each other and truly wanted the best for each other. But she was several years older than I was and she worried about that. Given that I was so much younger and not nearly as mature as she was, I worried about my ability to be the person she needed.

After months of painful confusion where sometimes we felt right about it and at other times one of us did not, we finally ended the engagement. I moved out of the ward to allow us both a new start. On my first Sunday in my new ward, I felt sad, out of place, and completely uninterested in getting involved in any kind of relationship. But there was a young woman in the ward who took an immediate interest in me and made it clear she wanted to begin a relationship with me. I was just not ready for that, and so I called my friend David Pace, who had been the Mission Secretary in the mission office with me, and told him I had just ended my engagement, had moved to a new ward, and asked if I could come to church with him the next Sunday. He said sure and told me where they met.

That next Sunday I went to the large Stake Center on 9th East Street across from Deseret Towers, where I had lived my first year at BYU. David met me and led me into the chapel. He explained that this was not really a ward but a Sunday School program for single adults in the Oak Hills Stake that met each week. As we sat in the chapel during opening exercises and announcements David quietly pointed out various members of the ward who were children or grandchildren of a number of well-known BYU professors and administrators including sons of former presidents of BYU (and future LDS apostles) Dallin H. Oaks and Jeffrey R. Holland. David himself was a son of George W. Pace, well-known and beloved BYU professor of religion. I was intimidated at being with all these kids of people who I respected and admired. Again, I felt out of my league with such a group of wonderful Latter-day Saints.

Then David pointed out a lovely young woman sitting in the middle of the chapel and whispered, "That is Mary Kimball, she is President Kimball's granddaughter. She just returned from a mission. You know, Dave, you would really like Mary. You should ask her out."

I said, "She looks like a very nice person, but I'm not ready to date yet."

David said, "Seriously, Dave, you really should ask Mary out. She is a wonderful person and I think you would really like her."

I said, "Thanks, but I'm just not ready yet. Besides, I don't deserve to date the granddaughter of the president of the Church."

David insisted, "I mean it. I just really feel like you should ask her out."

I glanced back again and noticed that sitting next to Mary was a tall, handsome, athletic guy with his arm around her. They both looked very happy and he looked quite possessive with his arm on the back of the pew. I said, "It looks like she is already involved with someone."

David said, "They just barely started going out."

I said, "Well, it looks like they are getting pretty serious. Again, thanks for thinking of me, but I am just not ready and, even if I were, I don't want to break in on something like that." David again said that he thought they had just barely begun going out and that I really should meet her. Again, I firmly declined and that was the last we talked about it.

The next day I went to my work at the MTC and Brother Ward, my boss, told me he would like me to go watch a new media presentation that had just been developed for sister missionaries. He said it was about poise and manners and stuff like that. I said I had a lot of work to do on the modular presentations we were writing. He said he knew I was busy, but wanted me to go see this presentation. I asked what a presentation on manners for sister missionaries had to do with my work. I said again that I felt pressed to work on my project given our deadlines, and asked if I really had to attend it. He said he did not know why, but he just really felt I should attend the presentation. When I again demurred, he said, "Dave, I am your boss and I want you to get down to that meeting right now!"

I grudgingly walked down the hall to the room and entered a large meeting room filled with sister missionaries. I sat in the back feeling very out of place. The media presentation was a kind of "Miss Manners" for sister missionaries and discussed a number of issues that Sisters should know, including how to do their hair and make-up, how to sit down and stand up, how to cross their legs, how to engage in conversation, and how to eat. There were photographs of young ladies of sister missionary age illustrating the points being made. I could not believe I was sitting there watching this stupid presentation when I had so much to do. I could see no possible value in what was being discussed for the work I was supposed to be doing. I could not wait for this thing to end so I could get out of there and get back to work.

But then there was a photograph of a lovely Sister illustrating "poise." I was certain it was that young woman, Mary Kimball, that David Pace had pointed out to me the day before and kept insisting that I meet. As I looked at the picture, I had a very clear and strong spiritual impression that I needed to ask her out. It was as strong an impression as I had ever received in the five years since I first learned the Book of Mormon was true.

Now I knew that this was why my boss had inexplicably felt so strongly that I should attend this presentation; and I had learned to immediately follow through on such impressions. When I got home from work that day I called David and told him that I would like to meet Mary after all. He was thrilled and said I should come to church the next Sunday and he would introduce me to her.

On Sunday, November 28, 1982, I went to the Oak Hill Stake Center again. It happened that Mary was teaching one of the two Gospel Doctrine classes that week. I attended her class and David attended the other one. I was impressed with Mary's spirituality and her scriptural and gospel knowledge. I was also completely smitten with her. After the class a number of people gathered around Mary to chat about the lesson and other things. It was clear that everyone liked Mary and enjoyed her company. After a few minutes, David introduced me to Mary, mentioning that we were in the mission field together. There were still a number of people that wanted to chat with her so there was really no time for us to talk at that point.

David and I went off to strategize about what the next step should be. David told me that Mary was fairly reserved and traditional, so we decided that the best thing would be to go on a double date. We discussed whether I should ask Mary directly for a date or whether David, who knew her, should let her know that I would like to go out with her and propose a double date. We decided that it might be more comfortable for Mary if David spoke with her. He said he would call her later that day. As I drove home, almost immediately I began feeling that I should ask her myself. When I got home, I called David and told him that I thought it was better if I called her and asked her out directly. David gave me her phone number and I called her.

Since she had only met me briefly and was a reserved and traditional person, I decided that when I called, rather than immediately ask her out, it would be best if I told her a little about myself so she would know something about me before I asked her out. I called her house and asked to speak with Mary.

When she came on the phone I told her I was Dave Dollahite, David Pace's friend who she had met earlier that day. She remembered meeting me and so I spent some time telling her a little about me. Now, this is the only part of the story where Mary and I have divergent memories of what happened. I recall that I did not want to take more than five to ten minutes telling her a bit about myself before asking her out. Mary recalls that I talked to her for about forty-five minutes before I got around to asking her out. Given what I know of Mary's good memory and my gregarious personality, I must admit that her memory of what occurred is almost certainly more accurate than mine.

When I finally asked her to go out with me on a double date with David Pace and his date, she accepted! I mentioned that I had never seen the lights on Temple Square and that David and I thought we could go out for dinner in Salt Lake City and then go see the lights. We set the day and time we would pick Mary up. We went on three dates in the next couple weeks and on the third date became unofficially engaged. Those three amazing dates are a story in themselves that I share in the next Chapter.

TENDER MERCIES & LESSONS LEARNED

The Lord was extremely kind to me in making it crystal clear to me that I should get to know Mary. I was in a state of emotional and spiritual confusion following the break-up of a relationship that I had thought would end in marriage. I lacked the motivation and confidence I would have needed to ask Mary out, so the strong impression I was given at the MTC gave me the emotional and spiritual boost I needed to be willing to ask out the granddaughter of the current president of the Church. From this experience, I learned that often our most difficult challenges bring the greatest spiritual blessings. I later learned that the photograph of Mary was taken by a woman in Mary's ward who had been asked to do the slide show on Sister Missionaries. The woman thought that Mary was just the person to illustrate poise. So, quite an amazing series of events led to my seeing a photograph of Mary at the MTC. But that was only the beginning of amazing events.

CHAPTER 27

Amazing Dates & Eternal Decisions

FIRST DATE: SPAGHETTI & MISSION STORIES

On our first date, we planned to go to Salt Lake City to have dinner at the Spaghetti Factory and then see the lights on Temple Square. My '70 Chevy Impala had some major mechanical problems and I had not driven it for a few weeks so David drove. David and I knew that since we had served together in the mission field it would be easy for us to regale the girls with a bunch of mission stories; but we decided to avoid talking about our missions. However, since Mary had also served a mission it turned out to be a natural conversation topic. David's date had not served but she seemed to be interested in our stories.

The restaurant was packed and we had to wait almost an hour just to be seated and then it took an extraordinarily long time for us to be served. But we were happy to have the chance to get to know each other. But then dinner took so long that just as we drove up to Temple Square all the lights were turned off. That was disappointing but we just headed home, telling more mission stories on the way.

When I brought Mary to the door she mentioned that she played viola in the Mormon Youth Symphony and that in a couple of weeks they had a concert at Temple Square. She invited me to attend the concert so I could see the lights on Temple Square. Given how impressed (and smitten) I was with Mary, I happily accepted her invitation and mentioned that date, December 17, was my birthday. I did not remember that that night was also the night of the Holiday

Bowl football game in which BYU was to play the Ohio State Buckeyes. I had become a big BYU football fan and really had been looking forward to the bowl game.

The next Sunday I mentioned to my bishop that I had a big dilemma. I told him I was really torn between either watching the Holiday Bowl game with my buddies or going on a "date" in which my date would be playing a classical concert and I would be sitting by myself in the Tabernacle. My bishop advised me to "go on the date." I said that it really would not be a "date" since we would not even be together and that I could ask her out for another date where we would actually be together. He again advised me to "go on the date." I responded that it was my birthday and why should I spend my birthday sitting by myself listening to a stupid classical music concert when I could be with my friends eating a feast of goodies and cheering on the Cougars? Again, he counseled me to "go on the date." I decided that, no matter how much I wanted to watch the game, I would follow the counsel of my bishop and go on the "date." I'm glad I did.

SECOND DATE: HOLIDAY CONCERT & THE HOLIDAY BOWL

On the day of the concert (my birthday) I received a package from my mom. As a birthday present, she sent a white dress shirt as she knew I wore these types of shirts to church. I was touched that my mom, who had taken great pains not to support my mission and made it clear she was not supporting my church activity, was thoughtful enough to know that a white dress shirt would be helpful to me. I had the feeling I should wear the shirt on the date. I immediately rejected that thought since I had a nice, cool, colored shirt that I had planned to wear and I did not think a white dress shirt was cool enough and I wanted to impress Mary. But the feeling persisted, so I wore the white dress shirt.

Since I could not afford to fix my car, Mary suggested that we drive to Salt Lake with her car pool, some friends of hers who were also members of the Mormon Youth Symphony. When I came to Mary's home to pick her up, she was not quite ready. Her mother invited me to have a seat at their dining room table. She began asking questions about my personal and family background. While most questions were about my immediate family, she also asked me about my grandparents, aunts, uncles, and cousins. She pulled out a piece of paper and began making a diagram of a "family tree" based on what I told her.

Except for my grandpa Iver, who was the only grandparent I actually knew, I did not know much about my grandparents. I am ashamed to say I did not even know their names. I knew a little about my uncle, who was an Episcopal Priest, but not much about my aunts and other uncles. And I knew very little—including even names—about my few cousins. She asked questions about my parents' family backgrounds, occupations, religious involvement, and other things. It felt like this was some kind of a test; and I felt like I was flunking badly. Thus, I was very relieved when Mary appeared and we began our date.

With two or three others in the car, Mary and I rode in the back of a small older car surrounded by instrument cases including a viola and a cello. Mary had made a chocolate birthday cake for me which we ate on the way to Salt Lake City. I was impressed both with her thoughtfulness and with her baking skills. But I must admit that once or twice on the ride up, as I listened to Mary's friends discuss various aspects of classical music, I felt culturally inferior and out of place and wished I was home getting ready to watch the Holiday Bowl.

We arrived at Temple Square an hour early so they could rehearse with the orchestra before the concert. Mary and her fellow symphony members went into the Tabernacle and I walked around Temple Square to kill the hour before the concert began. As I was walking toward the South Visitors' Center, I again wondered what I was doing on this "date" when the game would be starting in a little less than an hour. As I walked, I spotted Sam Dawson, a friend who I knew from my freshman year at BYU. Sam had lived on my floor at Deseret Towers. I called out, "Sam!" and Sam also recognized me.

"Hi, Dave."

"So, Sam, what are you doing here?"

"I'm a custodian here on Temple Square. What are you doing here?" he said.

"Oh, I'm on a date." He looked at me kind of funny and I continued, "She is playing in a concert in the Tabernacle and is rehearsing before the concert starts." Then Sam asked if I would like a "backstage tour" of the Tabernacle. I said, "Sure, that sounds fun."

Sam pulled out his big key ring and said, "Okay, let's start in the lower levels." He then took me down below the Tabernacle and showed me a few pretty cool things including the room where people translate General Conference into various languages (live, as it is airing) and an underground tunnel connecting several buildings including the temple, the Hotel Utah, and the Tabernacle.

Then Sam opened a couple doors to a storage room containing dozens of large maroon upholstered chairs. He said, "This is cool," as he pulled one of the chairs out of the storage room and said, "This is President Kimball's chair. It has speakers in the wings so security can communicate with President Kimball, if needed. Here, have a seat."

"I'm not sitting in that chair," I said.

"Come on, Dave, we all sit in it."

"I'm not sitting in that chair."

"Come on, it's no big deal. Just sit down for a second." Sam kind of pushed me down into the seat so I gave in and briefly sat in the chair. Little did I know then that I would later have the chance to spend a number of evenings with President and Sister Kimball in their apartment in the Hotel Utah. Then Sam put the chair back and said, "Okay, let's go upstairs."

As we were walking down the hall toward an elevator I noticed a number of people dressed in white shirts and ties that I assumed were members of the Mormon Youth Chorus who were also performing in the concert. Then I saw a fellow teacher at the MTC who was looking frantic. I called his name and he recognized me and came over with a distressed look on his face. I said, "What's wrong?"

He said, "Oh, man! I wore the wrong shirt. I thought we were wearing our blue tuxedo shirts and if I can't find a white shirt to wear I can't sing in the concert tonight."

I said, "I've got a white shirt. We're about the same size. Would you like to wear mine?"

He said, "Really? That would be great. Do you mind wearing my blue tux shirt?"

"Not at all." So, we went into a bathroom and traded shirts. I was now wearing a blue polyester shirt with large ruffles on the chest and big puffy sleeves and a large collar. We made arrangements to meet after the concert to trade shirts again.

Sam brought me upstairs and into the greenroom in an area behind the stage where we noticed a number of performers standing in groups chatting. I saw Mary and went over and said, "Hello."

She looked stunned and said, "Dave, what are you doing here?" I introduced her to Sam and explained that he had been giving me a tour. She looked at my shirt and asked, "Why are you wearing that shirt?" I told her what had happened and she still looked very surprised to see me standing in that room wearing that shirt. Then a bell went off and Mary said she needed to get on stage for the concert. I wished her luck and said I would see her after the concert.

Sam said he had one more place to show me and took me around to a little room just off the stage. He said this was the sound room where they made recordings of the concerts. There were a couple of guys playing with dials on sound equipment. There was also a man sitting in the room who introduced himself as Terry Hill, the associate conductor of the symphony. I told him one of the members of the symphony had invited me to the concert. He asked who and when I told him he said, "Oh, I was Mary's high school orchestra director. She is a wonderful person," and began telling me a bit about Mary.

One of the sound guys turned around and said "Hello" and I said "Hi" and then I noticed a small television sitting on the counter and the Holiday Bowl logo came on and I said to the sound guy, "So you guys are going to watch a little football while taping the concert? Nice!"

He said, "Yep. We wouldn't miss it. Hey, would you like to join us?"

I said, "Are you serious? I'd love to. Would that be okay?"

"You bet! We'll just pull in another chair. We've got plenty of room."

Then Terry said, "And I can tell you more about Mary!"

Sam said he needed to get back to work and I thanked him profusely for the tour and wished him well. They got me a chair and I sat and listened to the concert with perfect sound piped in. Mary was sitting facing the sound booth perhaps twenty feet away and so I had a perfect seat to watch her play. Terry told me a lot about Mary and what a wonderful person she was. He also told me about orchestras, which was great for me. I knew nothing about classical music or orchestra and I was happy to learn about what was obviously a big part of Mary's life.

I learned from Terry that Mary was also in the BYU Philharmonic Orchestra. He asked how I came to be wearing one of their concert shirts so I told him about my friend who sang in the chorus. He also asked about my background and wanted to hear about my conversion to the Church. We also watched the game, but it quickly turned into a complete blow-out with Ohio State killing BYU.

During intermission Terry took me into the room where the musicians were. Mary saw us and we walked up to Mary while chatting like old friends and again Mary looked extremely surprised to see me backstage during intermission with her high school orchestra director and Mormon Youth Symphony associate conductor. She asked what I was doing there and I told her what had happened. Terry told her I was a great guy and that we had been talking all about her. Mary had this very quizzical look on her face while we chatted.

Then the bell went off again and Mary and the other musicians had to get back on stage. Terry and I headed back to the sound booth. Terry told me more about Mary and about music. We also watched the Cougars get killed in the second half as well (the final score was 63–7). The game became less and less interesting to me and I was very glad I had listened to my bishop and gone on the date. After the concert was over I met up with my MTC friend and we traded shirts back. Then Mary, some of her Mormon Youth Symphony friends, and I spent a few minutes walking around seeing the Christmas lights on Temple Square.

When we got back to Provo, I took Mary to her door and asked her if she would like to attend a BYU basketball game with me the next week. She said she would and mentioned she was planning to start jogging so I asked if she would like to jog together in the afternoon before the game.

This was, by far, the most interesting, unique, and amazing date I had ever been on. I was able to help a friend, see an old friend, and make a new friend. Most importantly, although I was never actually alone with Mary during the entire date, I learned a lot about her and how important music was to her and came to understand a little better what an incredible person she was. And, it turned out that Mary had learned things about me that she mentioned on our third date—the one where we became unofficially engaged.

THIRD DATE: ARE YOU FOR REAL?

The day of our third date, David Pace called and asked if I had been out with Mary again. I told him we had gone out a couple days before and were going out that evening. He said, "Whoa, Dave! Slow down! Mary is a very traditional person, and very reserved, and you are going way too fast. You are going to scare her off." I said he was probably right since she did seem like the kind of person who did not rush into important things. I told David I would slow down and not ask her out again for a couple of weeks after our date that night.

With my Chevy still out of commission, we drove Mary's parents' old Ford Ambassador to the game and had fun cheering for the Cougars. After the game, we went to take me home. I pulled up in front of the house near campus in which I was renting a room and I turned off the ignition. Mary then reached over and put her hand on top of mine and said, "Dave, are you for real?"

I said, "What do you mean?"

She said, "Does everything just go your way? Like on your mission and on our date at Temple Square, is that how your life goes?"

I said, "Well, ever since I joined the Church, the Lord has been extremely kind and generous and has answered my prayers in wonderful ways. So, yes, I do live a blessed life."

Mary said, "Dave, I've spent years looking for the person I wanted to marry and dating a lot of great young men. But I don't think I need to look any longer."

I was stunned but thrilled at this extremely surprising development. I briefly thought about David's comment about how cautious Mary was. I said, "Well, I feel the same way." I wanted to say more, but, somehow, I knew this was not the time for me to talk but rather to listen. Mary went on to talk about how her parents would not really understand how quickly this had come about and said that we should probably wait for a couple months before we became officially engaged. I said that was fine. She talked about how long it would be good to be engaged for and about a spring wedding.

TENDER MERCIES & LESSONS LEARNED

It did not occur to me or to Mary until I was writing this account several years ago that Mary and I actually had not been alone together, other than for a couple minutes at the door, until we sat together in the car after our third date. We had not realized that we got unofficially engaged the first time we were alone together for any length of time. I was taking classes in marriage preparation and family relations at BYU and this was not what I was being taught about how to properly engage in the courtship process. Mary really was and is a very traditional, reserved, and cautious person and her family and friends were stunned when they learned how quickly she decided to get married to someone she barely knew.

Over the years, as Mary and I have reflected together on our "whirlwind courtship" it has always been clear to us that the Spirit was guiding the process from beginning to end. The Lord brought me from the confusion and self-doubt of a broken engagement to the joy and peace of an eternal relationship in just a couple weeks. This was, after my conversion to the restored gospel of Jesus Christ, the tender mercy that has made the most difference in my life.

It was out of character for me to "ward hop" (attending somewhere other than my home ward) but if I had not been willing to attend David's ward I would likely not have ever met Mary. I believe the Spirit was leading me since I could have done any number of other things besides calling David Pace. The Spirit clearly led my boss at the MTC to insist that I go to a meeting that really had nothing to do with my work for him. The Lord had guided the woman who made the slide show to ask Mary to pose for pictures, and the Spirit clearly manifested to me that I should date Mary. And I am not sure I could fully recognize the number of ways the Spirit led me on our second date to have me end up watching Mary's concert (and the football game) from the sound booth dressed in a blue Mormon Youth Chorus concert tuxedo shirt.

As Mary has tried to understand her seemingly out-of-character behavior (making a decision on what most people would consider very little information), she has concluded that it was a combination of having dated many young men and recognizing what she wanted in a husband—and following the Spirit in expressing her feelings.

From this experience, I learned again how much the Lord is in the details of our lives. I cannot fully recognize nor comprehend how much guidance I have received in various aspects of my life. But the guidance was clear and unmistakable in this most important of decisions (after the decision to follow Christ). I realize that many people do not receive such clear guidance in their courtship and again, I believe that the Lord was manifesting His tender mercy to a new convert to provide me with such a blessing. I am eternally thankful to the Lord for His tender mercy in guiding me to Mary and in making it clear to her that she could be happy with someone like me when there were many guys, far better than me, who courted her and wanted to marry her.

CHAPTER 28

Engagement & Early Marriage

Sitting in my room after this amazing date ended, I could hardly believe what had just happened. The most wonderful and incredible person that I had ever met had just told me she wanted to marry me. This amazing woman, whom David told me was reserved and cautious, had basically proposed to me on our third date. I really had intended to wait a couple weeks before asking Mary out again. But now we were effectively engaged! This was hard to take in. It all happened so fast. In a matter of days, I had gone from the deep confusion and sadness of a broken engagement, to a clear impression to date someone to whom a couple of weeks later I was unofficially engaged.

I called David and told him what had happened. He did not believe me. He thought I was pulling his leg. It took several minutes of convincing from me before he accepted that I really was not kidding him. Then he became worried about what he had done. It was he, after all, who had been so insistent that we should meet and date. Now he felt somehow responsible for our relationship. As the weeks and months went by, every time I saw David he asked how we were doing and always seemed relieved when I said we were doing great. He said that if we were to break up he would feel responsible for inflicting pain on us!

Although this time in my life was incredibly exciting and our courtship and marriage proceeded in a wonderful way, there were some challenging times ahead as her parents tried to fully accept the idea that their daughter, after so little time, was planning to marry a recent convert from California who in high school had spent his time playing sports and had been completely uninterested in religion, academics, classical music, or any of the other things Mary's life had revolved around. And rather than marrying someone who was going to be a professor, doctor, lawyer, or successful businessman, he was planning to be a marriage and family therapist (whatever that was).

In almost every way, I was just not the kind of guy Mary's parents (and most people who knew Mary) thought she would marry. Given how incredibly bright, spiritual, beautiful, and accomplished Mary was, as well as the fact that she came from a distinguished heritage in the Church, most assumed she would marry one of the many similarly accomplished young men from a similar background who had courted her.

Mary was someone who had developed her talents in wonderful ways. She had always been a very faithful Latter-day Saint young woman whom everyone liked and respected. She was kind, humble, and fully committed to the gospel. She was a returned missionary and knew the gospel and the scriptures well. Musically, she had sung in her high school's *a cappella* choir, played viola in three orchestras, played violin and piano, and had taken many music courses at BYU. She had traveled and spent time in many countries.

In addition to her full-time mission in Finland, she had done a semester abroad in London during which she was able to travel in Europe and the Middle East. Academically, she was an honors student in high school and was in the honors program at BYU. Mary majored in English at BYU and also studied great literature including Russian language and literature. After graduating, she intended to attend law school at BYU. In addition, she had developed a wide range of practical skills including sewing, crocheting, needlepoint, and cooking.

The more I came to know about Mary, the more I had to agree with those who thought that I did not compare favorably with the many wonderful LDS men who had courted her. As I thought about it objectively, I could not help but think that Mary deserved someone much better than me. Of course, this played into my natural tendency to think of myself as a second class Latter-day Saint. In other words, not only was Mary way out of my league, she was, in fact, practically perfect. She was full of faith and spiritual wisdom. She was optimistic and perfectly honest and without guile. She never spoke negatively about anyone (in fact in the thirty-four years we have been married I have never heard her say anything uncomplimentary about anyone).

I had seen the movie Mary Poppins for the first time just before meeting Mary and I thought the line about Mary Poppins being "practically perfect in every way" very accurately described Mary Kimball! I realize that someone reading this may think I am doing the typical guy thing and exaggerating how great Mary is. But I assure you that she was and is all this and more. It would be very difficult for me to overstate the extent of the wonderfulness of Mary!

As our courtship moved along I learned that she and the young man she had been sitting with in church had indeed just begun dating but that Mary had hoped they would become more serious. Had I come along even a couple of weeks later it may have been too late. I learned that she turned down dates from various guys while we were dating and unofficially engaged. I learned that one of Mary's mother's friends told her that she had had a revelation in the temple that Mary was supposed to marry the woman's grandson.

Mary's parents were understandably very concerned about how quickly things had progressed with us. When Mary returned from her mission she told her mother that, in response to a challenge from her mission president, she had set some goals for her post-mission life. One of those was that she would meet the man she would marry near the end of the year and be married the following spring or summer.

We had met in late November and when we became serious so soon, Mary's mother suggested to her that she was just trying to fulfill her goals.

Mary's parents insisted that Mary meet my family before becoming officially engaged. So, we planned a trip to Edmonds, Washington—where my parents had moved during my mission—so Mary could meet my parents. My parents were also surprised that I had met someone I wanted to marry so quickly after breaking off my engagement but they were thrilled for me and nothing but supportive of my marrying Mary. Mary and I flew to Seattle and my parents drove down from Edmonds to pick us up. We enjoyed a wonderful few days with my parents. Of course, my folks loved Mary and were very happy to welcome her into the family.

Now we could become officially engaged! Among Mary's many wonderful traits, she has a deep sense of Mormon Pioneer frugality and practicality. She said she did not even want a diamond in her ring, but an opal or just a band. But, because of my male ego, and from what I had observed in the LDS and BYU cultures of courtship, I felt that it was my duty to buy my fiancée the most expensive diamond engagement ring I could afford. Given that I was a poor student needing government loans and working part-time at the MTC, I could not afford to buy a really nice ring for Mary.

In fact, the only diamond I was able to afford (from a discount dealer) was dwarfed by the setting tongs and thus barely visible. But, hey, it was a diamond, and so I felt I had done my duty. Of course, when anyone asked to see the ring they had to look closely to see the diamond. I always felt inadequate as a true male provider of nice things for my sweetheart.

A couple weeks into our courtship, I moved into a basement apartment in a home about three houses down from Mary's home and was thus able to attend Mary's ward. Mary and I were called to team-teach a Sunday School class.

Because my car had broken down, yet again, a couple weeks before I met Mary, we walked to and from BYU most days. Although I would have liked to have been able to drive her to and from campus, Mary preferred walking and very much enjoyed this time in our courtship.

So, when I met Mary, not only was I a poor college student with thousands of dollars of student loans, but I also was without a car. Of course, my male ego was seriously impaired by this state of "carlessness" but it did not seem to bother Mary at all. She was happy to drive around in her parents' old Ford Ambassador.

One of Mary's friends from the Oak Hills Stake, Steve Clegg, was taking a class in auto mechanics at Utah Technical College n Orem (now Utah Valley University) and offered to work on my car for free (of course I paid for parts). He then worked on the car for several weeks, doing a number of things that needed to be done. Steve was not only a great mechanic but a great guy. I was very grateful for this tender mercy and I consider Steve one of those amazing automotive angels that have blessed my life.

A short time after we were engaged, we went to Salt Lake City so Mary could introduce me to her grandparents. By this time, in the spring of 1983, President Kimball's advanced age and declining health had required him to spend most of his time in a suite in the Hotel Utah under constant medical attention. President and Sister Kimball were most gracious and welcomed me warmly. They were very affectionate people. One of the greatest experiences of my life was when President Kimball hugged and kissed me on the cheek.

Sister Kimball insisted that I call her "Grandma." At first this was difficult for me but she was such a grandmotherly person to me that I was able to do so. I had not known either of my own grandmothers, so this was a wonderful tender mercy from the Lord to allow me to have such a marvelous adopted grandmother. President Kimball asked me to call him "Grandpa" but this was extremely difficult. He was such a towering figure in my life as a new convert that I struggled mightily to use such a familiar term for this man that I loved and respected so deeply—but from a distance. I was only able to do so after some time and with some ambivalence.

Sadly, for Mary and me, President Kimball's declining health prohibited him from performing our sealing. Homer Ellsworth, one of Mary's mother's cousins, performed our sealing and it was wonderful.

My parents were very unhappy with the idea that they would drive all the way from the Seattle area to Salt Lake City and then have to sit in the lobby of the temple while their son was getting married. We wanted my parents to have good feelings about the wedding, but there was no question that we would marry in the temple. So, we thought of ways to try to respond to my parents' understandable feelings about being excluded from the wedding itself.

Since exchanging rings is not part of the temple sealing ceremony, Mary and I decided to exchange rings at our wedding breakfast following the sealing. My parents could not afford to pay for a wedding breakfast for a group the size of Mary's extended family so Mary's parents generously offered to arrange for us to have the wedding breakfast in the Empire Room of the Hotel Utah (now the Joseph Smith Memorial Building). My parents seemed happy with our efforts to consider their feelings.

At the beginning of the wedding breakfast, conducted by Mary's father and mother, Mary and I stood and talked about eternal marriage for a few minutes. Among other thoughts, I mentioned that Joseph Smith, in a sermon to the Saints, had held his wedding band up and said that in the same way that a wedding ring has no beginning or end, so marriage was intended to be eternal. We then exchanged rings. Given that my parents were aware that many contemporary couples were now writing their own wedding vows and getting married in a variety of settings, our exchanging of rings seemed enough "wedding-like" to my parents and they were very happy.

After our wedding, Mary and I honeymooned in Marin County. The Leiningers (my "Mormon parents") allowed us to use their home and car (they were away on vacation) and I was able to show Mary around the area I grew up in. I was able to take her to the seven places we had lived in Fairfax, the schools I attended, the places I worked at, the various courts and fields where I played sports, and, most importantly, the place I first attended church and was baptized.

I now owed Jim Lowell, my best friend and tennis buddy from high school, a case of champagne. On the day of my high school graduation, I was being teased about getting married to my high school girlfriend and I proclaimed that I would not be married until I was at least thirty years old. Jim said he would bet me a case of champagne that I would be married before then. We shook hands and made the bet. When we sent Jim the wedding announcement, I included a note saying that as a devout Mormon I would be happy to buy him a case of non-alcoholic champagne to settle our bet. He politely declined and wished us well.[1]

When we returned from our honeymoon Mary began law school and I began my graduate program in marriage and family therapy

---

1. When I went to my 40th high school reunion in August of 2017, I bought Jim a case of champagne to finally settle my bet with him. It was six small bottles but I learned that six is a case for champagne.

(both at BYU). About once a month during the two years Mary and I lived in Utah (before moving to St. Paul to attend graduate school at the University of Minnesota) we brought dinner to President and Sister Kimball and spent the evening with them in their apartment. It was a marvelous blessing to be able to sit with the President and Sister Kimball for a few hours each month, serve them, and bask in their love and warmth. One time I was sitting on the couch with President Kimball and he mentioned how much he loved the Saints and wished he could be "out with the Saints" bearing witness of the gospel. He said, "Please tell the Saints that I love them and wish I could be with them."

Another time I was sitting with President Kimball, holding his hands, and he looked in my eyes and said, "David, I love you." I felt like I had been adopted into the Lord's family. Not only did I have a wonderful wife who loved and accepted me but, also, I had a grandmother and grandfather who loved and accepted me. With her wisdom, practicality, and patient longsuffering for my many weaknesses, Mary has been the perfect wife for me and the perfect mother to our seven terrific kids.

TENDER MERCIES & LESSONS LEARNED

Now fulfilled was the marvelous promise I received in my patriarchal blessing that, "You shall, in due time, be privileged to take into the Holy Temple of God a lovely daughter of Zion, a stalwart handmaiden, who shall be of joy unto you and there you shall be sealed together for time and all eternity. Your union shall be one of happiness and joy." It surely has been.

We have now been married for over thirty-four years, have seven terrific kids, and are grandparents of David, Edward, and Eliza (kids of Rachel and Collin Lambourne).

In short, we have lived quite happily ever since.

However, the early months and years of our marriage were wonderful and challenging. Like all newly married couples, we had to learn how to solve problems, how to serve each other, and how to compromise with each other. We share a lot more about those challenges and how we have addressed them in APPENDIX B.

CHAPTER 29

Planes, Floods, & Sacred Cows in India

I will share one last experience that is a full-circle kind of occurrence where the Lord took me from one place to a very different place with a series of tender mercies. I love to go to new places and meet new people and be a witness of Christ in whatever ways I can. But because I am not good with directions or details or maps, I easily get lost and thus I sometimes become quite anxious when trying to get from one place to another. This is especially true when traveling in other countries as I have been able to do a few times for my work. The time when this was most profound was when I was invited to be a visiting scholar in India and spent two weeks there giving lectures and consulting with faculty and students at a university.

In 2005, I was invited to spend two weeks as a visiting scholar at the Maharajah Sayajirao University (MSU) in the city of Vadodara (formerly Baroda), India.[2] I was invited by Professor Rajalakshmi Sriram (Raji), Chair of the Department of Human Development and Family Studies, one of the leading family studies programs in India. I came under the auspices of their Jawaharlal Nehru Chair (Jawaharlal Nehru was the first President of India) program for bringing "distinguished scholars from around the world" to visit MSU and spend a couple weeks giving lectures, consulting with faculty and

---

2. en.wikipedia.org/wiki/Maharaja_Sayajirao_University_of_Baroda

students, and planning and carrying out collaborative research with faculty and students.

MINOR MIRACLES IN GETTING TO INDIA

Soon after receiving this invitation, and several months before my visit, I called a BYU travel agent to make reservations for my trip and left a message on her voicemail. When I didn't hear back for a week or so I called another agent and again left a message that I'd like to make a reservation for India. When, after a few weeks, the second agent had also not gotten back to me, I began considering that perhaps this was "a sign" of some kind. Since BYU agents had always been very good about getting back to me, I thought that perhaps I shouldn't make the trip to India. So, I prayed and let the Lord know that I certainly did not want to go if, for some reason, I was not supposed to go, and I prayed for guidance and protection in all aspects of my travel plans. I waited another couple of months before making my reservations, felt good about going, then called and made the flight reservations.

On July 26–27, just five days before I was scheduled to arrive in India, Mumbai experienced the eighth worst rainfall in its history (thirty-seven inches of rain in twenty-four hours) with the worst flooding Mumbai had ever experienced. More than 1,000 people died as a result of the flooding and, according to Wikipedia, "The term 26 July, is now always used to refer to the day when the city of Mumbai came to a standstill due to flooding. . . . For the first time ever, Mumbai's airports were shut for more than 30 hours due to heavy flooding of the runways, submerged . . . from early morning of 31 July, with increase in water logging of the runways and different parts of Mumbai, most of the flights were indefinitely canceled."[3]

A couple days before my trip, when I went to register my trip on the American Embassy web site, there was a notice pleading with travelers to stay away from Mumbai for the next several days. A friend and colleague had read reports about the flooding and more than once he expressed his concern by kindly questioning whether I really should be traveling to India at this time.

I thought back on the fact that, when I had first tried to make reservations, twice I experienced what could be thought of as a bureaucratic "stupor of thought"[4] from two calls to two travel agents never returned.[5] However, I prayed and I felt that it would be okay to go on the trip so I continued with plans to go. In the weeks leading up to my going to India, I remembered telling the BYU travel agent that I would like to fly out of Utah on Saturday morning, July 30, so I could have a full week's work before leaving for the trip.

Because I "knew" I was leaving at 6:20 a.m. on Saturday, I didn't even look at the itinerary I was sent a few days before I was to leave. And even though Mary had asked to see the itinerary a few times

---

3. en.wikipedia.org/wiki/Maharashtra_floods_of_2005

4. In Mormon lingo, a "stupor of thought" refers to mental confusion, forgetfulness, or mental distraction which may be the Lord's way of suggesting that what you are currently thinking about doing may not be a good idea, meaning not the right thing to do.

5. I later learned that both BYU travel agents were on vacation when I called and they sincerely apologized they had not returned my calls as they had never failed to do so before.

in the week leading up to my departure, somehow, I kept forgetting to give it to her. So, I arrived at the Salt Lake Airport on Saturday morning at 5:00 a.m. for a 6:20 flight. The clerk told me I was not on the flight and on further checking she said that I was actually scheduled to leave the day before (Friday). I said that I was sure I was to leave Saturday, but I pulled my itinerary out of my pocket and, sure enough, my reservation was for Friday the twenty-ninth. Then, and only then, did I remember that we had needed to schedule my departure on Friday to get me there in time to start on August 1, the date on which Raji wanted me there.

I asked if there was any way I could get the same itinerary today and she did some checking on the computer and said that the flights were all booked and, even if she could make reservations, I would have to pay for all new tickets which would be several thousand dollars (BYU had already paid $2,200 for the tickets). She said she was sorry but gave me the toll-free number for British Airways. Of course, I was stunned, confused, and totally embarrassed since this meant that I would have to tell everyone at BYU, and my family and friends, that I had not made the trip because I showed up a day late to the airport. And, of course, it would be a terrible professional discourtesy to not go to India when I said I would.

So, I went into the bathroom and prayed. I told the Lord that if it was the Lord's will that I not make the trip, I was okay with that and I was sorry that I misinterpreted the earlier "stupor of thought." I also said that if He would like me to go to India, then could He please make the way open for me to go.

I came out of the bathroom and called British Airways and explained my situation. The agent called up my itinerary and said, "Hmm, that is interesting, it already has you on the flight from Utah to Chicago."

I said, "Are you sure that is not for yesterday?"

She said "No, it has just been changed for today." Then she said, "Let's see, the flight from Chicago to London is full . . . oh, wait, this is your lucky day, an opening just now occurred. So, ok, now we've got you to London and in a first-class seat."

I said, "I cannot afford to pay for first class," and she said it would be no extra charge.

Then she said, "Oh, that's too bad, the flight from London to Mumbai is also full so, hmm, let's see . . . oh, wait, this is your lucky day, a spot just became available on that flight. Ok, we've got you to Mumbai. Let's see . . . it looks like there is room on the flight from Mumbai to Vadodara. So, I guess you are all set."

When I asked if there would be any charge she said no, and that, with the major flooding in Mumbai, they were changing a lot of tickets to there so it would not cost me anything. I barely had time to dash through security and get to my flight just as they were getting ready to close the doors!

BEING IN INDIA

The flight across the Pond in first class was incredibly comfortable (I've not flown first class before or since). London to Mumbai was another long flight (the entire trip from Utah to Vadodara was twenty-four hours). However, when I arrived at the Mumbai airport it was complete chaos. Because of all the delayed and canceled flights, thousands of people had been sleeping on the floors there for days to get on flights. They were still canceling flights left and right but somehow my flight arrived on time. I later learned that ours was the first flight they had allowed into Mumbai since the flooding. And everyone there told me how lucky I was that I had not tried to come in the day before as I would have been stranded in London or in the airport in Mumbai.

I almost got stuck in Mumbai since they had given me a boarding pass for another airline but couldn't give me a ticket and so I had to get one there. But they wouldn't accept credit cards, only cash, and I had only $75 in cash. But with the airport closing and all, the agent simply gave me a ticket and asked me not to tell anyone.

When I called Raji to tell her that I was in Mumbai and about to get on an airplane to Vadodara, she said, "Oh no, David, you cannot be in Mumbai. I just saw on the TV that our Minister of Transportation said there are no flights in or out of Mumbai." I told her that actually I had just landed in Mumbai and would land in Vadodara in a couple of hours, she again said, "No, David, I'm quite sure you are not in Mumbai, perhaps you are at another airport in India." I again assured her that I was in Mumbai and about to get on a plane to fly to Vadodara. I'm not sure she actually believed me, but she was there to meet me at the airport.

The roads in India teem with all manner of vehicles, some cars and buses but mostly "auto-rickshaws" and bikes and bike-rickshaws and hundreds of men on motorcycles and women on mopeds and motor scooters and some entire families (3–4 people) on motorcycles. There are hundreds of cows, dogs, pigs, monkeys and goats just walking in and lying in the street and cars just go around them (the cows have the right away since cows truly are sacred in India) and the pace and craziness on the roads is quite disconcerting. Even though Raji was experienced in driving in all this chaos, I expected to be in an accident any second every time I was on the road. My hosts told me I was seeing India at its absolute worst because of the incredible rains and flooding (they had nine feet of water throughout the city less than a month before and there was extensive and widespread damage).

Hindu Temples and a Personal Sacrament Meeting

I attended a number of Hindu, Jain, and Sikh temples while I was in Vadodara. At one Jain temple (Jainism is sort of a subset of Hinduism), the four students who brought me, and several folks at the temple, were very excited to tell me all about Jain beliefs and practices and how the temple fits in. This is very much like how a visitor to any LDS temple visitors' center finds herself surrounded by excited people enthusiastically sharing their fundamental beliefs. There were eight main symbols carved into the stone pillars that they said had been there for hundreds of years. They said these symbols were "given by God." One was the Hindu swastika which I knew about, but the second one was a Star of David (the Jewish six-pointed star) and nobody knew what it symbolized but that it was just "given by God." When I explained that Jews have the exact same symbol and mentioned what it meant (the triangle pointing up represents humanity looking to God and the triangle pointing down represents God blessing humanity), they were interested and one of the older men said that he just remembered that it meant something quite similar in Jain belief. It was very interesting to see the symbol of Judaism on a Jain temple in India and a swastika on the pillar next to it. My theory is that a community of Jews had settled there hundreds of years before and their symbol was included by the religiously eclectic Jains. Of course, I have no idea if this theory is correct.

At temples, you leave your shoes outside the temple before entering. Since this temple was downtown with thousands of people (including many poor folks and beggars) walking by I asked, "Is it the case that no one will take the shoes of people visiting temples?" I was told that sometimes shoes are stolen, but, if they are, then it was because some bad thing was going to happen to you and now it will not happen. So, I figured my size-13 Nike running shoes were probably safe. The shoes were still there—if somewhat wet—when I came out of the temple.

Then they took me to the Haveli Hindu temple of the god Shree Nat Jee, who is one of the Avatars (incarnations) of Lord Krishna (who himself is an avatar of Lord Vishnu, one of three main gods of Hinduism). Each day they dress up the idol (their word) of the god (a black statue) in different clothes with a different color. They gave me the grand tour of the temple, explaining all about it as they led me around. As the time for the unveiling of the idol of the god came (it is behind a screen and they bring it out with great ceremony at an appointed time (8:00 p.m.) they made sure I was in the center with the best view. People were looking at me, this tall American, with expectant eyes hoping I would be impressed. It was very beautiful. Then on the way out of the temple they offered me some fruit and cornmeal to eat. It was offered to the god so is sort of like the Christian Holy Communion or the LDS Sacrament. Although the New Testament says you should "refrain from meats offered to idols" I decided to eat it since they believe the gods are just manifestations of the Great God (Brahman) and they offered it in such kindness and expectancy that I didn't want to offend by refusing.

On another day, they took me to two temples on the army base just outside of Vadodara. The first was another Hindu temple, this one dedicated to the worship of Shiva, one of the main Hindu deities (there are millions of Hindu deities, but Shiva is worshiped by a large proportion of Hindus (there are over 1 billion Indians and 80% are Hindu).

The second was a Sikh temple. Sikhs are an interesting blend of Islam with Hinduism. I'll describe some of the major features of their temple worship. Both men and women remove their shoes and socks and both must have their head covered. The women with a veil/scarf and the men with their turbans or, in my case, any type of hat (I wore my BYU tennis cap). As was the case in every temple I went to, I found the worshipers to be sincere and devoted.

With prior permission from my bishop, on Sunday, August 7, I held a personal Sacrament Meeting. I suppose it was the first sacrament meeting held in Vadodara. I brought some bread home and used a small paper cup for the water.[6] I sang an opening hymn ("O My Father") and offered prayer. There was no business to conduct so I read from the Book of Mormon about the covenant of baptism (Mosiah 18) and pondered about that great message. Then I sang a Sacrament hymn ("In Humility Our Savior") and prepared the Sacrament and blessed the bread and water and partook of each. Then I read from 3 Nephi Chapter 18 where the Savior provided the Sacrament for his disciples and the other Nephites. I pondered and prayed about the Savior's words about the Sacrament. Then I sang a closing hymn ("Redeemer of Israel") and offered a closing prayer. In my journal, I wrote:

The Lord was extremely kind and poured out His Spirit on me in great abundance. Although I was alone in a dingy room half-way around the world from those I love I felt the presence, power, and loving care of the Lord. Indeed, it may have been the most powerful outpouring of the Spirit I have felt since the day I first read the Book of Mormon. I have prayed and wept much since being here and never have felt the Lord's loving-kindness and presence more than I have

---

6. Mormons use water in place of wine or grape juice for the Sacrament (what other Christians call the Sacrament of the Lord's Supper; Holy Communion, or the Eucharist).

here. I know with a sure knowledge born by the power of the Spirit that God lives, that Jesus is the Savior of all, including me, and that there are spiritual realities and beings that can bless us in our most challenging times. So, although this has been the most difficult and lonely week of my life I have felt the sweet comfort of the Comforter. (Vadodara Journal)

UNIVERSITY, MARKET, & DINNER WITH AN INDIAN FAMILY

In a talk to faculty and students in the School of Social Work they "opened with prayer" in that they had a student come up and sing a "prayer" (called a Mantra or Shloka) in Sanskrit. Of course, I commented how wonderful it was to have a talk begin with prayer and how comfortable it made me feel since I begin all my classes at BYU with prayer. After the talk, when talking to faculty, I asked about the prayer and learned it was a prayer to Ganesh, the Elephant God (body of a man and head of an elephant) who is the god of auspicious beginnings. Whenever some new beginning occurs (marriage, birth, school, job, etc.) they pray to Ganesh for success and give the person a Ganesh idol. I asked for the gist of the prayer and this is it:

> We ask you O Ganesh of the tilted face [tilted is positive for disfigured], who has a huge head and great large belly and who has power [aura] like a billion suns—may this task we are undertaking be performed without any hindrance.

Here is the rest of Ganesh's story: it seems that he was a normal boy until his father, a god (Shiva) who was away on a long trip (many years), returned to find a young man in the area where only women and children were allowed and, not recognizing his son, took him for an intruder and cut off his head. Shiva and his wife, Ganesh's mother Parvati, were so upset that Shiva told his servants to travel off and cut the head of the first animal they saw. They did and the first animal was an elephant so they brought that head and Shiva put it on Ganesh and restored him. Indian lore is full of such stories of gods and goddesses.

One of the social work faculty members, Anil Navale, gave me his business card and I asked what the non-English writing in the university's logo said. He said it was Sanskrit and meant "Truth is close to God and is good" which sounds a lot like the motto of BYU which is "The Glory of God is Intelligence." And the social work faculty were fasting. During the month of August, which is an auspicious and religious month (kind of like Ramadan), many fast from breakfast and lunch and just eat one meal a day. In terms of the comfort level with religion around here it was very similar to BYU.

One day, the Sriram family took me for a ride around the city for a couple hours. We went down to the central market and it was a site I'll never forget. Unbelievable numbers of people were selling an incredibly diverse range of foods, clothing, spices, etc. It was Sunday so I didn't shop. There were some beggars but not nearly as many as I thought there would be. The level of poverty, filth, disorder, chaos, noise, pollution, raw sewage, and crowding is stunning and hard for those of us from wealthy nations to comprehend and deal with. I am incredibly grateful that I can raise my family in the amazing freedom, abundance, and cleanliness of America. On the one hand, I wish all of my children could see it first-hand for there is no way I can adequately describe the conditions there. On the other hand, if any of my children had been with me I would have been a complete basket case worrying about their safety. In many ways, I hope my children will never have to see that kind of deprivation although I know it would help them feel immense gratification for what they enjoy in America.

On my last full day in India, I had a great treat as one of Raji's recent master's students (Nivedita) invited me over to her home for a traditional Indian meal. Traditional Indian families don't eat around a dining room table. That is a recent (thirty years) custom from the West. They sit in chairs or on the floor and have the food served to them; this father was very traditional so he wanted to do it the traditional Indian way. They were extremely gracious and formal in their hosting. It is the host's job to encourage, urge, push, and otherwise insist that the guest eats more and more and you really have to practically run from the home to get them to stop trying to get you to eat "just a little more" so I went away very filled.

They serve you on a large plate and give you small amounts of everything arranged in a circle on the plate. You are supposed to eat clockwise and there are seven different kinds of foods. Each was wonderful and the little coconut pastries were especially delicious. Nivedita's mother didn't speak any English but her father, who is a banker, spoke fairly well and was extremely eager to share the traditional beliefs and practices with me.

Nivedita's fiancé was there for dinner and Nivedita was particularly keen to be sure he was well served. In fact, at one point she tried to get him to take more and he refused by pushing (gently and kindly) her hand from laying more food on his plate and then she went and asked her mother to go and offer him more and, of course, he couldn't refuse his future mother-in-law. I later said to her that was pretty interesting how she got her mother to get her fiancé to eat more and she smiled and said, "Yes, very tricky."

STRANGER IN A STRANGE LAND

I was in India for two weeks and did not see another white person. Now I have a better sense of how people of color feel in Utah or at least at BYU. Wherever I went I was stared at and heard whispers in Hindi (probably saying something like, "Look at that fat, old, bald, tall American guy"). I'm kidding, the Indian people are very gracious and polite and deferential to others. They love everything American there and very much look to the West for culture, clothing, technology, and music. Of course, their culture (music, dance, theater, film) is a very interesting blend. I'm saddened to see how much the worst parts of US culture (sex, violence, worship of pop and sports figures) has completely permeated Indian culture. Indian culture is thousands of years old and it troubles me to see faddish, superficial, and faith- and family-hostile Western culture embraced so enthusiastically by those who may not really know the damage it does leading to drugs, divorce, out-of-wedlock pregnancy, suicide, AIDS, etc. And all these things are steeply on the increase in India.

After a week in India, I wrote the following in an email to my wife and children:

> I love each of you very much and miss you more than you can know. I really do have a better sense for what Abraham must have felt when he said he was "a stranger in a strange land" and wonder how different the "culture" of this world is compared with our heavenly home. I think if we could remember what it was like there we would be terribly homesick all the time. Perhaps that is another reason our merciful Heavenly Father has placed the veil over our minds: so that we don't have to feel such an ache of longing in every moment on earth. And

*this experience has given me a bit of a taste for what it might
be like to not be sealed to one's family in the eternities and be a
lonely wanderer yearning for family members that you cannot
be with — ever. Now THAT indeed would be hell. I now
have a much better sense for what our missionaries in foreign
developing nations must feel like and how hard it must be for
them having to go out and confront that culture each day.*

*I had it quite easy on my mission since even though we lived
in very Spartan quarters and lived on very little money at
least we had all the comfortable infrastructure of America, we
spoke English, and we used U.S. currency for what we needed.
Thus, I can see why a mission to another culture would have
incredible growth-producing potential for our missionaries. And
I can much better understand how the parents of missionaries in
faraway foreign lands must worry about their children each and
every day and yearn for their return while still being extremely
grateful and proud they are serving the Lord under such
circumstances. (Vadodara Journal)*

EXCHANGING SCRIPTURES & GOING HOME

On one of my last days in India, one of the master's students,
Harpreet, gave me two religious books on the Sri Aurobindo faith
that she practices along with Sikhism. So, I gave her my triple
combination.[7] It had my name embossed and is leather so she was very

---

7. In Mormon lingo, a triple combination is three of the four LDS Standard Works
(canonized scripture) and includes the Book of Mormon, Doctrine and Covenants,
and Pearl of Great Price.

hesitant to take it but I told her it would give me joy to give it to her. In India, it is considered polite to refuse ANY offered gift or favor at least once if not twice before accepting it. I learned that I have to insist most strongly to do anything nice for or give anything to anyone. They have a saying that "The Father is a god; the Mother is a god; the Teacher is a god" and so they treat their teachers with great respect. On certain occasions, they bend down to touch the feet of the teachers to show great honor and respect. She said she would read it and keep in touch via email with me about her questions.

A couple days before I was to fly home, I sent the following email to Mary:

> *This morning I thought I'd check the news and one of the lead stories on MSNBC was a major strike at British Airlines that has shut down Heathrow Airport which is, of course, the one I'm flying into the day after tomorrow. I can only hope and pray that either the strike will be over or that they can reroute me through another airport or on another airline but I probably will be in Mumbai when I have to do all that and if I have to wait there longer than the 6-hour layover that will be hard.*
>
> *The news report said people were sleeping in the airport and the airline put about 4,000 people up in hotels in London but were also telling passengers that if they left the airport they might never see their checked luggage again. Needless to say, I'm anxious about what will happen once I get on a little [airplane] in Vadodara and head to Mumbai. I will trust in the Lord that I and my luggage will reach home in good condition and in a timely way.*
>
> *I'm not sure what to make of the fact that I came through Mumbai two weeks ago three days after their worst flood ever*

and after the airport had been closed for three days and they were still canceling flights and now two weeks later I'm going to an airport that is closed because of a worker's strike that may or probably won't be resolved by the time I'm in the air. I place my trust in the goodness, mercy, and generosity of the Lord.

I know that since coming here I have also felt fearful, anxious, and stressed and that I have turned to God in prayer frequently and have felt his sustaining and protecting influence over me. I have not felt impressed to try to teach Mormonism to these people in any formal, direct way but rather have tried to act in Christian ways and share in a non-preachy way about my faith and our beliefs and practices. I have made some friends and colleagues here and hope that in time some might have a desire to learn more about the restored gospel. I didn't feel it appropriate to preach to my gracious hosts since Hindus have serious problems with Christian proselytizing among Hindus and there has been much violence with Christians being killed, beat up, churches burned, missionaries imprisoned, etc. so I hope that my low-key approach might pave the way for further opportunities to share the gospel.

Often, I would make a brief comment about how this or that Hindu, Sikh, Aurobindo, Muslim belief or practice was similar to Mormon belief and practice and leave it at that. I noticed that a number of students would ask me questions about what Americans or Christians believe about this or that and I would always try to give a generic American perspective, an honest and generous Christian perspective, and then mention what my own faith tradition thought/did about that. Since many were fasting during this month it was possible to talk about our fasting practices quite naturally. I don't think I offended anyone and

*hope I represented the Lord and the Church well. I tried to fulfill
my covenant to "be a witness of God at all time[s], in all places,
and in all things" without being offensive or preachy. (Vadodara
Journal)*

Soon before I was to head home, I learned that the British Airways
strike was over.

TENDER MERCIES & LESSONS LEARNED

When people at MSU heard that I had come through Mumbai on
the day I did, they were amazed my flight arrived and left on time.
Some said they know people whose flights were delayed many hours
or days and the Minister of Travel was on the TV every hour or so
telling everyone not to travel through Mumbai because of the floods.
My main host, Raji, was extremely surprised I made it through
"unscathed" and on time as she was monitoring the situation closely
and was certain I would be delayed significantly. And when I told
them that I actually was supposed to come a day earlier and was able
to arrange for all my flights the next day, without paying additionally,
they were stunned. The Lord was extremely kind and generous and I
am very grateful.

As a result of all this, I revised my interpretation of why I had not
been successful in making reservations months previously. I decided
that likely I would have made reservations for earlier than the 29th or
at least had more time to get the itinerary to Mary and would have
planned to leave on Friday and thus been stuck in Mumbai. And I
credit my not remembering it was the 29th, or not getting the itinerary
to Mary sooner, to the Spirit of the Lord helping me avoid having
my first experience in India be sleeping in the packed, smelly, unsafe,

airport for a day or two. I am extremely grateful to the Lord for His tender mercies and gentle guidance during this entire challenging and fascinating trip.

The faculty and students at MSU were wonderful and treated me extremely kindly. Although I am only a somewhat well-known scholar in the US family studies field, they treated me like a visiting celebrity. I was introduced as a "distinguished professor" and my counsel was sought by many faculty and students and a steady stream came to my office for consultations.

I always try to be respectful of all faiths and I see much good in Hinduism. It provides a billion people with a spiritual path that brings them closer to what they understand God to be. However, I am so incredibly grateful for the restored gospel of Jesus Christ which I believe, from the Spirit of the Lord, to contain the fullness of the gospel and Heavenly Father's plan. While I see good principles and practices in all the faiths I've studied, they all are lacking in major areas of truth and they lack the authority the Lord restored to the prophet Joseph Smith by sending angels who held that authority anciently. I used to think that the most difficult group to bring the restored gospel to would be the Muslims but I now see that it will be the Hindus who are probably the most difficult since their religion is so incredibly different from Christianity, Judaism, and Islam, much less Mormonism.

FULL CIRCLE

A couple years after my trip to India, I was able to host Raji at BYU for a conference on family policy issues that she wanted to attend at the law school. She was in Provo for several days and seemed to enjoy her time at BYU. Just a few days before she got on her plane to come to Utah, she fell and broke her ankle. She had rented a wheelchair that she used while in Utah but could not take it back to India with her. She said it would be very difficult once she got off the plane in London and for the rest of her trip to her home. She also said it would be very difficult and expensive to get a wheelchair in India.

We took Raji to see some LDS sites including the Salt Lake Temple and the LDS Humanitarian Aid Center at "Welfare Square." While there, we heard about their program of donating free simple wheelchairs to people in various developing countries. While Raji was in watching a film about LDS humanitarian services, I explained to the volunteers about Raji returning to India the next day without a wheelchair and asked if there if there was a chance they could donate a wheelchair to her. They said that was not normal policy, and they did not currently have the parts needed but the volunteer said she would talk with her supervisor. She did, and the supervisor said they would see if they could quickly make one for her. They were able to cobble together a chair with spare parts. When Raji came out from watching the film, they presented the wheelchair to her as a gift. They asked that, when she had finished using it, would she please donate it to someone in India who needed the wheelchair. She was incredibly grateful and touched. She cried for several minutes at this turn of events. It was nice to send her off with a tangible token of LDS humanitarian concern for people around the world.

The trip to India was one of those times in my life when I experienced a number of tender mercies from the Lord. As I have told friends and colleagues about the experience, I am reminded that "the Lord is in the details" of our lives and delights to bless us. I came to love the people of India for their faith, humility, hospitality, and generosity.

CHAPTER 30

My Concluding Testimony

The Lord is good to all: and his tender mercies are over all his works.
—*Psalms 145:9*

The Lord has been good to me and blessed me with His tender mercies throughout my life. He has blessed me far beyond what I deserve in all things, both temporally and spiritually (Mosiah 4:26; D&C 14:11). When I was a new and young believer and my faith was "yet tender" (D&C 86:4, 6), the Lord was especially tender, merciful, patient, and gracious. The tender mercies I have recorded here are only some of those I have recognized, remembered, and felt comfortable recording for the benefit of my posterity, my fellow Latter-day Saints, and my friends of other faiths.

I am deeply and eternally grateful for His gracious kindness to me. I am certain that I recognize and comprehend only a small proportion of those tender mercies. I have the sense that when this life is over we all will be shown the many thousands of tender mercies the Lord showered on us during our lives. I look forward to seeing and being able to express gratitude for these as-now unseen and unknown blessings. In the meantime, I have covenanted to be a witness of God's tender mercies "at all times and in all things, and in all places" (Mosiah 18:9) and this book is one way I can witness of God's goodness and power in my life.

Among the greatest of God's tender mercies are the good people He places in our lives. He has been most gracious to me in this way. My parents taught me to try to be a person of honesty and integrity and the kind of person who seeks and accepts the truth, no matter what that might mean. The LDS people who fellowshipped me during my investigation of the Church, who were my leaders and friends, and missionary companions and leaders made a huge impact on my life during those early years when I was tender in the gospel.

I have discussed how, at times, I used to wish that I had been raised with the gospel under the divine influence of wonderful LDS parents and grandparents. Although I did not enjoy this great blessing, the Lord provided me with wonderful "Mormon parents" in LoDonna and Ray Leininger, and with wonderful LDS parents-in-law Edward Lawrence Kimball and Evelyn Bee Madsen Kimball. And although I only knew one of my grandparents, I was greatly blessed by having the privilege to spend some tender and personal time with Mary's grandparents, who loved and accepted me as their own. And He especially blessed me with an incredible wife and marvelous children, the greatest blessings and tender mercies I have received in this life, excepting only the Atonement of the Lord and the fullness of the restored gospel.

Above all, the Lord has blessed me with an overflowing measure of His Spirit to change, heal, warn, inspire, guide, and help me. At times, He even has sent visitors from the other side of the veil when that was needed. I felt the direct and tender protection and interest of angels on my mission. He has been longsuffering with me in my weaknesses and stupidity. He has been beyond generous with me when I needed blessings. He has been merciful to me when I have forgotten to seek Him, when I have not followed His tender prompting, when I have willfully chosen wrong, and when I have, through laziness, not done all I could have done to serve Him.

Given what I personally experienced, it is impossible for me not to believe in a living, loving God who is "over all his works" and who is "in the details" of my life. I believe that any thorough and objective analysis of the events of my life would show far too many times when my prayers have been answered in ways that cannot be explained away as mere coincidence or chance.

I have family members and friends who do not believe that God exists or that, if God does exist, He is not involved in the details of our lives. I understand how such views can be held. The world is a difficult place: There are senseless wars and crimes. Children die by disease or accident. Adults abuse children. Good people die young and evil too often seems to go unpunished. Had I experienced some of the things that others have, I am certain my faith would be tried as theirs has been. I have only compassion for those who, because of tragic personal experience, have lost their faith or have not been able to come to faith in God.

Others have been kept from developing faith in God because of the "mists of darkness" (1 Nephi 8:23; 12:17) that sometimes shroud the tender mercies of God from view. There are many who are led away through "philosophies and vain deceit" (Colossians 2:8), and "doctrines of devils" (D&C 46:7) and "the subtle craftiness of men" (D&C 76:75; 123:12) that keep many from the truth because "they know not where to find it" (D&C 123:12).

I believe that when we "leave this frail existence" (LDS Hymn: "O My Father") we will be shown the true and full record of our life including all the unseen, unknown acts of those on the other side of the veil in our behalf. I believe we will then know in full that throughout our lives and in all aspects of our lives, "the tender mercies of the Lord are over all those he has chosen" (1 Nephi 1:20) and "the Lord is good to all: and his tender mercies are over all his works" (Psalms 145:9).

I have learned that the Lord blesses us according to our faith, need, desires, and in His own due time and way. I have learned that the Lord is in the details of our lives and that He delights to bless and protect us. I have learned that the Lord responds to frequent, fervent, and faithful prayer. But, certainly, not necessarily in the way and at the time we might prefer were we in charge of those blessings.

I believe that it is important for us to try to recognize the Lord's tender mercies in our lives and to record our spiritual experiences and share them with others—especially our family members. Through the process of remembering, retelling, and writing these spiritual experiences my own faith has been strengthened and deepened. As I have written this record I have seen even more clearly how God's hand has guided and protected me and how His tender mercies have been with me in every situation, at all times, and through the various changes and challenges I have experienced in my spiritual journey to this point.

For any of you who struggle with your faith or testimony for any reason, I hope and pray that reading about my experiences has strengthened your faith or helped you to develop at least a "desire to believe" (Alma 32:27). I hope that you will look prayerfully and carefully on God's tender mercies in your life and put your trust in Him. He is kind, merciful, patient, and full of love and He will bless you with what you most need if you humbly and patiently turn to Him in faith.

From these experiences, I know for myself that God, our Eternal Father, lives, that He loves us with a depth and power we cannot fathom, and that He answers our earnest prayers.

I also know that I am not the star of the experiences I have shared but merely a grateful recipient and witness of the love of God. My experiences have been a result of the profound love and tender mercies of God toward someone who must have needed such experiences to convert and stay faithful. All I did was be willing to receive eternal blessings when they were offered. All glory and honor and praise be to the Eternal Father and His Beloved Son.

The dramatic experiences received by the prophet Jonah, Saul of Tarsus, and Alma the Younger—not to mention Laman and Lemuel—demonstrate that God, in His mercy, sometimes provides dramatic spiritual manifestations to those—like me—who, because of pride or unbelief, really do not deserve to receive them. To the apostle Thomas, who had required a dramatic manifestation in order to believe, the Savior said, "Blessed are they that have not seen, and yet have believed" (John 20:29).

Personally, my spiritual heroes are not those who have experienced dramatic spiritual experiences. I most admire the many marvelous Saints I have known who continue in faithful devotion and service to God despite never having experienced an overpowering spiritual witness.

My friends, wherever you find yourself spiritually, I say to you in love and humility: I know that God lives and will answer your sincere prayers. I know that Jesus is the Christ. I know that only through faith in Christ and His atoning sacrifice can sin be washed and burned from the soul.

My intention has been to point you upward to prayerful communion with your Eternal Father; downward into deep study and pondering of the Book of Mormon and other scripture; inward into the depths of your soul, where you will find an eternal being yearning for the things of eternity; outward to sharing the glorious gospel of Jesus Christ with others; and forward to a future of faith and devotion to the Lord Jesus Christ and His restored gospel.

The Lord has been most gracious to me. He has granted to me a testimony of the restored gospel of Jesus Christ that has changed and blessed my life in more ways than I can possibly express. My testimony is the most precious thing I possess. It transcends all earthly things in importance and meaning to me. It is the "pearl of great price" (Matthew 13:46) spoken of by the Savior and is of such infinite and eternal worth that giving up all earthly things in order to obtain and retain it is only reasonable.

I have been blessed to be able to bear my testimony of the restored gospel of Jesus Christ many times, in many places, to many people. I have felt the power of the Spirit witness to my soul many times as I have borne my testimony of the truth. I conclude this account with my testimony. I do so in humility and solemnity and testify to you that I know these things for myself, independent of any other human being. I share my testimony with you as the greatest gift I can offer you.

From my own experience, I know that there is a God in heaven who is the Father of the spirits of all human beings. I know that our Heavenly Father called us together in a great council before the earth was created and chose His only begotten Son to atone for the sins of all of us. I know that we are on this earth as part of a great and eternal plan designed to test us and help us grow spiritually.

I know for myself, from my own experiences, that God knows us perfectly and responds in kindness and patience to our deepest yearnings, desires, and prayers. I know that God answers our prayers in His own time, His own way, and according to His own will, but in ways that are to our greatest eternal good.

I know that Jesus of Nazareth is the Son of God, the Savior of the world, and the only perfect and sinless being to have ever lived. I know from my own experience that through faith in Jesus Christ we may have our sins forgiven and our souls cleansed of all iniquity. I know for

myself, that, through the Savior's Atonement, we can be granted peace
of conscience—one of the greatest of His tender mercies. I know that
it is possible to be given a new heart and a new soul; to be born again
as a new person with no more desire to do evil. I testify that these
spiritual blessings are more real than anything in this world.

From the witness of the Holy Scriptures and from sacred personal
experiences, I know that the Lord Jesus Christ will come again in
glory to reign as Lord of lords and King of kings. I know that He is
full of compassion, love, and patience. However, I also know from my
own experience that He is full of justice and that it is possible to grieve
the Spirit so that it withdraws from us and we are left to our own
power and wisdom. And when we are left to ourselves we are pitiful,
weak, foolish, and prone to all kinds of follies and errors.

I know from my own experiences that the Book of Mormon is the
word of God. I have spent the last forty years studying many hundreds
of books in religion, social science, literature, philosophy, history,
science, and family relationships. I know that by diligently and humbly
studying and faithfully living the teachings of the Book of Mormon
a person can get closer to God than through any other book. I know
that the Book of Mormon is a miraculous witness of the divinity of
Jesus Christ.

I know that Joseph Smith was a prophet of God. God has
witnessed to me by the power of the Holy Ghost on more than one
occasion that Joseph did, in fact, see God the Father and His Son
Jesus Christ in vision. I know that Joseph Smith holds the keys to the
Kingdom of God in these last days. I know that the Church of Jesus
Christ of Latter-day Saints is a restoration of the church that Jesus
himself established on the earth during His mortal mission.

I know for myself, from many spiritual witnesses, that the Church
of Jesus Christ is led by living prophets and apostles who receive

continual revelation from the Lord. I know that the president of the
Church of Jesus Christ of Latter-day Saints holds all the keys that God
has restored in these last days and that he is literally God's prophet on
earth. I know that the Holy Priesthood was restored to Joseph Smith
by angelic ministration.

I know from my own experience that God has power to heal,
inspire, reveal, and bless His children, particularly through the holy
priesthood of the Church of Jesus Christ of Latter-day Saints. On
dozens of occasions, I have felt the power of the priesthood flow
through me to bless others. Under its influence, I have heard myself
speak words of truth and power to those I was blessing that I could not
possibly have known for myself. I have heard myself say things about
their past, present, and future that they later told me no one could have
known.

I know that the sealing powers of the holy priesthood are real and
binding. In the sacred sealing rooms of the holy temples of the restored
church I have experienced for myself, through the power of the Holy
Ghost, the witness that what is bound on earth is bound eternally
in the heavens. I know from my own experience that, through the
Atonement of Jesus Christ, it is possible to be reconciled to our family
members if we become distant or separated from them for any reason.

I know that any person who goes to God in faith and humility
and persistence will be blessed with those things they most need and
righteously desire. I know that His tender mercies are over all His
works. I am a witness of the goodness, the mercy, the loving kindness,
and the gracious care of God.

I bear this testimony in the name of the Lord Jesus Christ,
Amen. ✺

APPENDICES

APPENDIX A

Sharing Sacred Experiences

In this appendix, I reflect on the process of writing sacred experiences, provide my views about the nature of sacred experiences like the ones I will share, and discuss some of the challenges of sharing and receiving personal accounts of sacred experiences. I do so to provide some context for the experiences I share. At the end of this Appendix, I discuss some thoughts or tips on what to do (and not do) when recording and sharing your own sacred experiences with others. I do this in hopes of encouraging you, dear reader, to record and share your own sacred experiences.

When I use the term *sacred experiences* I mean experiences that are deeply important and meaningful in one's life. While the scriptures include accounts of those who have seen divine beings (God and angels) with their eyes, I have not. Though I know people who have, I have never heard the voice of God audibly. Thus, when I say I will share a number of my personal "sacred experiences" I am referring to times when I felt powerful spiritual influence (e.g., spiritual guidance, comfort, warning, inspiration).

Many of the experiences I share in this book were times when I felt like the Lord intervened in some way in my life. I realize that not everyone who reads these experiences will agree with me that God was involved in that series of events that I report. One person's sacred experience might be another person's silly coincidence. A reasonable person could say that I experienced a fortunate coincidence, a happy accident, or a lucky break. When it comes to coincidences, I am tempted to refer to Leroy Jethro Gibbs of the TV show NCIS and his Rule 39: There Are No Coincidences. However, I am willing to grant that there are some coincidences in life; but I believe that the sacred experiences I share herein are not among them.

Nearly everyone who knows highly religious people has heard someone share an experience that the person sharing thought was a clear example of God working in their life. If we ourselves believe in God, and believe that God can and does communicate with people and intervene in their lives, we are more inclined to accept someone's story of divine intervention at face value. However, even those of us who, because of our own beliefs and experiences, are inclined to believe in such things, have likely heard of someone's "spiritual experience" that we find troubling or hard to believe for some reason. One of the things I love most about the Church of Jesus Christ of Latter-day Saints is that it teaches that we don't have to rely on the word of someone else—even the word of prophets, apostles, or even God—but rather we have the right and privilege (and responsibility) to ask God to reveal the truth of religious teachings to us and that God will do so by the power of the Holy Ghost.

CHALLENGES INVOLVED IN SHARING SACRED EXPERIENCES PUBLICLY

Sharing and hearing stories of sacred experiences is part and parcel of being a member of the Church of Jesus Christ of Latter-day Saints. The LDS Church began with the prophet Joseph Smith's religious experience in the Sacred Grove in Palmyra, New York. Joseph wrote multiple accounts of his First Vision. Our missionaries share one of Joseph's accounts of that experience—the first one published—in the lessons they teach to those who want to hear more about Mormonism.[1] Furthermore, the Book of Mormon consists of many stories of sacred experiences written by prophets. Latter-day Saints are enjoined to write their own personal histories including a record of their sacred experiences.[2] Latter-day Saint prophets and apostles share sacred experiences in conferences. Across the earth, local LDS leaders and members share sacred experiences in meetings and classes and Family Home Evenings. Indeed, a distinctive and essential part of being a Mormon is to listen to, record, and share sacred experiences. However, there are some challenges and limitations in this process that I think are important to mention in a book, like this one, that consists largely of an account of sacred experiences.

My goal was to create a record of the Lord's tender mercies toward me in my early spiritual development, of many of my most important spiritual experiences, and to reflect on what I learned from them. Given that this is a record intended for the spiritual edification of my posterity as well as others, I desire that it be as accurate as possible. To ensure the greatest amount of accuracy I have consulted various written materials (journals, diaries, newspaper clippings, calendars, emails, etc.), as well as, where possible, conversations and interviews with those whose memory and records would supplement—and in some cases, correct—my own. I cannot claim there are no errors. Indeed, given the fallibility of my own memory, the limitations of my own perspectives, and my tendency to attend to some things better

---

1 See essay on accounts of Joseph's First Vision at: lds.org/topics/first-vision-accounts

2 See excellent article from the Encyclopedia of Mormonism on the importance of record-keeping at: eom.byu.edu/index.php/Record_Keeping

than others, I am certain there are errors. I believe they are minor and
hope they will not detract from the overall message of this volume.

I wish I had kept a regular, detailed journal of my experiences
throughout my four decades in the Church. Except for sporadic efforts
in my first year in the Church, and an all-too-cryptic missionary
journal, I have not regularly kept a personal journal. I am sorry to say
that a couple of years after joining the Church, I allowed a statement
by a priesthood leader I greatly respected to discourage me from
keeping a journal. When I told him that I was having a hard time
getting into the habit of keeping a regular journal he said, "Well, I
have never kept a journal. I never want to look back." Something about
that greatly appealed to me and I decided I wanted to be the kind of
person who "never looked back" and so I never really made myself
develop the incredibly valuable habit of keeping a journal. However, I
have told a number of these experiences numerous times over the years
to various individuals and groups so they have remained fresh in my
mind.

I have done my best to remember and accurately record the
experiences I was blessed with, but I am sure I have forgotten or
overlooked important things and made some mistakes. I have learned
over the years that my recollection and others' recollections of the same
events do not always perfectly match. I have also learned that I forget
or misremember things and exactly what was said by whom. In telling
my experiences, often I will use "remembered dialogue" or my memory
of who said what to whom. My memory is imperfect, however, and
while I do my best to record what others and I said to each other, I
am sure I do not always provide a completely accurate account of what
actually was said. All I can do is be as careful as possible and record
my recollections to the best of my ability. Again, I apologize to anyone
to whom I might have "put words in your mouth" that you did not

actually say or impute motives to you that were not actually there. My intention was always to be as generous as possible.

While I will not excuse myself from any errors that remain, I admit that I take some comfort from Joseph Smith's statement about the Book of Mormon that this sacred book was the "most correct" book on earth (but he did not say it was perfect) and from the scriptural statements of prophet-authors in the Book of Mormon itself that there may be "mistakes" (Title Page), "imperfections" (Mormon 8:12; 9:31), and errors (1 Nephi 19:6), and who apologized for their own "weakness in writing" (Ether 12:23–25).

I find it meaningful that even in sacred scripture the titles of various books typically include the name of person who wrote the record so it is, for example the Book of Nephi (not Book of What Actually Happened to Nephi), or the Book of Alma (not the Book of God About Alma), or the Book of Enos (not the Factual Account About Enos by His Guardian Angel), or the Book of Mormon (not the Book About Moroni's Actual Behaviors). In other words, much of sacred scripture are personal accounts of people's personal sacred experiences rather than Objective Facts About Sacred Events.

While some may think of scripture as consisting mainly of long sermons, lists of commandments, and boring history, the Book of Mormon is filled with deeply personal accounts of individual and family joy and sorrow, success and failure, righteousness and wickedness, and patience and anger. Indeed, the level of intense personal expression in the writing in scripture is profound. Some examples include: Nephi's Psalm (2 Nephi 4: 16–35) in which Nephi says, "Oh wretched man that I am!" (verse 16) and "my soul grieveth because of mine iniquities" and "my heart groaneth because of my sins" (vs. 17–19); or Alma the Younger's poignant and detailed account of his conversion to Christ where, for example, he said, "I was racked with eternal torment, for my soul was harrowed up to the greatest degree and racked with all my sins" (Alma 36:12) and, "Oh, thought I, that I could be banished and become extinct both soul and body" (Alma 36:15); or Enos's deeply personal account in which he writes about the "wrestle which I had before God, before I received a remission of my sins" (Enos 1:2). Among the most poignant stories is when Moroni wrote, "And my father also was killed by them, and I even remain alone to write the sad tale of the destruction of my people (Mormon 8:3) and then mentioned, almost in passing (Mormon 8:10–11) the marvelous sacred experience of being visited by translated beings (the Three Nephites). For me, these and other prophets in the Book of Mormon, are examples of personal expressions of honesty and vulnerability in writing about one's sacred experiences.

On August 1, 2017, the Deseret News (a newspaper owned by the LDS Church) published a story about much-loved and respected Apostle Jeffrey R. Holland's telling of a missionary experience to missionaries at the Missionary Training Center. It turns out that some of the parts of the story that Elder Holland heard and then retold were embellished by the person from whom he had heard the story.[3] Embellishing stories is a profoundly human activity and the vast majority of human beings are liable to participate in this process. Keith Erekson, Director of the LDS Church History Museum was quoted in this article saying, "Maybe this is an opportunity to invite people to tell their stories so we have more of them on the record."

Sadly, this also is a regular occurrence in our church meetings. It is likely that we all have engaged in this process in one way or

---

3 See story at: deseretnews.com/article/865685840/Elder-Holland-withdraws-Church-News-missionary-story.html

another. For example, when my wife and I were newly married, we attended a ward (congregation) of young married students at BYU. In a Sacrament Meeting, Mary and I heard a wonderfully inspirational—indeed miraculous—story. The person who shared the story indicated that the experience occurred to "a friend of my mother." We shared the experience with Mary's family that evening. Mary's father [4] was a careful LDS historian and said that he had heard a similar story shared by someone else. He suggested that we ask the person who told the story if they could request their mother to ask her friend to write down the experience with as much detail as possible. We did so. Our ward member got back with us a few days later and mentioned that the mother said that the experience actually happened to "a friend of a friend" and when she asked her mother to try to identify the person it actually happened to it turned out that nobody really knew the person to which the experience happened.

As we, and other religious people, and other human beings, often do, we share stories of great experiences and, almost inevitably, we consciously or unconsciously add or subtract from what we heard or read. In telling our own experiences we all know how easy it is to embellish certain details just a little. And then the next person that tells the story might misremember or, perhaps consciously or unconsciously, embellish a detail or two here or there. And pretty soon we have a "faith-promoting rumor" (to use the popular LDS term for such stories).

Since this experience, I have tried to be much more careful in what I am willing to share of sacred experiences that I do not know for certain occurred—either to me or someone I know and trust

---

4 Edward L. Kimball, LDS author of numerous biographies.

who said the experience happened to them (not to a friend or family member). I have also tried to be much more careful to not embellish the story—either of my own experience or someone else's. Human beings are story-telling beings and we love—indeed live for—a great story. But as religious people, we need to do our best to tell the truth when we share sacred experiences. We owe this to the Lord, to those we share experiences with, and to ourselves.

SUNDAY SCHOOL CLASS ON WRITING SACRED EXPERIENCES

One of the sweetest and most sacred experiences I have had in four wonderful decades of membership in the LDS Church was the two years I spent teaching a Sunday School class that the bishop allowed me to develop on Writing Sacred Experiences. The class fell under my calling as a Ward Family History Consultant. My approach was to have class members take turns reading from our personal histories those parts that recounted sacred experiences and then counsel together about what we can learn from what we heard about how to record our own sacred experiences.

During the class, I was able to read much of an earlier draft of the text of this book to students so those who had never written their spiritual experiences would have an example of one way to approach doing that. I also shared my thoughts and facilitated class discussions on ways to handle challenging situations such as writing about less-than-ideal (read: very challenging, discouraging, depressing) times and circumstances and experiences from our lives. Some class members had very troubling childhoods that included very negative experiences (e.g., abuse, neglect, dysfunctional families) and understandably struggled to know how and what to write about that. Others had a variety of spiritual challenges such as unanswered prayers or blessings, religious doubts and faith crises, or difficulty identifying inspiration and revelation. We all struggled with how to write about tough times and experiences in ways that were "faith-promoting" or "uplifting" or otherwise helpful to our intended readers.

It was wonderful to counsel together under the direction of the Holy Spirit about how to think about these challenges. I tried to avoid offering easy answers to these challenging questions and dilemmas and to remind us that there is no simple formula for addressing such quandaries. But the Spirit can guide each of us in our own circumstances to fulfill the divine invitation to keep sacred records. Each Sunday, we read and briefly discussed the different ways to understand some passages from the Book of Moses about how Adam kept a sacred record.

And a book of remembrance was kept, in the which was recorded, in the language of Adam, for it was given unto as many as called upon God to write by the spirit of inspiration; And by them their children were taught to read and write, having a language which was pure and undefiled. Now this same Priesthood, which was in the beginning, shall be in the end of the world also. (Moses 6:5–7)

These verses are full of meaning for those of us in these latter days but the one I want to mention here is, "for it was given unto as many as called upon God to write by the spirit of inspiration" since that promises us that when we undertake to record our sacred experiences we can have the blessing of spiritual assistance from the Lord if we earnestly seek it.

As you read the accounts of sacred experiences found in this volume, I sincerely hope that you will be reminded of those times in your own life that the Lord has blessed you, guided you, inspired you, warned you, protected you, taught you, sent people to bless and teach you, and in every way shown His tender mercies to you. I hope that this book helps encourage you in your own efforts to record your sacred experiences for the benefit of your family and friends. I hope that by seeing my weak efforts to write the things of my soul that you will know that if I can do it you can too.

Over the four decades since I converted to the Church of Jesus Christ of Latter-day Saints in my late teens, I have been asked many times to tell about my conversion and early experiences in the Church in various settings. Often those who heard my story encouraged me to write my experiences for the benefit of others. I was asked to write my conversion for a book called *Converted to Christ Through the Book of Mormon* edited by Eugene England (Deseret Book, 1989). That book contains a brief account of my initial conversion but nothing about the months and years that followed. I was asked to give a BYU Devotional[5] and, in the limited time I had to speak, shared parts of my conversion experience. Until preparing this volume, I had not made a more complete account of the many tender mercies the Lord blessed me with in the first several years of my membership in the Church. There are various reasons why accounts may vary including different audiences, growth of our understanding and perspective over time, different purposes for each account, and time constraints; for example, my BYU Devotional was limited to twenty-five minutes so I had to leave out a number of things that happened during my conversion while attempting to reflect in depth on what happened.

Over the years as I have worked on the accounts of the sacred experiences I share in this book I have revised the accounts as new information has come to light (typically from hearing others talk about their part of my experience) or as I have thought more about the

---

5 See speeches.byu.edu/talks/david-c-dollahite_receiving-the-eternal

experience and, often with the help of the Holy Spirit, remembered some part of the experience that I had forgotten. Also, as I thought about the possible effect of my words on others, each time I revised I tried to be more careful, more generous to others, more sensitive to others' perspectives and experiences, and more humbly grateful for the Lord's part in the experience.

Two (or more) people can have the "same experience" or witness the "same events" and, for a variety of reasons, have different experiences, recollections, attitudes, and emotions about that experience or event. In fact, in a court of law, if multiple witnesses' stories are too similar in details and expression, it often is assumed that they are colluding on their testimony (they have agreed together what story to tell). About the varied accounts that Joseph Smith wrote of his vision, the Gospel Topics essay on First Vision Accounts on the official LDS website states:

> *The various accounts of the First Vision tell a consistent story, though naturally they differ in emphasis and detail. Historians expect that when an individual retells an experience in multiple settings to different audiences over many years, each account will emphasize various aspects of the experience and contain unique details. Indeed, differences similar to those in the First Vision accounts exist in the multiple scriptural accounts of Paul's vision on the road to Damascus and the Apostles' experience on the Mount of Transfiguration. Yet despite the differences, a basic consistency remains across all the accounts of the First Vision. Some have mistakenly argued that any variation in the retelling of the story is evidence of fabrication. To the contrary, the rich*

*historical record enables us to learn more about this remarkable
event than we could if it were less well documented.* [6]

I have benefited by reading and hearing others' perspectives on
our shared experiences. My first mission companion, Wayne Buhler,
allowed me to see his journal from when we were together. He kept a
much more detailed journal than I did and this allowed me to add or
correct some information from my own journal and recollection.

When people record and share their own sacred experiences it is
incumbent on them to attend to certain issues. Inspired by President
Gordon B. Hinckley's list of "Bs" given to the youth of the Church[7],
I would suggest that those of us who record and share publicly sacred
experiences try to attend to the following:

- **Be honest.** Avoid embellishing the story and just report
  what actually happened. Also, try to "speak the truth in
  love" so that you are an authentic but inoffensive witness of
  the goodness of God.
- **Be careful.** Try to get the facts (names, dates, places) right
  so that you place your experience in context and make it
  easier for others to connect with your experience.
- **Be humble.** Remember to give glory to God and to other
  people who were involved in your sacred experience.
- **Be faithful.** Share your experience in a way that builds
  faith in the living God and turns the hearts of your readers/

---

6 lds.org/topics/first-vision-accounts

7 See: lds.org/ensign/2001/01/a-prophets-counsel-and-prayer-for-youth

listeners to their Heavenly Father and the Lord Jesus
Christ.

- **Be compassionate.** Be aware of the implications of
  your experience for others who have not yet obtained
  the blessings you are writing/speaking about and be
  compassionate toward those who, for whatever reason,
  might be hurt, offended, or otherwise bothered by your
  story.
- **Be generous.** Give others who are involved in your
  experience the benefit of the doubt about their motivations
  and intentions — especially when the experience was not
  necessarily a positive one for you.
- **Be open.** Remain willing to revise your account of the
  experience in order to be more consistent with what
  you learn from others who might have been part of the
  experience and have different recollections, feelings, or
  thoughts than you about what occurred or what it means.

I would like to say that I perfectly follow my own advice in every
account of my experiences in this book; while I tried to do so, I'm
sure that I have failed in some instances. My intent is to provide an
accurate and honest and open and faithful account of my own sacred
experiences to bear an authentic witness of the goodness of God in my
own life. If you are aware of mistakes and errors in this volume of any
nature, I invite you to correct me privately and/or publicly. I welcome
having the record set straight on any aspect of what I have written.

I hope that reading this book has prompted you to think of times
in your life when the Lord and His servants have touched your soul,
enlightened your mind, sent others into your life to bless you, and
helped you recognize the workings of the Holy Spirit. I invite you to

record and share those sacred times when you have received the eternal into your life. Doing so will be a blessing for you, for others, and for future generations.

My whole intention is to lift and build people. If anything that I have written in any way offends any of the people I have mentioned or their friends and loved ones, I apologize and ask for your forgiveness. I would love to be able to do so personally and/or publicly. Please let me know how I can do so.

Please feel free to email me at: davidcdollahite@gmail.com.

APPENDIX B

Creating Marital Unity
Despite Differences

If you have made it this far in reading this book, you deserve a little break from all the serious sharing of spiritual experiences. Mary and I have some fun in this appendix sharing stories and ideas on how we learned to build marital unity despite us being very different from one another in many ways. We hope you enjoy it and perhaps learn an idea or two that might help you in your marriage or that you might pass along to someone you know to help them.

This appendix is adapted from a talk that Mary and I were invited to give at a BYU Women's Conference. It provides a view into the way we have dealt with some differences in the experiences, perspectives, personality, and communication styles that we brought into our marriage. This appendix retains the format we chose then of taking turns speaking, lightly edited for a reading audience.

MARY

Our discussion centers on how to create a union not merely between husband and wife but a partnership with God. LDS Apostle Russell

M. Nelson said, "Marriage has been divinely designated as an eternal and everlasting covenant. . . . That union is not merely between husband and wife; it embraces a partnership with God."[8]

A few years ago, one of our now-grown children watched over a few days while my husband, Dave, and I were working through something. She asked me as I drove her to school why I "put up with" that disagreement, when it wasn't easily resolved. I said something like, "You don't understand. What you don't see is the whole story."

This talk is the longer answer to that question about the reality that eternal marriage is more important than one moment in time.

I was born to a fifth-generation, large, Latter-day Saint family living in Montana. Granddaughter of Spencer Kimball and Camilla Kimball. My father was a university professor of law, and my mother was a full-time homemaker who had double majored in sociology and psychology. Quite an academic family. I was the third out of seven children—a full dinner table. I grew up playing the piano and the violin, climbing trees, playing softball, reading both fairy tales and the scriptures, and playing math games at the dinner table.

DAVE

I've been asking that same question our daughter asked, "How does Mary put up with me?" our entire marriage. While Mary was growing up in a large, Mormon, academic family, I was growing up in Babylon in California. I was born to an Episcopalian couple. Actually, my mom's dad was raised Lutheran and her mom was raised Catholic and

---

8 "Nurturing Marriage" in April 2006 General Conference of the Church of Jesus Christ of Latter-day Saints: lds.org/general-conference/2006/04/nurturing-marriage

my dad was raised Baptist and they met in the middle in the Episcopal Church, and I was baptized and an altar boy in the Episcopal Church. My father was a police officer and my mom worked in a doctor's office. I spent my time playing sports and skipping school and avoiding studying, hanging out with friends, and goofing off. Not the kind of LDS family that my wife grew up in.

MARY

When my family moved to Provo, I attended Provo High and then BYU. I served in the Finland Helsinki Mission then returned to BYU.

DAVE

When I was in my first semester at a junior college in California, I joined the LDS Church and came to BYU to prepare for a mission. I didn't come to study as, at that point, I was not interested college or book-learning or things like that. I only came to BYU because they said that was the best place to prepare to be a missionary. So, I served a mission in the Massachusetts Boston Mission and then returned to BYU.

MARY

When Dave and I met, it seemed we had quite a bit in common: my dad worked in the legal field and his dad worked as a police officer, we both loved the Gospel, we both had served missions, we both attended BYU, we both loved learning. But best of all, we loved each other!

Dave and I wanted to begin our marriage at the altar in the temple of the Lord. We wanted the Lord to bless our marriage. Little did we realize how great that blessing would be, this covenant with the Lord that included inviting Him into our marriage.

We each—man and woman, soon to be husband and wife—bring to the altar our best selves. We have grown up enough that our parents might actually miss us. We have—or will soon—shed baggage like self-centeredness. We bring our habits of prayer and scripture study, church attendance, and honoring parents. We bring to the altar a desire to covenant to begin the becoming of an eternal family.

And we bring it ALL: we bring debts, talents, skills, hobbies. We bring our weaknesses.

Then out of all that, the Lord begins to work with our desire and willingness to bring the unity, the work of becoming one, into the realm of the possible. This is one of the great miracles of the Atonement, that two very different lives can come together as a son and a daughter of God and start working together toward an eternal life.

I attended my home Single Adults Sunday School. Dave happened to ask a missionary friend who also attended the class if Dave could attend with him. I happened to be interested in another young man at the time. But I was team-teaching the lesson and at the end of the lesson Dave asked his friend to introduce us after Sunday School.

Just to cut the story very short, we got engaged and he moved into our ward boundaries—

DAVE

—She proposed to me on our third date.

MARY

We're not going into those details, Dave. That was a distraction.

DAVE

Sorry, I didn't mean to throw you off there, Mary.

MARY

Okay, Dave, we're going to talk about similarities, not eccentricities. We both believed the Gospel to be true, and we both had a full mission time of teaching the Gospel. If you'd asked us at the time, we would have said, "Yes, we are equally yoked."

While we were engaged, we were called to team-teach a Sunday School class. Dave and I found we approached the lesson material differently. We carefully divided the sub-topics in the lesson manual. Then, during class, he would share experiences and share more experiences. And when it was my turn, I stuck closely to the lesson manual. And when there was a question I would ask it, and pause until someone responded. A pause is time for thinking, right?

DAVE

No, a pause is time for me to tell another story.

MARY

We both loved teaching the Gospel on our missions. Why, then, were we having difficulty melding ourselves for teaching a simple Sunday

School lesson? We actually felt a little relieved to get married and get out of that calling! However, during that time, in our preparations, we made a specific goal. We knew what our weakness was and we decided that during our marriage, one of the main things we would work on was the ability to teach together. Someday—in the far future when any children we had would be grown—we would be able to teach together so we could serve a mission for the Lord together. How in the world would we be able to do that?

Good question! We each bring our own script to the marriage. Hopefully we each soon realize that we (husband and wife) want to and need to write a new script together. The ideal is when we ask the Lord to be our script editor. It's tempting to take the easy route and let our growing-up scripts, or cultural scripts, or the media be our guides. However, eternal families require an eternal script.

DAVE

I received training as a marriage and family therapist, and one of the things we learn is that people come into their marriage with a different script, a set of expectations for how things in marital and family life are supposed to go. Those who have been married for a while have learned that there are many ideas and expectations about how things should go in marriage and they often are not consistent with what your wonderful spouse thinks and expects.

These expectations are based primarily on one's family of origin (family you grew up in). It is rare that a husband and wife's expectations will be the same about how to do finances, and birthdays, and vacations, and so forth. This can cause frustration and conflict when the expectations are unmet. The set of expectations people bring to marriage about marriage and family life are called marital scripts. Marital scripts provide each person with an internal guide for how things will be or how things are supposed to be. An important part of developing marital unity (and avoiding conflict) is to get your marital scripts aligned by talking about what your expectations are for something, and asking what the other person's expectations are, and then to find ways to work together to bring unity despite those differences. This usually involves some kind of sacrifice on each person's part.

MARY

We would like to share several examples of rewriting a personal script into a marital script. We will highlight what it is we each placed on the altar and what eternal blessing we received together from our sacrifices. As an introduction: Dave has found that he is an extrovert in a family of introverts. He came from that kind of family and he married into one. As for myself—I love people. I just get anxious when in a group of, say, more than five.

I really love a gathering of family and/or friends. In high school, friends would gather at each other's houses for talking, making cookies, homework. My friends would support whatever activity one of the others wanted to organize. For example, one time I organized a play reading.

Dave spent most of his public-school years after school at friends' houses playing ping-pong or door-bell-ditch, or driving to the beach.

Whenever I thought about my (now our) wedding, I hoped to avoid a reception. I knew myself that I would be exhausted by traveling from Provo to the Salt Lake Temple, the gathering and greeting of my aunts and uncles and many of my dozens of cousins in addition to my parents, six siblings and two in-laws, and then driving back to Provo.

Also, Dave's family (mom, dad, and brother — three) had driven all the way from Seattle to be with us.

Dave enjoys a party. But kindly he let me use as an excuse for a reception the fact that the raw numbers of guests would be so uneven between his family and mine. If it had been reversed and I had been outgoing and he reserved, the two-to-three-hundred-plus friends on both sides might have required a reception.

So, we were sealed, held a wedding breakfast, then immediately boarded a plane for our honeymoon.

DAVE

Elder Eyring suggested that we each have a blessing journal.[9] You might think of what we share as an example of some of the things that we've learned over the years and we hope that some of those experiences we share might help you to find greater unity in your own marriage.

MARY

I'll begin with this story: When we married, we were both busy in graduate school — Dave studied for a Master's in Marriage and Family Therapy and was a research assistant and taught a family class at BYU. Dave also worked at the MTC in the Jewish Culture program. I studied at the law school and taught a freshman English class at BYU. And we NEVER had enough time together to talk about everything we wanted to.

---

9 lds.org/ensign/2013/08/recognize-remember-and-give-thanks

More often than not, we shared late into the night. Amazingly, we agreed most of the time. When we disagreed, we could usually talk and figure out that we were simply using different definitions or understandings of words or coming from different backgrounds. Then we enjoyed moving the discussion to learn more about the other.

DAVE

However, unfortunately, sometimes I became a little disagreeable—sometimes a lot. And here is how we learned to solve that.

MARY

I'm pretty analytical and frankly, he does talk a little bit more than I do. So, I was the one who would look at my watch and see what time it was. Amazingly, the commonality between the disagreements and being disagreeable was that being disagreeable generally seemed to be after 9:00 at night. There was something magical about 9:00. And so, we made a joint decision to not discuss anything possibly, conceivably, disagreeable or hard after 9:00 p.m. It was amazing because you have the scripture that says "don't let the sun go down on your wrath" and yet we found that if we did let the sun set on our wrath we would be okay but if we didn't then we would be up all night. We found that when we lost track of time and moved into a tough topic and . . . then one of us (I) would ask, "What time is it?" and it would invariably be after 9:00 and then we would postpone the discussion until either the next day or the day after that at lunch or some set time.

What we sacrificed was a little bit of pride, a lot of impatience, and a lot of satisfaction about finding out who is right. However, we did gain patience, trust in each other that we would come back to the subject, and the idea that our relationship was two people becoming not the other person but something better together.

DAVE

That little lesson has had a big impact on our relationship. We have since learned that we also don't want to have discussions about things that are difficult before I have eaten dinner as that didn't usually go well. I also learned that we did not need to resolve it NOW even though my training as a therapist and my personality cried out for us to spend whatever time was needed to deal with it now. Mary was more wise, mature, and patient than me and helped me learn that if we set a time in the future to resolve it usually we had a much more productive and calm interaction.

When we had been married for two or three months—living in a drafty fourplex south of BYU campus—Mary picked up the mail that day, saw that one envelope came from the credit union, pulled out the monthly statement, handed it to me and said...

Mary: "Here. Dave, I'm sure you want to see this."
Dave: "Why would I want to see this?"
Mary: "Well, you know, to balance the checkbook."
Dave: "Oh, I don't balance the checkbook."
Mary: "You don't . . . what!?
Dave: "I just, well every couple of months, I deposit a check and don't record it in the checkbook ledger. Then I know I've got more than I think so I'll never overdraw. So, I never balance the checkbook."

Mary: "Then how do you know how much money you have?"

Dave: "I don't really care how much money I have. And I know that I have more than I think I have. So that's good enough."

Mary: "Okay, Dave, so I've got a question for you. How were you able to buy my engagement ring?"

Dave: "O, I just assumed that there was going to be money in there for that."

In fact, I had a few hundred dollars more than I thought—just enough to buy Mary a diamond ring with a VERY small diamond (you could barely see it down there between the four prongs). Later, Mary lost that diamond (it dropped out of the ring) so we got her a wedding band. Actually, all along she only wanted a band but with my stupid male ego noticing how every engaged BYU coed seemed to be sporting a large rock, I stubbornly had to buy Mary an engagement ring and wedding band. After that discussion, we decided Mary would handle the checkbook.

MARY

And that was when we had no mortgage, no credit cards, no car payment, and we grocery shopped together every shopping trip. Talk about joined at the hip. My personal family script was that my dad balanced the checkbook to the penny, every month. And he still has all those checkbooks. Christmas was equal to the penny for each of the seven children. And I married a man who didn't even balance his checkbook—ever!

This was the blessing: we finally had that temporal, financial discussion that we should have had before marriage. And I learned that Dave knows that God always provides. And Dave learned that I know that we need to be careful with what God provides.

DAVE

Well, to be fair, I have learned at least seventeen important things from my wife for every one important thing she has learned from me.

MARY

The next one is a very personal script to me. The first two years we were married we rented an apartment in an old-fashioned fourplex in Provo south of BYU campus. We attended a married student ward on Sundays and spent the weekdays (and many Saturdays) on campus in classes, in the library, and Dave working. The rhythm of our lives didn't seem to change much on paper from the weeks of our courting. We still did all we had been doing during our courtship and engagement.

But—inexplicably—on Sundays after Church meetings and a meal I'd start to become sad. The whole first year I would just get sad on Sundays. After a few weeks of this, I tried to anticipate my sad mood by planning a walk, or scripture reading or letter writing. Those didn't work—even when Dave shared those activities with me.

Finally, I spent some time in introspection (a specialty of introverts) to compare details of Sundays as married versus Sundays as single. I realized then that the bottom line was that every single Sunday I became homesick.

Now, my parents only lived two miles away. So I was trying to figure out how that matched.

Dave knew what to do about that. He said, "There's an easy solution, Mary! Let's go spend Sunday afternoons with your family."

But I wondered how I could learn to be married and not homesick on Sundays if I always went home. I wanted to build a Sunday for the two of us.

Then Dave tried to find out what it was my family did on Sundays that I was so homesick for so that we — the two of us — could do that.

I searched my memory and could not think of a specific thing my family did that Dave and I weren't doing: attending Church and sharing a special meal. For the first time, I put into words something I hadn't known: my family didn't DO anything on Sunday that I was homesick for. We just *were*. We were together, safe, content. Reading in different rooms or playing board games or word games, or discussing a lesson, or making a cake or cookies in the kitchen. I had felt peace in being a member of my family. In being. Not necessarily doing.

This was what we sacrificed: Dave sacrificed by having a homesick wife every single Sunday for a whole year. As for me, I was obeying the commandment to leave father and mother and to choose the rhythm and enjoy the rhythm of Dave's and my new family.

Our blessings: even though I had intentionally spent the year following my missionary service living at home expressly in order to learn everything I could from my parents about their marriage (they have a great marriage), I now learned that there was one more thing for me to learn and that was simply not all the "doings" of a family but the "being" of a family. I was, I hope, able to bring that into our marriage a little bit.

DAVE

Another story about different scripts: So, I grew up in a family where—obviously—what you do on Christmas morning is that the kids wake up way before dawn, then the kids wake up the parents, and then rush in and immediately open up all the presents as quickly as possible. It takes about thirty-eight seconds to get them all opened and then you spend Christmas day playing with the presents. That is how Christmas is supposed to go.

So, the first Christmas I spent with the Kimball family was a big surprise. It was like a pageant or a play. Everyone sat in a circle in chairs with many of the presents neatly organized in a pile by each person's seat. Mary said that Christmas was carefully choreographed since her mother spent all year shopping and the presents were arranged so you would get the "least" presents first then work your way up to the "best" presents. Her father sat at the tree (to hand out the final presents—often coupons of promises in envelopes!) and her mother sat in a chair directing the entire operation.

In addition, you did not simply open up the present. Oh no. You had to rave enthusiastically at every phase in the process. First, you raved about the wrapping, the ribbon, the bow, the name tag ("Oh, Mother, where did you find this incredibly colorful wrapping? And the ribbon, it matches perfectly!"). And then Mary's mother would tell a story about where she got the wrapping. Then you raved about the box the present came in ("Oh, I remember this box from last year! Wasn't this box originally from Grandma?"). Then a story about the box. Then inside the box is the paper the present was enclosed in (usually the Sunday comics) and you raved about that. It took about five minutes for each person just to open the present. Then you had to rave about the present, the thoughtfulness that went into the present, and how much fun you were going to have with the present.

They spent the entire day opening Christmas presents! I thought I had died and gone to someplace bad. Mary—Admit, after a while the children did beg their parents if they could please take a break and have some lunch.

So, in our own family, we had to find a way to somehow bring together those completely opposite approaches to Christmas day. We experimented for several years as our kids came along and got older. Like all couples, we had to see how things went and we evolved into an approach to Christmas that was somewhere between what my family did and what Mary's family did (a lot closer to what her family did, I have to say).

MARY

So, Dave, what is your take-away from that?

DAVE

My take-away? Rave about the wrapping. It's a really good thing to do.

MARY

So, what is the eternal lesson that you took away from that?

DAVE

When God gives us gifts, we should be grateful for the wrapping they come in.

MARY

I'm going to move us along with another series of stories: In Minnesota
for graduate school, we lived in a townhouse with two bedrooms
and a bath upstairs and one big room with a kitchen downstairs. We
moved in three of us. Just over a year later there were four. One day I
decided to surprise Dave (and this was before Pinterest) by having all
the toys picked up before he came home. Then the kids and I made a
game of "watching for Dad" through the window as he was going to
walk across the large field before our apartment. When he arrived, he
came in the door, kissed each of the three of us, glanced around with
a puzzled look on his face, saw how neat and clean the house was, and
asked, "Didn't you have any fun today?"

Another day, in the same place, Dave arrived home as I was having
a very serious conversation on the stairs with our oldest daughter. He
smartly left us to finish our conversation. He heard that the outcome of
the discussion was a new family rule—something about no toys on the
stairs or sharing with the baby, I don't remember. But I do remember
later that night Dave said, "Mary, you're here most of the time. You see
what rules need to be made. You just make them and then tell me what
they are so I can be consistent."

One example is a rule I made years later. I determined (and ruled)
that no child could babysit the child next youngest (made in Utah
when Rachel was about eleven years old and I started leaving them for
maybe one or two hours).

Some things that we sacrificed were: having a clean house, and
the predictability of house rules (he never knew when he was going to
come home and find a new house rule).

But I have become very empathetic to the fact that I was blessed
to see a lot of firsts in our kids' lives that Dave missed so I needed to

be very understanding of the blessing to me of his desire to be very involved with them and facilitate that to the best of my ability.

DAVE

Ninja Pork Chops.[10]

This is a little longer story. Although I was raised in an Episcopalian home, I cannot say that I ever noticed a relationship between our religion and food, except, of course, for the consecrated wafers and wine at Holy Communion on Sunday morning. I do know that high church Episcopalian practice does not include storing large quantities of food against a time of emergency. We were squarely in the middle class, but my mother aspired to the lifestyle of the affluent Episcopalian gentility. Thus, she was not especially prone to practice frugality in general, nor food frugality in particular. We ate out often, were the first in our circle to own a microwave oven, and ate a lot of fancy TV dinners. And, most importantly, we threw food away when it was at all even approaching getting old.

I began my Mormon culinary journey in paradise, enjoying the delectable cooking of Sister LoDonna Leininger. Ray and LoDonna took their food almost as seriously as their missionary responsibilities, and I was the happy beneficiary of both. Therefore, at the same time I was feasting on the Word, I also supped many times at the Leininger's table before missionary lessons, home evenings, and firesides held

---

10 The part about "Ninja Pork Chops" is adapted from Dave's essay of the same title found in the book *Saints Well Seasoned: Musings on How Food Nourishes Us—Body, Heart, and Soul*, edited by Linda Hoffman Kimball (Deseret Book, 1998).

at their home. The food was plentiful, filling, and sweet. In a word, celestial.

For many years following, nearly every meal was only a shadow of the gastronomical glory I had experienced in my new-convert primeval paradise. I am ashamed to say that in my first few years of marriage I often spoke wistfully to Mary about my days in culinary heaven. Thankfully, she took all this in good humor. Mary is blessed with a cheerful confidence and a solid and nurturing family with pioneer heritage all the way back, on both sides, and is practically perfect in every way. She is also perfectly practical in every way, and sometimes Mary's pioneer frugality and my unrealistic culinary expectations have come into conflict. This occurred most sharply during what I call the "Ninja Pork Chops Era" of our marriage.

I sometimes tease Mary that she and her family live by the Articles of Frugality, which include: "We believe that all things may be saved, by obedience to the principles of frugality," "We believe in the gifts of coupons, yard sales, hand-me-downs, patches, Deseret Industries, and so forth," "If there is anything old, or used, or broken-but-repair-worthy, we seek to keep these things."

All this was fine with me when it came to things like hanging on to the old car a few more years, or using a thirty-year-old crib—given us by a fellow graduate student—through four children. But when it came to food frugality, I confess I had a harder time. Though I tried to get a practical testimony of this principle, it did not come quickly or easily—it came can upon can, pork chop upon pork chop.

In 1989, we had been married for nearly six years, living on the salary of a new assistant professor and paying off large student loans. One day during one of our visits to Utah, Mary's mother emerged from the food storage area in her basement with numerous huge cans of freeze-dried pork chops. Mary was thrilled with our share of the bounty: twelve #5 size cans, to be exact. This was no problem for me until I was told that the pork chops were originally packaged for the U.S. Army by the Oscar Meyer company in the early 1960s, and that these particular cans had been rejected by the Army as "not conforming to their specifications." Mary's parents' bishop, who happened to work for Oscar Meyer, had made the rejected food available to his ward, and Mary's frugal parents had purchased a good many cans for food storage at twenty-five cents a can.

I wondered: If the Army, not exactly known for its great food, didn't want them in the first place, why did our family have to eat them a quarter of a century later? I thought I remembered hearing something about the importance of rotation in food storage, and twenty-five years seemed like a long rotation cycle. I wondered aloud to Mary whether fossilized, reconstituted, freeze-dried trichinosis was as deadly as it sounded. Mary calmly called the State Agricultural Agent and found out that twenty-five-year-old freeze-dried pork chops were probably safe, although the agent offered no such assurance about their nutritional value, except as roughage. Some of the cans were bulging badly and Mary, in a flight of extravagance, did not make us eat those.

Each freeze-dried pork chop was about the size of a mall cell phone and the consistency and appearance of old, sturdy cardboard. Because of how they looked, their military origin, the martial-artsy sound of "chops," and the fact that I was sure they would be silent killers, I referred to them as "Ninja Pork Chops." I suggested to Mary that, rather than eat them, we should continue to store them so that when the last days came and marauding food-storage robbers showed up at our home to plunder our wheat and powdered milk, we could just hand these cans out to buy them off. Or, if really pressed, we could break out the chops from their cans, sharpen them, and use them like a Shuriken (those sharp-pointed metal weapons that ninja assassins flick at their victims). I told Mary it was my opinion that the second approach would actually be the more Christian thing to do.

Regardless, since my testimony of food frugality was not very strong, I did not believe I was being unfaithful to my religion when I told Mary that I would not eat twenty-five-year-old Army Surplus pork chops, nor would I allow my children to do so—devoted husband and moderately frugality-friendly guy though I was. Mary took my protest in stride and served them up anyway. She soaked them overnight to rehydrate them, let them simmer for several hours, and then made a casserole with condensed cream of mushroom soup and rice—the meat added "for flavor."

Despite my valiant and, I believed, legitimate protests, I knew that I had to eat those pork chops in order to prove to my in-laws, my wife, and my sixth-generation Mormon children that, although I was just a recent convert from California, I too could endure hardship for my religion. We then had a period of three or four months when, about once a week, we ate twenty-five-year-old pork chops for dinner.

This became a time in our marriage when mealtime meant much more to me than just coming home to eat, drink, and see Mary. I thought of those long months as my personal trek toward True Pioneer Mormonism. Mary's pioneer frugality not only gave us many inexpensive meals during a time of financial scarcity, but turned hard times into defining lessons. The blessing (grace) over dinner became much more important for me. I obtained a much better gut-level sense of how Ezekiel's "dry bones" could be made to return to life after such a long time (Holy Bible, Ezekiel chapter 37). And I saw that Mary had unwittingly acted in the pattern of the prophet Joseph Smith himself, by taking something very old and translating it for use by another generation.[11]

After all of this, however, I have a confession: Mary's Ninja Pork Chop Casserole actually tasted pretty good. In fact, it tasted really good, and I almost began to look forward to it. Of course, I did not dare tell Mary this, since I had no idea what else might be lingering in my in-laws' food storage. And not too many years after this, our food budget allowed Mary a little more freedom and our evening meals became a lot like those I remember from my early days in Mormon mealtime paradise. Mary's cooking was and is absolutely heavenly—in a down-to-earth, frugal Mormon sort of way.

So, I had to sacrifice my pride and my comfort, and frankly for a while there I thought I might have to sacrifice my very life on the Altar of Frugality. The blessing was that we got a number of good, inexpensive meals and I learned to become a True Pioneer Mormon!

MARY

I'm just so sorry that my mom had already served us all the Oscar Meyer ham and Lima beans before I met Dave so he missed out on that.

DAVE

Yes, I'm really sorry I missed that! (Not!)

---

11 In 1830, founding LDS prophet Joseph Smith published the Book of Mormon, a record of ancient peoples written in an ancient language, which he had translated by the gift and power of God.

MARY

Another instance in our lives where we could have had disagreements but decided to unify was about tithing. Dave and I have always agreed on paying our tithes and have agreed how to pay tithing. We did disagree, however, about children paying tithing on small amounts from their allowances or extra chores when that tithing would amount to cents, nickels, or dimes. One of us (Dave) thought amounts of less than, say, one dollar was imposing on the Ward Clerk's time. In addition, the point was made that anything less than maybe 50 cents cost more in paper and envelope than the donation. The other one of us (Mary) felt strongly that a tithe is a tithe and should be practiced small (10 percent is always 10 percent, but sometimes 10 percent can seem small and sometimes big). Ward Financial Clerks are clerks for the entire congregation and not one (to my knowledge) has ever complained about paperwork for small cash amounts. And, I must say, this discussion was pre-internet, when financial records were kept by paper.

The sacrifice, for both of us, was not steadying the Ark and the blessing was clear: our children have learned the importance of the law of the tithe and of being generous with fast offerings. I love when I have seen them filling out a donation envelope without my help.

DAVE

So, I'm a convert to the Church, which means I've had to become converted to every doctrine and principle in the gospel and this is one of many times when Mary has helped convert me, in a kind and loving way, to a true principle. I was wrong to suggest that our kids should not pay tithing even on a very little amount of "income." I had always paid tithing and wanted my kids to learn that principle and Mary helped me become fully converted by her great example and the way she taught and helped our kids to learn this principle for themselves.

Finally, as a BYU professor of family life, I would be shirking my responsibilities if I did not offer at least a few brief suggestions for how to align your marital scripts.[12]

- Expect that expectations will differ.
- Expect that most times it will not matter how you do things (e.g., toothpaste from middle or bottom; doing the dishes with rag or sponge).
- Expect that sometimes it will matter (e.g., do we have Family Home Evening, do our children pay tithing, what things are okay on the Sabbath day?).
- Expect that both ways of doing things (yours and your spouse's) are reasonable and effective.
- Expect that usually you and your spouse can work things out to your mutual satisfaction. (It is very sad when young couples with disappointed expectations start thinking that perhaps they married the wrong person.)

---

12 Here are some resources on marriage and family life that you might consider: Faculty in the School of Family Life has produced three edited books on LDS family life (all published by Deseret Book): *Successful Marriages and Families* (2012), *Helping and Healing Our Families* (2005), and *Strengthening Our Families* (2000). We have a website on fathering called FatherWork (FatherWork.byu.edu). This link brings you to a YouTube channel with talks I've given over the years on religion and relationships: youtube.com/results?search_query=david+dollahite+byu.

- In things that matter to only one of you, try to go with that person's way.
- In things that don't really matter to either of you, take turns getting your way.
- In things that matter a lot to both of you, try to find a way to try to honor both ways:
- Take turns when possible.
- Compromise on things that are not central.
- Combine to create new way that honors both.

MARY

We each bring to the marriage altar all the good and all the incomplete that we are. At the marriage altar, we covenant with each other and with God, whose purpose is to create eternal families. When we continue to bring to the altar all that we have and are—and we bring all in humility and sacrifice—we will be able to hear—individually and as a couple—how God would like us to proceed to unity with Him and with each other in our eternal marriage.

Nephi asks, "I would ask if all is done? Behold I say unto you, Nay; for ye have not come thus far save it were by the word of Christ with unshaken faith in him, relying wholly upon the merits of him who is mighty to save" (2 Nephi 31:19).

After more than thirty years of marriage, and seven children, and numerous teaching callings, and jointly teaching at least 1,600 Family Home Evenings, we have had a little more practice!

But a couple years ago, the Lord put us to the test. We were called to teach the Marriage and Family Relations class in our home ward. We got to teach Sunday School together again. We loved it!

And we're still working on our eternal marriage script. We're including our differences. I play the instruments and he plays the radio. I watch tennis and he plays tennis. I make the treats and he eats the treats. In the most important ways, though, we continue to both put our all on the altar.

DAVE

Mary has talked a lot about the marriage altar and I hope that you have been thinking about what that meant and means to you—if you are married—when you and your spouse knelt at the altar of the temple. As Latter-day Saints, often when we attend the temple we participate in the endowment ceremony. And that is great. However, I strongly encourage all married couple to seriously consider doing sealings [13] as often as you can together as a married couple. When you do sealings together, you get to spend an hour or so in a sacred place, dressed in white, in a beautiful and peaceful place. And, for the most part, all you say to each other during that hour is, "Yes" and "Amen." And those are very good things for spouses to say to each other as often as possible, both in the holy temple and every day in

---

13 "Sealings" are performed both for the living and, vicariously, for married couples who died without having the blessing of being married "for time and all eternity" (the phrase used in the temple) by the authority of the holy priesthood. Sealings are performed in a room in the House of the Lord—the temple—that contains a simple altar, a few chairs, and two mirrors facing each other in a way that when you stand together and look at your reflection in the mirror there is a never-ending series of reflections that wonderfully illustrate the eternal nature of the marriage relationship when sealed in the holy temple.

your marriage relationship. As often as you can, when your spouse asks you to do something, enthusiastically and sincerely say, "Yes!" And, as often as possible, when your spouse expresses the things of their soul, mind, or heart—as often as possible—say, "Amen!" and mean it. Of course, I don't really mean that you should say "Amen" every time but work to find ways to agree with them even if you might not initially do so.

We have learned from each other, helped each other grow, supported each other through challenges and changes, helped each other serve the Lord and His children, worshiped together, helped each other grow our testimonies of the restored gospel of Jesus Christ, and in a hundred other ways influenced each other. We are grateful that the Lord has been our constant companion throughout our married life. We express our appreciation to God, our children and grandchildren, and many other family members who have supported us in our marriage.

We have learned that marriage can be challenging hard work but we feel it is worth every effort to work together to turn our marital differences into ways to grow together in partnership with God.

APPENDIX C

Possible Discussion Questions for Book Clubs

- For the person who chose this book: What made you want to read it? What made you suggest it to the group for discussion? Did it live up to your expectations? Why or why not?

- What do you think motivated the author to share his life story? How did you respond to the author's "voice"?

- Do you think the author is trying to elicit a certain response from the reader, such as sympathy? How has this book changed or enhanced your view of the author?

- Compare this book to other memoirs your group has read. Is it similar to any of them? Did you like it more or less than other books you've read? What do you think will be your lasting impression of the book?

- How do you feel about the author's Appendix about the challenges of writing sacred experiences?

- Did reading this book influence your thinking about writing your own sacred experiences?

- Did you learn anything from this book that you could use to record your important experiences?

- What experience was the most pivotal for the book?

- Which experience resonated most with you personally in either a positive or negative way? Why?

- Has anything ever happened to you similar to the experiences shared in the book? How did you react to it differently?
- What surprised you the most about the book?
- Were there any particular experiences that stood out to you? Why?
- What did you learn from, take away from, or get out of this book?
- Did your opinion of the book change as you read it? How?
- Would you recommend it to a friend?
- Do you feel changed in any way as a result of reading this book?
- Do you have a different view of Mormons or the LDS Church as a result of reading this book?
- How did reading this book affect you?
- Was there anything especially surprising about the author's story?
- Were there any parts of the book where you would have liked more information?
- Did the book remind you of any other memoirs or biographies you've read?
- What did you particularly like or dislike about the book?
- Was there an overall lesson for LDS, non-LDS, or non-religious readers that could be taken away from the book?

www.ingramcontent.com/pod-product-compliance
Lightning Source LLC
LaVergne TN
LVHW051451080426
835509LV00017B/1735